Don't Mess with the Press

Don't Mess with the Press

How to Write, Produce and Report Quality Television News

Tony Seton

iUniverse, Inc.

New York Lincoln Shanghai

Don't Mess with the Press
How to Write, Produce and Report Quality Television News

iUniverse, Inc.

For information address:
iUniverse
2021 Pine Lake Road, Suite 100
Lincoln, NE 68512
www.iuniverse.com

ISBN: 0-595-28781-6 (Pbk)
ISBN: 0-595-74919-4 (Cloth)

Printed in the United States of America

This book is dedicated to all people who take journalism seriously. I've been honored to work with many who considered their work both a craft and public service. I have also suffered the loss of some important friends and colleagues who died while covering the news.

Joey Delisera was a sound man. One of the nicest fellows I ever encountered, Joey died when a helicopter in which he was riding crashed into the Caribbean.

Producers Dave Jayne and Larry Buchman died when their charter flight out of Beirut developed mechanical problems on take-off.

Producer Dave Kaplan was shot to death riding with other journalists through Sarajevo. He left a young wife, Sally, who also worked for ABC News.

Terry Khoo was a cameraman for ABC in Saigon. The week before he was to leave the country and relocate to the Bonn bureau, where he was to marry the secretary there, he went up to the front for a last look. He was shot and killed.

It was typical of field producer Kenny Luckoff to race after a story. Early one morning found him running across Los Angeles International Airport to catch a flight to Mexico City. He made it. When the plane tried to land in Mexico City, it hit a fuel truck on the runway; most on board, including Kenny, were killed.

Correspondent Bill Stewart was one of the true workmen in television news. He was in Nicaragua in 1977 covering the impending collapse of the Somoza regime. At a national guard checkpoint, he was ordered to lie face down in the street. For no apparent reason, a 17-year-old guardsman shot him in the back of the head. Because I had been traveling, I was unaware of what had happened to one of my dearest friends until I saw it that night on television.

The deaths of these men are reminders that there is always more to do. Journalists are targets of despots and common criminals around the world. Good journalists, that is. Most of those in the profession today tend to shy away from stories that mean personal danger. Those who hold out for the truth, often at personal risk, are among the true heroes of a society that means to be free. We won't have the world we want until the reporters are all safe.

Contents

Introduction

There are three phases of television news. You cover it, produce it and broadcast it. Or in the esoteric industrial vernacular you assimilate, manipulate and disseminate. The first task is to be aware of the news and to gather the necessary elements—information, audio and video components—to create a report. When you have all of the elements, you write a script, select the sound bites and cover shots, and then edit them together into a package. Then the report needs to be broadcast in a format that provides context for the viewer to understand and to value what is being reported.

It is very important that these three tasks—coverage, production and broadcast—all be performed and in order. When some news outlets—particularly the all-news cable networks—go live to cover a press conference or controlled photo op that has been packaged into a pseudo news event, they are ignoring the critical role of journalism—to make sure that what goes out on the public airways is thoughtfully considered and judiciously presented. Too often, the public is fed propaganda in the guise of a news event when with a little delay and some editing, an event could be reported in effective journalistic fashion.

Don't Mess with the Press outlines the purpose and challenges of each of the three phases of television news. There is also a fourth section on news management, which focuses on marketing quality television news. Because television is where the vast majority of Americans gets all of their news, it is vital to the well-being of the community—local and national—that a news operation be focused not only on garnering top ratings, but that it do so by informing their audience fully and accurately. Finally, the Appendix includes an alternative approach to network news coverage, some clues on finding work in television news, and the author's experience. There is also an extensive glossary of television news terms which may help to clarify some points raised in the text.

On line at dontmesspress.com are discussion points and practices for each chapter, as well as sample formats. You will also find there FAQs and an errata section, and you are invited to contribute to each as appropriate.

Preface

Fifty years ago, owning a television station was viewed as a license to print money. Not so today, where many stations are in crisis because the proliferation of satellite and cable systems has provided viewers with hundreds of choices; not to mention the advent of tapes and now DVDs. Margins have shrunk as the audience is split among more channels and a massive library of recorded programs. The only arena in which local stations don't face significant competition is local news, where in most markets only two or three other stations are competing for the same audience.

Television news was never an altruistic venture. Stations originally broadcast the news because it was required of them by the FCC to keep their license. A half-century after its inception, some stations are dropping television news altogether. One reason is because they can—the FCC no longer requires them to air news—but also, many stations have decided it's not worth the effort to compete with the other news operations. This is a dicey issue, because a news operation today, if it is successful, can produce well over half of a station's revenues.

In business terms, one can understand the decision of a station manager to cancel a newscast if it brings in less money than it costs to produce. But that station manager is on thin ice justifying that decision by saying that the community is served by other stations providing news. The fewer news organizations, the less competition, and that often means a decline in the scope and quality of the area news coverage. Usually there is enough local interest in television news for at least two stations to earn a big enough piece of the pie to make it worthwhile.

The business of television operates on the basis of the gross number of viewers. That's the way the sales staff sells the time. Maybe they've got 25,000 viewers for their early evening news compared to 21,000 for the second-rated station. Maybe there's a third station, which is drawing an audience of only 15,000 viewers.

But GRP—for gross ratings points—is not the whole story for the advertiser, the buyer of the commercial minutes you're selling. If they're advertising a lube shop or fast food drive-thru, they may be fine just counting the total number of eyeballs that may catch their commercial during a newscast. In truth, they're probably better off at the quantity end of the viewer spectrum. But what if they're a Lexus dealer or a stock broker or they're marketing a graduate school? Then they need active minds behind those eyeballs, and that means they need to be drawing a higher-end audience.

So you may be the number three station, capturing only 60% of the number of viewers watching the number one station, but if you're attracting the educated, consumer-oriented, community-aware people with money, you may be in a position to charge significantly higher rates for a smaller but more valuable audience. This is especially true during weaker economic times, when the buying power of the less affluent diminishes and those with money tend to keep spending.

Happy Talk

Let's harken back to the olden days again for a moment. There was a time, back before mini-cams and satellites, when news was a serious business. Back in the 1960s, for instance, every newscast was anchored by a straight-laced white male who delivered the news in stentorian tones. But then a radically new format came on the scene; it featured talking between the anchors, and among the anchors and reporters. The classicists pejoratively termed it "Happy Talk" and it took off like a rocket.

News consultants sold the chit-chat style as more engaging—the viewer was family, or at least a friend—and it soon became the dominant format. But when everyone was using the same format to snag viewers from the competition, some stations went further to make their banter more enticing, specifically hiring anchor "talent" who would charm the audience; journalism credentials were secondary. Because it was easier to attract a larger audience with personalities, local news was soon less about news and more about entertainment.

Revolution in News

Thomas Jefferson said that our nation probably would need a revolution every twenty years. Well, for the last twenty years, television news has typically been defined by the chatty, viscerally-oriented newscasts that target emotion rather than intellect. Most stations are wallowing in this format. They cover news in the same way and promote their coverage and personnel in like fashion. It's time for a revolution in television news.

Imagine what would happen in a market with the appearance of quality television news—intelligent reporting on significant issues presented in a comprehensive manner that demonstrated respect for the audience.

Consider how quickly an audience could develop for a newscast that was assembled and presented based on journalistic principles; it would look wildly innovative in most parts of the country. It would be startlingly different enough and would generate enough buzz to invite at least a look. Providing clear and concise information without hype and staged banter, such a newscast would offer measurably more content, from the number of stories to the substantive interviews to the scoops. It would be the news the newsmakers watch.

It probably wouldn't take long for the quality television news to draw a winning audience. Maybe not the most viewers, but certainly the ones who cared to be informed, and those are the folks with money. Even for the station manager who was just interested in the bottom line, quality television news would be a more viable approach.

That's because quality television news is less expensive to produce. It requires fewer people and less facilities than the typical news operation. The work environment is simultaneously more focused and rewarding, which translates into people working better together and remaining at the station longer; both are critical factors in the corporate profit picture.

Don't Mess with the Press explains how to write, produce and report quality television news, as well as how to manage and promote it. It might hastily be added that what you can learn from this book will benefit everyone considering television news as a profession, no matter what kind of news operation they might choose to join, since the better they know how to perform the essentials of news-gathering, production and presentation, the better equipped they will be in any news operation to handle whatever is thrown their way.

Notes

—In the days before gender equality, writing was generically masculine, e.g., you wrote of mankind, he, him and his, and didn't worry about offending half the population. Today, one has to be careful, because a good thought could be lost behind the cushions of a bad couch. I thought of switching back and forth between gender appellations, but not going so far as to use terms like reporteress, correspondente, or anchorette. However, upon reading the text, I found that I myself was getting confused. So I decided to move from the third person singular to the second person generic where I could and it wouldn't seem stilted.

—There is some repetition of ideas in these pages because many of the subjects overlap, e.g., writing, reporting and anchoring, and it was anticipated that some readers would not read the whole book.

—There are a number of personal stories mixed in with the instructive text, and appended to some of the chapters. They are included to provide some illumination of the principles of television news coverage, but also to share the excitement. Because as Marshall McLuhan observed, education and entertainment are inextricably entwined.

—You can get the latest updated information, corrections, and FAQs on-line at http://dontmesspress.com.

—Thanks to all those over the years who contributed to my education. Greg Dobbs, Richard Jett, Tim O'Brien, Bob Sirkin, Phil Starck, Pete Simmons and Paul Cleveland are singled out for special appreciation. Finally, my deepest gratitude to Charles Bierbauer and Doug White for their meticulous reading of an early draft. They made it much more pliable for the rest.

I—Gathering the News

If a nation expects to be ignorant and free, in a state of civilization,
it expects what never was and never will be.

—*Thomas Jefferson*

A television news broadcast is a slice of life. On any given day, some stories you cover are on-going, e.g., a trial, and need only to be updated with new information, visuals and/or sound. Some stories are new and need to be assembled from scratch. Still other stories will rely primarily on file footage, as in an update on a zoning conflict. Some stories, like a ground-breaking or news conference, are planned events. Others—crimes, accidents, acts of god—are complete surprises.

Before any of these stories can be delivered to the audience, they first must be covered. Significant breaking news usually warrants sending a reporter and/or photographer. Other stories can be assembled by a writer working with file footage. It is the function of the assignment desk, usually in conjunction with the news director and broadcast producer(s), to see to it that all of the essential elements of the stories are gotten in house in time to be prepared for broadcast.

What are the elements that must be gathered to produce a news story? Information is the first. Even if you have no pictures or sound cuts—maybe you don't even have time to pull file footage or put up a graphic—you can always get on the air with a story if you have the facts. But if you don't have the facts then you don't have a story.

What are facts? The truth about a situation. Often the facts are incontrovertible, but when there is some question about the truth, then Job One for the reporter is to ascertain the who-what-when-where-why-and-how, before you go on the air. This involves checking with authorities, and with other sources, to make sure that you doesn't say or imply anything you doesn't truly know. To insert "maybe" or "probably" is not "usually" enough.

The second element to be gathered is video. It may be apocryphal, but today we say that a picture is worth a thousand words. In fact, the ancient Chinese expression was that a picture is worth ten thousand words. Does that say something about the nature of editing? Dunno, but it definitely underscores the

1

importance of the visuals. Television is a visual medium. Many people watch with the sound low or off. Of course, you can go on the air without pictures, but then you could be doing radio instead.

The third element is sound, as in sound bites and the noise that news makes. It might be a criminal's confession, the roar of a hurricane, or the relative silence of a normally-busy street that has been closed due to a water main break. It should be obvious that just as you can go on the air with pictures but without sound, there are times when you can go on the air with sound without supporting pictures, e.g., a phone report from the scene of a breaking story, before pictures are available.

Section One outlines how news coverage is executed, starting with the issue of what is news, and goes on to explain the function of the Assignment Desk and how coverage is planned. Also discussed are the roles of the different players in the assimilation of the news. From assignment to investigation to reportage, coverage is the journalistic heart of any serious news organization.

1. What Is News?

News, said Edward R. Murrow, the dean of broadcast journalism, is that which interests and affects the largest number of people. News is information that is significant to the viewer, whether he knows it or not. A snowstorm that closes our children's schools is of interest, but the decline of our public schools, if less obvious, is far more important.

One of the bright young men who worked with Murrow at CBS in the Fifties was Av Westin, who became one of the major shapers of television news in the Seventies. Then, with 20 years of television news history behind him, Westin, the Executive Producer of the *ABC Evening News,* said a viewer is watching the news to get answers to the following four questions: "Is my neighborhood safe? Is my country safe? Is my world safe? What else should I know?"

I agree that both of those definitions of what is news are worthwhile, and I would add a third. The purpose of news is to help the governed monitor their governance. The electorate needs to understand current events so that they can elect the right people to resolve the issues that face us. So I propose that the news should strive to clarify the most important issues facing the community, reporting the facts and exploring potential solutions.

I suggest that the five most important issues in the community—national or local—be a foremost topic of discussion in determining what is the news of the day. What happened or didn't happen during the last news cycle to move us closer to resolution of these five issues? It's not that every broadcast should lead with an education watch, a health watch, an economy watch, et cetera, but by merely covering the events of the day, it is easy to let the critical issues disappear from view.

Too often, politicians, bureaucrats and business and civic leaders who are mindful of coverage cycles will simply wait until a story slips down to the bottom of and then off the news digest, which in a rapidly-changing world can be just a day or two. This underscores what I believe is a vital function of the news—in any medium—and that is to make sure that vital matters stay in public view. It is irresponsible to let these matters drop, simply because there isn't an immediate news peg. How else will they get resolved if they don't have public attention?

Certainly there is an endless stream of events to fill a newscast—national or local—but there is more to news than reporting events. There is the context of our lives. If a news organization fails to keep critical issues before the public, they won't get resolved. So many of our politicians are conflicted over voter attitudes that they choose to do as little as possible on the major issues for fear of offending one side or the other and risking the loss of an election. So there remains for the serious news organization the need to keep vital issues before the public, so that our elected leaders don't lose sight of our priorities.

This is not to suggest that spectacular events—e.g., multi-car collision or a colorful parade—that aren't related to the five important issues should be ignored, or buried at the bottom of the newscast. Rather, it is to remember the balance between what is important and what is eye-catching. If an accident ties up the freeway, it may not be important in the general scheme of things, but if lots of people couldn't get to where they were going on time, that accident was very much news to them, and the failure to report it would be a mistake. But keep events in perspective; most happenstance requires little time to illuminate and explain, and accidents are part of daily life.

The primary purpose of news is to inform us about what we need to know about the matters that affect our broader lives, i.e., what is being done to remedy past mistakes and to prevent others.

Cause and Effect

Economics and foreign policy may not seem interesting to most people, but they certainly affect us. As much as public surveys show an alarming disinterest in world affairs, the fact is that what happens in the Middle East has ramifications on all of our lives, viz., the terrorist attacks of September 11th 2001. The latest Israeli elections may not seem important, or as visually stimulating as a three-alarm fire that consumes an empty warehouse, but it is the obligation of the journalist to make those elections relevant to the audience, if you are serious about keeping your viewers fully informed.

On another level, news organizations that report crimes but not their causes are failing to illuminate the areas on which the people must focus their attention to find solutions. It is like reporting that a large segment of the populace is suffering from running noses and neglecting to note that there is a flu epidemic; and what might be done about it. All too often stations report horrendous crimes—or everyday street crimes—and while they might go into the background of the victim to engage the viewer through pathos, they rarely look into why the perpetrator became the person he did.

In many markets, news directors have become gun-shy about prying too deeply into such issues, since in many situations, it is violence, brutality and ignorance that breeds crime. But, they fear, if they were to report the facts they would be accused of racism. And rather than face and face down such criticism, they let the story slide, and the problem fester.

(What is news is sometimes determined by what kind of newscast is being produced. For instance, time limitations restrict the number of stories that make it on the air, and the number of acts in each story that get reported. For instance, on a nightly newscast, most copy stories or readers are delivered in less than twenty seconds and most reporter packages are less than a minute-thirty, while in a documentary or magazine format, ten minutes or more are devoted to a single story. Does this mean that the producer of the nightly broadcast should ignore stories because they are too complex to be reported quickly. Of course not. If the story is important, you have to find the time to report the essential facts, in context, because it's news. The question of what is news also pertains to the order in which stories are reported, presumably by importance, and how much time is given to report them. These subjects will be addressed in greater depth later.)

News Judgment

Can news judgment be taught? Probably not. Can it be learned? Probably. The top journalists I've known have an instinct about news. They know while scanning the wires which items are going to turn into substantial stories. They can sit through three hours of a press conference and recognize the important sound bites as they go by.

While there may be something genetic in the make-up of a journalist that gives you this acute sense of the news, the trait can be enhanced. The more you expose yourself to the news, the more you are likely to understand. And to further enrich your news judgement, it is valuable to expose yourself to perspectives from people who hold viewpoints that might seem at least somewhat at odds with your own.

It is also a good practice to try out the soundness of your thinking, off the air, on friends and colleagues; this can illuminate any fuzziness in your thinking. Remember, most people think their opinions are as valuable as anyone else's, regardless of the focus and information that form their thoughts. Many people, without doing any of their own thinking, take blusterous pride in parroting the bombast of radio ranters.

It's one of the crosses to bear in this profession that most members of the GP (general public) don't really think of journalists as professionals. They don't give them any more credit for their views than they would give the mailman for his. So it can be particularly frustrating for a journalist to endure a sermon—on the radio or at the dinner table—when the speaker relies on voice level to cover his misconstruing and misinformation. On the other hand, even speaking from ignorance, people can bring attention to where a line of thinking might have derailed, and therein can help the journalist avoid making the same mistake.

Critical Role of News

News is the critical link in our society between the government and the governed; it is the Fourth Estate in democracy; Shakespeare's fool; the observer; the conscience. When the press is not vigilant, when the media—print and electronic—fail to report clearly, comprehensively, and accurately, they undercut the ability of the people to monitor the government.

It is essential to the health of a free press that those covering the news keep their distance from the newsmakers. As I. F. Stone observed, you can't report honestly on people with whom you play tennis. As top television news salaries have soared into the millions of dollars, the people who pocket them are clearly in a very small class of Americans. They, and those with whom they share the wealth, have a vested interest in the status quo. This can translate into acquiescence to the way things are, and tacit endorsement of current policies. It can be tough when you make a friend who might be in the news. It comes down to personal integrity, and if there's any a question that the public might perceive a lack of it in your reporting, hand off the assignment to someone else.

Because the people who deliver our news socialize with the nation's government and business leaders, they are in danger of toeing the company line. It would not be deliberate deception, but whether through omission or commission, it would be an act of complicity. It is the story of the emperor's new clothes. One can almost see the network anchor booths perched along the parade route as the emperor marches by, naked and proud, being cheered by the frightened populace. And in the booth, the color commentators speak knowingly about the colors and patterns of the royal garb.

News is more than a business. It is a calling.

2. What Is Television News?

Television news comes in a many different shapes and sizes. From the announcer reading a script he doesn't have to understand over a station ID slide just before they play the national anthem at sign-off to everyone involved in live coverage ala September 11th 2001. Between these production extremes are the scheduled daily newscasts, which might be the premiere evening news involving dozens of journalists and technical people or a morning news cut-in, written, edited and reported by the new guy on the block.

Just as the products vary, so do the television news operations that produce them, from the big time at the network to the smallest markets in rural America. The differences are not only huge, but they determine the nature of the work for everyone involved. If you start at the top, you can miss a lot, while if you start in a small station and work your way up, you can be particularly well-equipped to handle a network position. Consider the variations:

The networks will send five people—producer, correspondent, camera, sound and lights—to cover a story, while small market stations will assign a single reporter. You will put a chalk mark on the sidewalk so you know where to stand when you focus the camera to shoot your own standupper.

At the networks, only a few correspondents are on the air every night, while at local stations a reporter may be shooting a package or two every day, and picking up sound cuts and b-roll along the way.

At the networks, a correspondent and producer work together with researchers to develop stories. At a local station, a reporter will pick up the gist of the story from the newspaper and scrounge for the rest of the news you need on your cellphone on the way to or from the scene.

At the network, couriers will pick up tapes and scripts from location shoots, while in small markets, a reporter is responsible not only for recording as much video and audio as possible, but also for delivering it all to the station in time to prepare it—you may well edit it your self—for air.

At the networks, a separate control room with audio, video, director, associate director, technical director and supporting engineers will pre-package reports. At a smaller local station, the one control room might be staffed by one person.

And it is all called television news. Most people in The Biz never work at a network, or even in the top ten markets. Most slough it out in smaller and middle-size markets until they find another profession that looks more attractive. And there are also some people who work all their professional lives at the same station, and love it.

Those who do climb up to the top tier learn most of what they know in the streets. Those who take the time to absorb the lessons along the way have a far greater understanding of the craft and a greater ability to produce quality television news. Journalism school and good books are valuable. Mentors can be invaluable. Also, expose yourself to different people and new ideas. And give yourself time to digest and reflect.

Watergate

With the Watergate affair now blurring in history, it is bemusing to remember the frantic pace of the times. So many people were telling so many stories that it was sometimes hard to keep track of what was known, what had been admitted, and what was simply being reported. There were also a lot of players, including a slew of Republican staffers for CREEP, the Committee to Re-Elect the President, and the FNC, the Nixon campaign finance committee. Plus, the White House people, the

Cubans and The Plumbers. And then all their lawyers. Depositions were being taken right and left.

One afternoon in September of 1972, shortly before the Watergate story really broke loose, former Attorney General John Mitchell—known to many at the time as Martha's husband—was to appear at the office of eminent D.C. attorney Edward Bennett Williams, who was trying to figure out whom to sue on behalf of what was left of the Democratic National Committee. I was assigned to capture Mitchell on film, with correspondent Sam Donaldson and two film crews. (This was very unusual, having two crews, perhaps due to pressure from the higher-ups because ABC was not getting their share of scoops.)

Donaldson and one crew parked themselves with what looked like half of the Washington press corps at a street corner, waiting for Mitchell to arrive in his limo. I went into the building with the other crew and hid out of sight near the elevators. At the expected time, Mitchell arrived, got out at the wrong corner, and then led a mob of reporters and camera crews into the building.

When he was about twenty feet from the elevator, I stepped out from hiding with the crew and positioned us between Mitchell and the elevator. Suddenly everything stopped. The former attorney general had nowhere to turn but to me. I realized that I could wait for Donaldson to push his way through the crowd, but what if he couldn't get through or the elevator arrived to provide an escape? I didn't want to stand there limply waiting so I threw three questions at Mitchell. They were the questions of the day: When did you know about the break-in? What was your connection with Gordon Liddy? Did you approve the break-in?

Mitchell blustered and hawed, denouncing the "charges" as scurrilous, et cetera. I felt sorry for the man, even at the time; everything was going wrong for him. He was probably more upset with what the Nixon Administration was doing in the cover-up than with the insanity of the initial plan itself. Wouldn't it have changed things if he had suddenly had a change of heart, put down his briefcase and said, "Kid, I've got a story that'll knock your socks off. Can we go somewhere and talk?" The stuff of dreams.

*   *   *   *   *   *   *

The heroics were not always heroic. The next spring, when ABC decided to get footage of John Dean—no one had fresh shots of the man—they hatched a plan that consisted of four cars tailing Charles Shaffer and Bob McCandless, Dean's two attorneys. I was stationed somewhere in suburban Maryland at the entrance to a cul-de-sac where Shaffer lived. I was to follow him when he left in the morning, staying in touch with the bureau by walkie-talkie. (Walkie-talkies were a place that ABC saved some money; I was unable to reach the camera crew a half mile away.)

I must have seemed pretty obvious, being the only car on the street, and with a whip radio antenna on the back of the car. It didn't matter. When Shaffer left the cul-de-sac, I followed him. He drove a hundred yards down the street and then into a neighbor's driveway. Not wanting to be completely obvious, I drove past the driveway. Then he pulled back out and started following me. When we reached a fork in the road, I took a right—away from where I thought he might be going—and he continued to follow me. Finally I pulled into the driveway of a monastery. He pulled into the bottom of the driveway behind me, waited a few moments to mock my efforts and then drove off to his office.

*   *   *   *   *   *   *

It was this nonsense that drew much of the attention to coverage from the actual news. There was much that was uncovered during the spring and summer of 1973 that was over-looked or got lost in the shuffle. Like the reports that White House "dirty tricks" chief Charles Colson, within hours of the shooting, tried to send his operatives to check out the Milwaukee apartment of Albert Bremer, the man who shot George Wallace. There was another story about a $350,000 illegal campaign contribution to Nixon from one labor official to get himself out of jail, and another contribution of equal size from his union to impose restrictions on his labor activities. It underscores the danger that you can be too taken with a single story to be on top of all the news.

3. Staying Current

Though it is easy to disparage the quality of today's news coverage—broadcast and print, local and national—the fact is that most of the important information about current events is readily available—to journalist and news-junkie alike—and if you have a context for it, you can stay fairly well informed. To create that context, you need to stay current. That means you need to have a working knowledge of a broad range of subjects and perhaps some depth in a chosen few. That requires monitoring different media and different sources.

For instance, as rich as is the news content of the Reuters wire service, it tends to under-report some stories of particular interest to an American audience. The AP news wire, on the other hand, appeals to a broader audience, with more focus on sports. *The New York Times* is more intellectual. CNN is less. So sampling several wire services, together with listening to the radio, watching television and reading the local paper(s) should give you a wide variety of inputs. It's time-consuming, but if you enjoy watching history being made—and that's what attracts many journalists—you love the work.

People who aren't as interested in the news don't understand how some of us can check the news wires every twenty minutes, or have the radio tuned to an all-news station, which we turn up at the top and the half of the hour for headlines. In some of us, there is a basic need to know how the world is doing, how stories are developing, what progress is being made, and what challenges loom ahead and over the horizon.

It is also useful to judge how different sources cover different stories, and different kinds of stories, as noted above. Reuters is stronger internationally. AP tends to get on domestic crime stories faster. CBS radio news, which used to be more serious, seems to be edging toward the more stylized format used by ABC. CNN may get the first pictures, but the broadcast networks usually bring more depth to the coverage. Gaining a perspective on how the different media report which stories is interesting in itself, but it also provides a framework for more effectively assimilating a breaking or in-depth story.

There are excellent regional and local news digests available on the Internet, as well. Most news outlets—radio, television and newspaper—have websites, but of varying quality. Some smaller papers simply plug in a wire service together with local weather. Some update their sites only a couple of times a day. Others make a real effort at staying current, though the resources required for such currency are usually beyond news operations in all but the largest markets.

(In California we have Rough & Tumble (rtumble.com), which daily reports several dozen headlines and lead story lines from newspapers and information services about and affecting California. It is an invaluable source for any reporter interested in news of The Golden State.)

What can be learned from "reading in" is not only what other reporters are saying about a story, and how they are aligning their facts, but also what are their perceptions of their readers, listeners, or viewers. Presuming that the reporters know what they are doing, they will indicate in their fact selection and script what they believe the audience already understands, what's new to them, and how to integrate the new with the known. You may not agree with their perceptions of their audiences, but at least you have a point of demarcation. If you're reporting to the same audience, you can more carefully tune your reporting to better reach your audience.

It probably doesn't need to be said, but the more you are up on the news, the better position you will be in to cover it. The more you have assimilated, the less you will have to learn fresh. This is true not only about on-going stories, but also breaking stories. The more background you have on a community, the better—and more richly and quickly—you will be able to provide a context for the current event. For instance, if you already know that a jurist now charged with corruption has long been playing footsy with the rules, or if you are familiar with the voting record of a politician who suddenly changes sides, you are in a position to provide a valuable context for your viewers.

Generalist & Specialist

There are basically two types of journalists—the generalist and the specialist. The generalist will cover stories of any sort. Some reporters are particularly adept at covering the top of a story instead of going for depth. They make good generalists. The specialists focus on a particular field, like medicine or business. They will report major developments in their areas, and be called on to report on a breaking story that requires a particular expertise. Of course, it takes a larger roster and budget to afford specialists, which is why at most smaller and middle-market stations, most reporters have to be ready to cover any kind of story.

This doesn't mean that they can't specialize—they should if that's their bent—but the more general awareness they have, the better positioned they are to take advantage of more opportunities.

Be warned that most reporters who focus on a specific area tend to let themselves off the hook for having to know about the world at large, and this can cause problems. Particularly if news from their chosen area has wider implications. A specialist on energy, for example, needs to have at least a passing knowledge about geo-petro-politics and business. A medical reporter needs to know the symptoms of poverty.

An important way to stay current, particularly if you are a specialist, is to pay attention to industry publications. Also, the better plugged in your are to people in your field of focus, the most likely you are to receive information early. People *in situ* can not only provide you with new developments but they can also provide you with a sense of the culture of a company or industry—in terms of personalities, priorities and habits—all of which can be most valuable in assimilating and reporting a story. (The next section deals with contacts.)

Keeping Your Edge

It's vital that you keep your edge. If you find yourself covering the same stories over and over again, you should be alert to the danger of taking the facts for granted. At least you should be looking for new people with new ideas to address a continuing situation.

Charlie Jones, an ABC cameraman operating out of the Atlanta bureau, knew that he needed a transfer when he found himself shooting a story on the annual fire-ant invasion for the twelfth time. He moved to San Francisco.

Don't let your head get stuck in television news. The news can be as seductive as it is scintillating; and television provides a lot of ego gratification. Keep your mind alive by participating in something, not just observing. Maybe you'd like to try your hand at writing fiction or poetry, which would not only be a good diversion but would also hone your news writing skills. Harry Reasoner—before he became famous—wrote a charming book called <u>Tell Me About Women</u>. It had more sensitivity to what the young man had to learn about women than any other source I ever found.

You might do better to choose something further afield than writing—maybe in sports or music or gardening, i.e., something that engages other pieces of you. The more well-rounded you are—and the more you are able to give your journalist's mind a rest—the sharper will be your journalistic skills.

4. Contacts

One of the most valuable tools of a journalist are his contacts. Contacts are people who can be called upon to supply information or to give direction toward an answer. They can be in government, business, community groups and even in the media.

The first thing a reporter should do upon relocating to a new market (or for someone embarking on a journalism career in her own town) is to get a clear picture of the who's, how's, where's, why's, when's and what's of the market. Sound familiar, as in your first writing assignment in the fourth grade? And yet when you parse news reports today, it is startling how often not all of these questions are answered, let alone raised.

The first sources for such basic information should be the local media. But take what you get with a grain of salt because you may not be getting the whole story. Especially in small or middle-size market, the people who manage the media—your station manager, for example—frequent the social circles of many business and civic leaders where friendships and business relationships often intertwine, and can sometimes be at odds with straight reporting.

Also, some media managers are big fish in a small political pond, which can invite serious conflicts for their employees trying to report the news cleanly. It's not that there is necessarily false information being deliberately reported, but sometimes certain facts are down-played, under-reported, or ignored.

Remember that most journalists, particularly in the smaller markets, are quite content to stay where they are and are not likely to rock the boat, especially when they might have concerns about their boss, who is Rotary pals with a contractor under investigation, or who sits on the school board which has misplaced some state funds.

That warning aside, the local news organizations are certainly the place to start gathering information. It is usually from these media that you can begin to see how the community operates, who are the leaders, what are the issues and goals and how all the pieces come together.

In many markets the news tends to be a video version of the police wire. Even where this is not the case, much of news coverage is of sudden and disastrous stories, making it crucial that you understand the dynamics of—and develop contacts among—the emergency services, e.g., local and state police, fire, paramedics, air/national guard, coast guard, etc; these are the players in many suddenly-breaking stories. Who's in charge? Who really knows what's going on? What are the planned responses in a likely disaster, e.g., hurricanes in the Gulf of Mexico or brush fires near Los Angeles? Having the answers to these questions will put you steps ahead of the competition.

Knowing who is running things at the regional, local and community level is invaluable in understanding and reporting the news. Politicians, union and religious leaders and other movers and shakers are the pivots around which a story can revolve. By understanding their positions and motivations, a reporter can get more deeply inside a story. Most public figures recognize the power of television and will respond to a reporter on and off the record. But many are not always good information sources, because while they may hold the title, they may not necessarily know what's going on. So many officials today are popular but unworldly politicians, and/or people vaunted to leadership by circumstances.

With any person who has political power, it is wise to be aware of their ambitions. Many of the powerful see it all as some kind of game, and if they haven't made the rules themselves, they have a sense of how it is best played for their personal benefit. Sometimes, the more experienced politicians will throw a bone to a new reporter. So you might ask yourself, if a bone should come your way, Why is this person-in-power handing this important information to you? What's in it for them? Why have you been chosen?

Often the key for getting inside information is the staff or assistant to the top people. An administrative aide, a secretary, a floor nurse, a ward heeler, a community group treasurer—all can be useful contacts. The less visible are often the more accessible. Ideally, you will want to connect with people you can call at home after hours; people who will call you at home, too.

You can't simply send out form letters asking "Would you like to be my contact?" Though there are many people whose egos would yearn for television exposure—as a manifestation of their importance—the most reliable sources are those who have more than ego invested. Often they will be staff people who are committed to their boss or to the ostensible cause. They are best chosen on the basis of who they are as human beings, and who they find you to be.

Contacts are also going to be people who are non-controversial, like the manager of a local supermarket. Television journalists need more than information, they need pictures. And the superior reporter will know where to go for the specific or generic pictures needed to flesh out a story, e.g., retail outlets (clothes, hardware, food and drink), agriculture (farms, tractors, cattle, crops), hospitals, warehouses, banks, etc. If you have access to the people who manage these places, you can shoot the footage you need, and in a hurry as is so often the case.

Your little black book or PDA should be something you keep with you at all times. Call them anal, but good journalists will hold onto the most obscure listings, because "you never know." My little black book contained the phone numbers, not only of the principals, but of their press liaisons and secretaries as well. I also kept information on a number of restaurants where I could set up a meeting and provide their address and phone number immediately; also flower shops (to send gifts), the airlines, car rental agencies, messenger services, police, fire and other emergency numbers.

When in doubt about the value of a name or number, write it down anyway; you never know when you might be able to use it again. Know where to find it, too. Come up with an information storage and retrieval system that works easily for you. Be diligent about keeping it up to date. It will come in handy over and over again.

5. Sources

Sources are the lifeblood of successful journalists. Unlike contacts who are public, sources are private and usually hidden. When Elvis Presley died, WHBQ scooped the competition because the assignment manager was a friend of a high police official who told her what had happened. And just think what would have happened if Woodward and Bernstein didn't have access to their high administration official they called "Deep Throat"; Richard Nixon might have finished out his second term.

Sources are useful for tips, and for background information, but they must be regarded as loaded weapons. Many reporters have used sources irresponsibly—out of gullibility or greed—and those guns have backfired. Remember, sources are people, human beings with a point of view they want aired.

Very often sources will only provide information on the condition that their identity be protected. They could be at risk for revealing information that conflicts with that of a superior. Others may want to float a new idea, or to publicly force someone to declare a position. Think of how many times reporters quote "a senior administration official" when the White House or State Department wants to stir up a political situation without becoming overtly involved.

Some of the greatest stories come from "whistle blowers," people inside an agency or in the private sector who value justice and want the truth to emerge. But they also may have their own ax to grind, which is why it is essential on all but the most obvious story—a criterion born of experience and common sense—to get outside confirmation. Especially if you are uncertain about the source's motives. Often people will give you half-truths, or couch what they say in a particular tone to elicit support or sympathy.

The issue of confirming sources extends beyond such huge news events as Watergate. In fact, every story should be researched as though your career depended on its accuracy; your reputation does.

If you think this is nit-picking, read or watch *All the President's Men*. In it both Woodward and Bernstein make an inference about the grand jury testimony of Nixon re-election campaign finance deputy Hugh Sloan. A simple misinterpretation of what Sloan said came out in print and gave the White House ammunition to seriously—if temporarily—challenge the credibility and undermine the efforts of the two *Washington Post* reporters.

And when dealing with opinion, have a clear understanding of the opiner's perspective. If the new highway is finally going to be built, you might go to the mayor for comment and likely expect that she will be happy about it. By the same token, you can't expect the contractor who will build the highway to volunteer the reasons why it shouldn't be built.

Common dictum has it that a reporter needs two sources to go with a hidden story; three, if the issues are controversial or the facts contestable. That's probably a reasonable starting point, but it's not a hard rule. Sources have their own value. Some have their own agendas; some use reporters more than the other way around. On the other hand, sometimes you only need one source, if he is trustworthy, or none at all if you are the witness. It all comes down to your own professional understanding of the story and your grasp of the facts.

Cultivating sources is an important aspect of most reporting. Like contacts, sources come from all strata. Some sources are just good for a single story; others will supply information for years. Many sources put their jobs at risk by leaking information, and reporters have to be careful to protect them. This often limits access; for instance, you may not be able to meet with them, or call them at their office. Respect your sources. Protect them. Make sure that they are getting something out of the relationship with you.

Sometimes flowers or a meal are appropriate. Often sources are satisfied with seeing the truth come out, but it should never be construed that you are buying information. In today's news climate, some operations are willing to pay their sources, sometimes outrageous sums, but when you buy information, you can never be sure that you place the same value on the truth as does the supplier.

Another place to find sources, though it is not as frequently talked about, is among non-competing journalists. A radio or newspaper reporter might be working on the same story and you could both benefit by sharing information. It's sort of like pooling, where news operations organize to cover an event together with one crew and reporter, e.g., a trial. Also consider that CBS and *The New York Times* do polling together. Knowing who are the other news gatherers in your region and what are their talents and predilections can be very useful.

So what do you do if you have your entire script ready to record, but you're waiting for that one phone call to lock it in. A call that won't come through, as it turns out, until the next day. Few news directors want to hear that, especially on big stories. In the old days, it was journalistic caution that would delay the release of a story; today, it's the fear of a libel suit. The result is the same. You can either report only part of the story or you have to kill the piece, at least until you get the confirmation you seek.

Most experienced reporters, at some point in their careers, have written a script two ways, waiting for a confirmation or a denial of questionable information. And not just about police or other legal matters; it could be a vote by the city council, or a medical prognosis.

As the clock races toward air time, the temptation to close out a story becomes very strong. For the reporter who knows the story is accurate and is looking for a confirmation or an official response, tracking down a spokesperson can be difficult. Many officials will avoid a reporter late in the day; they may simply be gun-shy because they earlier got the short end of a hurriedly-scribbled, out-of-context quote.

In some situations you can find another unrelated source with whom to check your facts. In other cases, you can cajole an assistant into a confirmation or denial. Sometimes you can read a controversial portion of a script and ask for a comment. But be careful if they refuse to say anything. It may not be a denial. They may not want to comment, or they may not have the information or the authority.

In our society, "No comment" is like invoking the Fifth Amendment, refusing to testify against one's self. Most viewers will infer that "No comment" is an admission of guilt. Be very careful how you take it and how you use it. Remember, too, that most people watch too much television and have their ideas about how they should deal with the press tainted by entertainment programs.

The fact is that too many times, the telephone will remain still on your desk, taunting you with its silence. And these are the circumstances that separate the top journalists from the pack.

Some reporters will pepper a script with "alleged" and "purported". Be careful. The power of the press to smear is greater than the power to clear. Think of the difference between implication and inference. You imply when you suggest something to someone. They infer when they make a presumption about what you are saying. The press has the power to imply to its audience, but not to control the inference.

Reporting the facts is not enough. Saying "Police want to ask Google O'Leary where he was on the night in question" implies Google is a suspect. Google might have a perfectly good explanation, but he is out of town visiting his sick aunt and doesn't know the cops are looking for him. If you go with your script the way it's written, even though it's accurate, you will hang Google with a large segment of your audience.

A responsible journalist will leave out the name altogether, just as police refuse to release the names of accident victims until the notification of next of kin. You have an obligation both to protect the people on whom you're reporting, as well as the sources who inform on them. It's a matter of judgment and consideration. If those criteria aren't enough, consider your reputation and the possibility that you might want information from these people at some point down the road.

Finally on the subject of sources, you are the best you have. Gut feelings are perhaps the most important source a reporter has. Your instinct is what can tell you whether someone is telling the truth; telling the whole truth. Don't go on feelings alone; it is the synthesis of brains and guts—the rational and the intuitive—that produces the most accurate and complete picture. Trust your intuition. A little paranoia is better than going forward and getting the story wrong. My criterion for judging the veracity of a story is that my head and gut have to agree. If I only think something is right, or only feel it is right, I won't go with it. Both have to be right; ergo, To Think + To Feel = To Know.

The Best Kept Secret

This book wouldn't be complete without the story of Ron Rotunda, one of the country's most respected Constitutional lawyers, legal scholars and teachers. When I met him in 1973, he was an attorney on the Democratic staff of the Senate Select Committee investigating Watergate. It was the Summer of '73, and I was an assistant producer covering the story for ABC.

We became friends during the course of the hearings. He never leaked anything, but he frequently helped me to understand some of the complexities of the processes, and he created context for some of the testimony.

On Monday, July 16th, shortly after noon, the day the cat would be let out of the bag, I ran into Ron and walked with him toward the hearing room. In a quiet but urgent voice he said to me, "You want to be on this afternoon."

I was shocked at his directness. We had talked a lot, but never had he virtually told me something large was looming. The problem he was telling me I had to deal with was that after the initial explosion in hearings coverage, the networks had started rotating the coverage of the hearings. They had all been on all the time, but then revenues pressures had kicked in and they had decided to take turns—ABC one day, CBS the next and NBC the third. The networks that were making money instead of featuring these historic events, were always ready to go on the air, they said, if need be, but it would have to be really serious.

That Monday was CBS's day and ABC was in normal broadcasting mode, soaps and game shows. Ron was aware what it would mean for ABC to suddenly announce that they were going on the air. But he was also aware of the importance of the witness who was to appear before the committee at one o'clock.

"Who is it?" I pleaded, knowing the case I'd have to make to the Executive Producer Wally Pfister.

Ron just shook his head. "I can't. But you'll find out at one o'clock. It's going to be the best kept secret in Washington for the duration."

"Ron, I can't get us on with your say-so. They won't do it. No offense."

"I understand," he said smiling wryly.

"It's not your word, it's mine. I know we should go on based on what you're saying, But they won't listen to me." I meant it; Ron was and is a man of impeccable integrity.

He just smiled. I ran down the hallway to the phones and called in. To no avail. People who wanted to witness history as it was happening were going to have to watch it on CBS.

On my way back to the hearing room, I spotted the witness. When I saw the initials on his briefcase I knew who it was, but I had no idea what he was going to say.

When he had finished testifying at 1:17, Alexander Butterfield had started the beginning of the end of Richard Nixon's presidency. He revealed the presence of a taping system in the White House. The hearing room was as silent as a held breath as Butterfield, reluctantly, explained how the taping system worked, and that it would have picked up the key conversations in the Oval Office. The tapes would authenticate the testimony of White House Counsel John Dean that his boss, the President of the United States, knew all about the Watergate cover-up.

When Rotunda mentioned that it was the best kept secret in Washington, he wasn't exaggerating. Butterfield's knowledge had been revealed three days earlier—Friday the 13th—at the end of a long day of staff investigations of witnesses for the committee. They were on the verge of wrapping up the pre-interviewing of Butterfield. It was already after 5:00. Don Sanders, ironically a Republican, was summing up. He asked Butterfield the standard pre-screening questions, including if there were any way to confirm or deny John Dean's allegations about the President. Butterfield took a deep breath and sighed. "I was afraid you'd ask me that." And then he told them the explosive information.

Somehow in that sieve-like environment, the secret held all weekend. Then that Monday the smoking gun was revealed. A month later, Judge John J. Sirica signed an order for President Nixon to turn over the tapes. It still took over a year of impeachment resolutions in Congress and a decision by the Supreme Court supporting Sirica, but Nixon finally resigned.

I was covering the courthouse the day that Sirica's original decision was handed down. After I phoned the news to the office, I went back to Sirica's chambers with a couple of other news people who had developed a relationship with "Maximum John," the man who stood up to the conspiracy and deceit from the highest levels with a calm determination that was a credit to the bench.

The legal baton had been handed up after an excellent run. I asked for his autograph, and he wrote "To my good friend Tony Seaton, from John J. Sirica" on a copy of the decision. For a number of years, I didn't get it framed because Sirica had misspelled my name. I grew up. Now the document is slightly fanned and double matted inside a simple bronze-colored metal frame. It now hangs in my office and is one of the first things I'd grab in the event of a fire.

6. Staged News

Statistics are like ladies of the evening; once ya get 'em down you can do anything you want to 'em. That, according to Mark Twain, allegedly. I used that reference in a talk a number of years ago, and later a woman came up to me and accused me of being sexist. I told her to complain to Twain, retorting that the issue was not gender but ownership. If you pay for the numbers, you can usually get them to say whatever you want.

I raise this point because so much of "news" today comes from news conferences and press releases. Regrettably, many smaller news operations simply rewrite press releases into what they consider a news story, and often do so without checking the facts or calling to find out who might disagree with them.

This often leads to flagrant errors, since nothing is deliberately released to the press that isn't at least partially slanted. No PR firm or corporate public relations person is going to deliberately raise any negative issues, unless trying to pre-empt the media getting hold of a worse story; their purpose would be to inure the audience to, or distract them from, more damaging information. It needs to be repeated: every press release is designed to improve the public image of the releaser.

Similarly, a press conference is most always called to release information favorable to the caller, or to spin negative information in such a way so that it will do the least damage.

A clue to a negative release is the timing. Most public relations people—they're often pejoratively referred to as flacks, not always a fair appellation—know that the best time to release a damaging story is late in the day, especially on a Friday; that limits coverage, and presumably, the consequent fallout. The late afternoon release works particularly well on the television news operations, which are usually too busy putting together their early evening shows to go out after a new story that occurs later than the middle of the afternoon. Since at many smaller stations the reporter or cameraman is also the editor, there are rarely extra bodies to go out to the business park or city hall at five o'clock, except for live coverage, and that has its own pitfalls.

The flacks also know that even if their news hits the wires, it's going to have to be a major story if an early evening show producer is going to take the trouble to shoe-horn the item into a formatted newscast. In most cases, the flacks also know, there is not a great deal of attention to the news wires while the show is in the final preparation and then on the air.

Another reason for the late afternoon news conference, from the PR people's standpoint, is that while the story may make it into the late evening newscast—with a significantly smaller audience—there's a good chance that it will probably die by the next day. Unless it's a slow news day, or the story is big; the producers of the next day's news usually wipe the story board clean every morning.

News that comes out too late on Friday for Saturday coverage may make it to Sunday, but it will rarely survive the weekend. Sometimes, much to the consternation of the instigator, a Friday evening release will pique the interest of the Sunday talk show hosts, and the issue will then be revived in the Monday papers.

This timing issue has been somewhat mitigated by the cable news channels and the Internet, but most news operations and most citizens are less focused over the weekend.

Be attentive to the way people release news. Remember that no one releases anything innocuous, unless it is perfunctory, like unsurprising corporate earnings. Or unless it is a smoke screen. Some flacks will release significant information but mask it with persiflage from all but the most discerning eyes. They will count on the sloth or ignorance of the recipients to overlook the important facts. An example is a politician talking about war and sacrifice while understating or ignoring the deleterious effects on the economy.

If you sense that there is more to the story than meets the eye, dig in a little bit. Push past the press spokesman. In every release will be the name of an executive who is claiming credit (or responsibility) for something. Insist that you speak with that person; you want to get a direct quote. You might want to ask, for example, why the release is coming out now, if that is germane, or how certain numbers compare to the previous quarter, or how their situation contrasts with that of their competitors. Another good question is how the numbers will affect output, profitability, future earnings, expansion, hirings and firings, et cetera.

At their 1979 unveiling of the much vaunted K-car, with lots of glitz and corporate glee, company president Lee Iacocca announced that Chrysler would be producing 270,000 or so of the cars. But, he was asked, don't you need to produce 315,000 to see a profit? The answer was yes, but Iacocca ignored the question. However, the fact that he "refused" to answer was picked up and used by other reporters in their coverage.

It may seem as though most news organizations are at odds with big business, especially in the post-Enron climate of business reporting. [Enron was a scandal-plagued energy company at the turn of the millennium.] Most businesses naturally like to be seen through rose-colored glasses; it means happier investors, and more of them. Also, many businesses have been seriously burned by the media, even when they have done nothing wrong. This is because many reporters have little or no understanding of business or economics, and they unintentionally mis-state and/or misconstrue.

This problem can be aggravated by reporters who are improperly given license to adopt a tone that reflects antipathy toward "the suits," a posture seen as attractive to some news directors, especially those who are pitching to a less discerning audience.

On the other side of the problem are the reporters who openly admit that they will not cover stories that put their parent company or a partnering firm in a bad light.

Protecting the Facts

A difficulty of another sort crops up when the person actually making and/or delivering the news—not a polished spokesman—lacks the skills to make an effective presentation. Engineers, in particular, show a remarkable inability to speak coherently for public consumption. The same is true of many academics, researchers and scientists. Also, many people who are normally reasonably articulate can freeze up and forget everything they once knew when a microphone is shoved toward them. They may have nothing to hide, but their verbal clumsiness, together with a deer-in-the-headlights look, can make a dramatically poor impression.

During the Senate Watergate hearings, Joseph Montoya, a Democrat from New Mexico, put Nixon counselor John Ehrlichman in a very bad light, and it wasn't Ehrlichman's fault. Montoya, an amiable fellow, was never well-briefed, and frequently mangled what facts he attempted to assimilate. Meanwhile, Ehrlichman, a deliberately contentious fellow despite the circumstances of the hearings, showed himself to be in control throughout most of his testimony.

But when it came to fielding questions from Montoya, he hit a snag. Montoya confused his facts. Ehrlichman told him so, saying he was mixing apples and oranges. Montoya erupted, not knowing that he himself was wrong, and he filleted Ehrlichman before the national television audience. Said Ehrlichman's attorney afterwards, a bad questioner can make even a good answerer look bad.

Which brings up the point that a journalist has an obligation to present the facts clearly, even if this means rescuing them from an inarticulate deliverer. The story is what needs to be reported. It is not the duty of the journalist to protect a person, or to hide any facts; the opposite is true. But if someone is merely inept at delivering the information, then it's up to the journalist to take that information and deliver it properly.

Of course, if the delivery is part of the story, then by all means show it all. This might be the case of a public figure who is inebriated, for example, or perhaps losing his faculties. Also, a poor press front might be indicative of a company or organization that is unraveling, and that, too, could be news.

Bypassing the Agent

It is always a good idea to have a working relationship with at least one executive at the major companies and organizations in your area. Preferably, this contact is someone other than the public relations spokesperson. You never know when a story will break that requires confirmation or fleshing out and you will want an inside track on the information. It may be a national story with local implications.

For instance, when the scandal broke over the high-living of the head of the United Way, local United Way organizations came under immediate scrutiny. When the Firestone faulty tire firestorm erupted, there was at least one tire dealer in every hamlet across the country who was affected. Not that you need to make a point of going out on your lunch to meet the local franchise tire dealer, but a rich contact list is an effective time-saver.

It shouldn't be necessary to say this but night, home and cellphone numbers and email addresses of these higher-ups are very valuable. You may never need them, but when you do, it's always better to have them at hand than to go looking futilely through the phone book. And when people give you a home phone number, respect their privacy and don't call unless it's urgent.

Good Public Relations

Late one night in November of 1979, ABC Business Editor Dan Cordtz and I traveled to Hershey, Pennsylvania. The chocolate company had announced a price increase that tested President Carter's guidelines. We arrived in town after one in the morning, and were shooting at the plant not many hours later. During the shoot in the factory, we watched as a woman stood at the end of the conveyor belt where the freshly-molded bars came out of the chilling box; she was ready to recycle any bars that weren't fit for the consumer. She had her finger on a button that could dump the row of eight bars back into the recycler, and in her other hand held she held a suction device for pulling a single bar out of the row and dumping it. She had done this, we were told, seven hours a day for fourteen years.

I remarked to the public relations fellow who had arranged the shoot for us that I didn't think I could handle her job for even an hour. He smiled at me and shook his head; he couldn't either. But, he noted, when she left work at four in the afternoon, she was done for the day. Whereas we had called him at home several times in the evening, and he'd worked late and come in early to facilitate our shoot. Still, neither of us would have traded places with the woman.

And this sidebar. After the shoot, when we were ready to chopper back to New York, I asked the fellow if we might go back with some chocolate for our executive producer. He hesitated, and then quickly apologized for not giving us chocolate before we asked, and he handed over several boxes. He said he had been reticent to offer us any chocolate for fear—in the post-Watergate era of squeaky clean respectability—of appearing to try to bribe us. They didn't make enough chocolate in a year to buy better coverage than we gave them, but only because the facts were on their side.

Making Effective Use of PR

Though most journalists will scoff at press releases, they are, in fact, a useful tool in a number of ways. First, they can actually announce a story worth covering, though the ratio of good stories to releases is rather low. Second, you can often get a sense of what's doing on the local business scene and in the community by how the release is presented. Third, you can find some potentially-useful phone numbers. And fourth, you can make contact with the publicists who occasionally come across a significant story.

If you don't put them down—as is the tendency among reporters because the professions are so incestuous—you may find an ally and friend among the ranks of the practitioners of public relations. It is true, however, that most flacks are more interested in the fact of the coverage than the truth. Viz, when est-founder/guru Werner Erhardt was about to do an interview with a reporter, his publicist set up his own tape recorder, explaining that he wanted to be prepared, "just in case Werner said something new".

The fact is that there are probably as many good PR people as there are good reporters, and whenever the twain shall meet, they can do some good work together. They share the same goals—to get information to the public—and when they work together, they will present the information clearly and completely.

7. Scoops

Being first with a story is always a thrill, but being first is not as important as being accurate. If you've got a good scoop, it isn't ready for air until it has been nailed down. Scoops can be very seductive. Sometimes news operations will unearth a story of little interest, but because they are the only ones to report it, they consider it a scoop. That's a looser definition of the term than some would use. Most journalists believe that a scoop (1) has to contain significant new information and (2) must be reported ahead of the competition.

Watergate was rife with scoops, many of them accurate. One factor was that Watergate was an umbrella that comprised a number of different elements, from the actual break-in at the Watergate building to The Plumbers, and the domestic spying program, Cointelpro. At several points during the Watergate coverage, a number of major leads would develop at the same time leading in different directions. The issues news organizations had to confront were, Whom to believe,

Who can corroborate and How long could they sit on a story before another news organization would get it on the air?

On one occasion, Sam Donaldson, ABC's lead reporter on Watergate went on the air with a report about a Watergate connection with someone named Harry Dent. I was an assistant producer on the coverage, and had developed my own sources, one of whom told me that Donaldson had gotten it wrong; that it was Frederick Dent who was involved. Unhappily, ABC had to air a retraction.

Elections reporting is all about scoops, all night long, and sometimes longer. The networks pushed their vote analyzers to call as quickly as possible, trying to call winners before the others, and have bragging rights for the "best" coverage. There can be a lot of struggling and squirming over projections, trying to be first, but also not wanting to make a mistake. Do they have enough data yet? Is there a chance the race could change direction? How close can their competitors be to calling with these same numbers?

The three major networks got their fingers badly burned in the 2000 presidential race in Florida when they called Al Gore the winner of the state fairly early and then had to retract the projection. [At the time, the networks received vote totals and projections from the Voter News Service.] It was believed that the fault lay in the vote counting service, which simply got some numbers wrong, and that the networks mis-processed them and passed them along to the world. Ironically, the voter information service had the right numbers, on the basis of exit polling, but because the Palm Beach County ballots were confusing, the intentions of the voters as registered in the surveys conflicted with the actual votes cast.

Accuracy is particularly important on a breaking story when your scoop might affect that story. Obviously, with all of the scoops that popped during Watergate, the results were that it pushed people to resign or be indicted. Eventually the coverage forced Nixon's resignation. When you are working on a story that can change events, it is even more important that you make very sure that it is error-free.

Another example of when scooping intertwines with events was in Afghanistan in 2001. At one point, eight foreign aid workers, convicted by the Taliban of preaching the wrong faith, suddenly turned up free in Pakistan. Everyone wondered how it could have happened. One report said the Taliban had freed them, which would have signaled a significant change in their policy. A second report said that U.S. Special Operations forces had staged a successful military mission to free the aid workers. But then a third report indicated that the eight had been liberated by locals after the Taliban had fled. Which ultimately meant that we had not yet seen any indication of a split among the Taliban, and that the war would continue to be prosecuted with full vigor.

Finally, the best scoops are those with legs. That is, when a reporter breaks open a story that will require continuing rather than single-shot coverage. Maybe it's a story of political corruption, or corporate misdeeds, but if you get on top of an important story alone, you can dominate the airwaves for days and even weeks, earning a reputation as an investigative reporter.

The Happy Rockefeller Story

In late fall 1974, I was working as an overnight assignment editor at the WCBS Television News desk, in between freelance producing stints there. It was two on a Sunday morning, and the overnight news writer had gone home early, entrusting the unlikely updates for the 2:42am voice-over slide newscast to me. [They used slides instead of computer graphics then.] In fact, I'd already had to rewrite the lead to report a major and bloody coup in Africa when the call came in from Trish Reilly.

Trish was a correspondent for WCBS who enjoyed the higher social circles. Though some might have dismissed her for her beauty, she was as bright as she was attractive. That night she'd been at a party in Connecticut with a man who was the head of public relations for a New York hospital. He told Trish that Happy Rockefeller, the wife the of Vice President of the United States, would be coming into the hospital that evening (Sunday) and would be undergoing her second mastectomy the next day.

Trish was as sure of the story as I was of her. But I made a few calls, including two to Rockefeller's top aide Hugh Morrow. I explained the information we had to the Rockefeller operator, and she informed Morrow. On the second call, she confirmed that Morrow had this information, and that she had relayed to him that we would go with the story if it weren't denied. She said Morrow understood but didn't wish to return the call. I asked the operator if she had told him everything. Yes, she said, she had.

That was good enough for me, what with what Trish had been told. It was implausible that the man would have lied to her, and even more unlikely that Morrow wouldn't block a false story about the Second

Lady of the United States. Especially such a story. So I wrote a new lead, with "WCBS news has learned...", and "It is reported that...." It was simple and clear, without any horn-tooting. Which was the way it should be, considering the nature of the report. And it went on the newscast; an announcer read the copy to the few folks who were watching old grade "B" movies at that time.

It turned out that one of those folks was at UPI, who called WCBS to confirm the story. I repeated what we had, but didn't reveal the source. I then passed on the information to the dayside editor at 8:00 that morning and headed home for bed. The phone rang an hour later. The office wanted to know where I had gotten the story. From Trish, I said; I had explained everything to my relief guy. What was the problem? I asked. The hospital PR director, I was told, had backed off the story.

Trish stood by what she had said and I stood by what I had written. I had only a brief flash of primal panic when I wondered how something of which I was so sure could have been wrong. It couldn't. The PR director must be lying to protect himself. The Rockefellers knew what we were going with and would have said something if it was wrong.

When WCBS went on the air with its regularly-scheduled newscast at 7:00 that night, the anchorman reported what had been reported 17 hours earlier, but observed that no one had shown up at the hospital. Listening to his copy, I could hear the station doing some backpedaling. With phrases like "When we first learned of this story..." and "but now the information...," they looked like they were trying to cover themselves.

And then, to many peoples' surprise, Paul Dandridge broke in on the anchor. He was the WCBS reporter at a live remote at the hospital, back in the days when live remotes were uncommon, and particularly so on a weekend. Dandridge reported—live and in color, as it happened—that the Rockefellers were at this moment coming through the door.

The relief was visible on the anchor's face, but there were no phone calls to me that night. Nor the next morning, and my fear sense was growing active. I made a phone call and found out that I was "in trouble." I called Marv Friedman, the assignment manager who supervised my desk work. "I'm sorry, Tony," Marvin said, probably meaning it, "I was told not to use you anymore. You're off the schedule effective immediately."

I attempted phone calls and letters to get through to News Director Ed Joyce, the person who had made the decision, but he never responded. I learned later that the reason why I had been fired was that I had failed to call him at home to get permission to run the story. Joyce went on to climb the CBS News ladder, and later slipped and fell. I sent to him a sincere note of regret, but never received a reply.

8. The Assignment Desk

The Assignment Desk is the first point of action for a television news operation. Whether there is a full-fledged operation such as at the networks, with a domestic editor, a foreign editor, and a host of supporting personnel, or it's another hat worn by the anchorman/news director who determines the coverage at a small market station, it is the assignment desk that usually first learns of a news story and then organizes the coverage. While the assignment desk doesn't have the glamour that sometimes accrues to reporters in the field, it is equally on their shoulders that the success of the broadcast rests.

Essentially, the purpose of the assignment desk is to determine what events are worthy of coverage by a reporter, with or without a videographer, and then to arrange that coverage. If the only news event on the schedule was only a fifteen-minutes news conference a block away at nine in the morning, it wouldn't be too complicated, but inevitably there are more stories worth covering than there are staffers to cover them. So the job of the assignment desk is logistics—moving people and equipment around to cover stories and to get the coverage back in time to prepare it for broadcast.

While there is often occasion for some snap decision-making, for the most part, the work of the desk is planning of coverage of scheduled events like public meetings, demonstrations, press conferences and ribbons-cutting. The assignment desk needs to understand the scope of each story—geography, time, subject matter—to know what is required to cover, in terms of time, equipment and personnel. Also, they need to know how important the story is, in case another, more deserving story needs coverage.

For instance, a press conference about the city master plan might require three hours of a reporter's attendance, but if most of the information is going to be covered in the script, rather than sound bites, you may not have to tie down a videographer for the whole morning. Another example of knowing the particular needs of a story would be a press conference at the chamber of commerce where you may be able to cover using the lights of another station's crews. There are also some stories that require no thought, like when the cherry trees blossom; at some point you'll get a videographer to shoot for fifteen artful minutes to capture all of the pictures you need.

Good desk people are those who understand not only know how to cover a story, but what footage will wind up on the evening news. They will spend the day acquiring that footage as efficiently as possible, while making sure that they are in position to cover emergencies, if need be, and to still have the necessary resources committed to live shots and evening coverage.

Some of these decisions are about equipment and travel time, but most are about personnel, and specifically the reporters and videographers. One of the most important factors in determining how well the assignment desk functions is how well they know the strengths and weaknesses of The Troops, the people they send out to get the news. Some videographers work better when they aren't rushed; others are cowboys when it comes to breaking news like fires or plane crashes but can be slipshod when it comes to shooting an interview. Some videographers just take pictures, while others capture the story.

The same is true of reporters. The desk needs to know which of the reporters work best under pressure. Some reporters are truly camera-shy and can barely get through taping a standupper, while others come alive when the on-air tally light on the camera turns red. Some reporters are more deliberate, and are best suited to shooting in the morning and having extra time to edit in the afternoon. Others seem to do better when they don't have a lot of time to think. At the smaller markets, few such differentiations exist; everyone covers as much as possible as fast as possible, often shooting and editing the stories they report.

Of course, no assignment desk ever has a full compliment of differently-talented people to send out to cover every story. So under adverse circumstances, the desk will want to send out a strong producer with a weak reporter, or a veteran reporter out with a rookie camerawoman. Ideally, everyone is a polished professional, but there is no ideal, even at the networks.

(Some producers, like ABC's Greg Dobbs and Mike Von Fremd, who have shifted to the front of the camera and become correspondents understand the larger picture; i.e., they can produce themselves. But few reporters have gone behind the camera to become producers; they like the glamour, and who can blame them. However, one of the best producers ever, Pete Simmons, did some reporting work first.)

It's also true that the more that people know, the more they are relied upon; which is why some people choose to hide their knowledge. But in strained economic times, it stands to reason that reporters who know how to produce and producers who know how to report are going to be in the greater demand. Even in the best of times, when you have a full complement of reporters and producers, the more multi-faceted are your people, the better backstopped you are in the event, for instance, that a story goes in two different directions.

Also on the issue of assigning people, you want to consider the personality of the people you are sending and on what kind of story. For example, some reporters are particularly good at covering crime and disaster stories, while others stand out reporting on the financial machinations in a boardroom. You also are likely to have reporters who do a better job in one neighborhood than another; someone who handles pathos with dignity, another who can elicit intelligible sound cuts from bureaucrats.

Again, it is important for the desk to understand the breadth of the story and to know as much as possible in advance what kind of coverage will be required. Is it a simple interview and a wrap-around standupper? Is a lot of b-roll—extra shooting, editing and writing—going to be necessary? On the first story, you can send anyone, but on the second, you are going to get better coverage from a videographer who thinks like an editor.

Stories whose events are going to be finished by lunchtime—a scheduled news conference, for example—can be delegated to a wider range of reporters and cameramen than can a story that doesn't begin to unfold until mid-afternoon, e.g., a jury returning with a verdict.

Another consideration is single-day versus continuing stories. The former can be picked up by an available body, whereas an on-going story with new developments should be put in the same hands every day.

Of course, there are few assignment desks with any real latitude. At the networks, where on a major breaking story money is less of a restriction, there are many more options for coverage. At a small local station, there are often no options at all. The reporter is also the shooter and editor, and is expected to deliver a full report for the five o'clock, plus a scripted voice-over for the eleven.

But given some room to operate, the assignment desk will approach its work in two ways, mainly as a recipient of news leads, and secondarily they will be going out to find the news. It's always a goal to generate footage on as many stories as possible, to provide the producer with as many options as possible, so they will take the calendar of scheduled events and pick out the most important for coverage. Where logistics allow, they will assign a second tier of stories. But these assignments are always made with an eye on what-if's; you always want to be able to get coverage of suddenly-breaking stories. This means knowing which crews will be where, how quickly they can move and what coverage will be lost if they do.

Then, beyond covering the planned events and breaking news, the desk needs to infiltrate the community through a deliberate outreach, so that people with news come to you, instead of going to other news outlets, or simply sitting on the information. Outreach consists of making sure that you have not only contacts, but also good relations, with business and civic organizations, unions and various social and political factions. A good relationship is not about toadying, but about having a reputation for quality news coverage. You want to be known as fair, both to the newsmakers in your community as well as to the average viewer.

Practically speaking, there are two ways to reach into the market or ADI (Area of Dominant Influence). One is geographic and the other is by subject. All other factors being equal, it would be grand to have different sections of the market assigned to different reporters. By making a particular community the responsibility of one person, it not only induces the reporter to focus on the individual beat, but it also enhances the station's identity in the area. There is an identifiable reporter on doings in that neighborhood; a person to call if there is a news story in that district.

The second division of the market would be by subject; one reporter for city hall, another for business, a third for cops-'n-court, et cetera. Few local stations have the staff to follow this approach, but it would certainly make sense if each reporter could be encouraged to develop a specialty. Then when the opportunity presented itself, the one with the greater expertise could be assigned the coverage.

Newsmaker Access

It has been said that the most important tool of the assignment desk is the Rolodex, and it's true; you want to have every newsmaker's business, home and cellphone number. You also want to have a history with these people, so when it comes to talking to the press, you are the person at the top of their call list. This is accomplished by reporters spending the time to make themselves known to the newsmakers.

Even the sleaziest newsmakers prefer better news coverage than poor, and they know that they will get it from the best journalists. They know that the merely pretty face reporters generally cover allegations in detail while giving short shrift to the denials; because it's easier. Real journalists leave the convictions to the juries.

Reporters can develop relationships when they are out in the field on stories. When they have time, it would be useful for assignment editors to go out themselves to public events and newsmakers' offices, putting their face to a name. They might drop off their business cards; in some cases with their home phone numbers handwritten on the back, for those people who don't want to call a news outlet.

(Business cards are a invaluable extra which you should get for yourself if the station won't. They don't have to be expensive—less than $20—and they come in very useful. You may find yourself next to someone you can't speak to publicly, but you can discreetly hand over your card.)

The serious news people make a point of meeting not only the newsmakers, but also their aides and secretaries; these are usually the people who control access to the principals. They are likely to be more help to the journalist who openly recognizes their importance and shows them respect.

This is particularly true when you have frequent and/or ongoing contact with a person or a company. Quick access to public or corporate officials can make the difference between scoring a coup or missing a story. If you've taken the time to visit the city manager's office and introduced yourself to his personal secretary, you're a long way ahead when it comes time to ask for a late interview.

Stringers

Though the practice seems out of vogue, setting up a list of stringers can pay off richly. Stringers are people who aren't on your payroll but do freelance work. Some of them in urban areas will cruise around, particularly on nights and weekends, listening to the police scanner, and pick up footage of fires, major accidents and crimes and sell it to local stations.

Some of the most significant footage ever shown on a network has been taken by freelancers who happened to be in the midst of a breaking story. Also, many amateurs have video cameras and produce some spectacular pictures; the attack on the World Trade Center and the destruction of the Columbia shuttle are good examples.

Stringers can be anyone and anywhere, and they can be particularly useful in outlying areas. A local station can reach out on the air and through its website for people who might be interested in stringing. It is useful to know about them in advance, perhaps even to have seen their work, in case you want to call on someone in an outlying area, for example, to cover a breaking story before you own cameraman can reach the scene.

(Indeed, with the proliferation of home video cameras, a news director would be well advised to find out who can shoot usable tape. This might be done by holding an amateur photographer's contest; perhaps managed in conjunction with local video store, which might buy a whole slew of commercial time for the visibility.)

On an August night in 1977 when the Son of Sam was finally captured, I had just returned on a late flight from an assignment in Chicago and was lying in bed waiting to fall asleep. I was listening to the WCBS radio news headlines at 12:33 when the bulletin came over that the killer had been arrested outside of the city and was being driven to police headquarters in downtown Manhattan. David Berkowitz—the Son of Sam, also known as the .44-Caliber Killer—had shot six people to death in New York City, creating, as one might expect, a lot of hype and fear.

I called the ABC assignment desk to make sure they knew—they didn't—and twenty minutes and a well-tipped cab driver later, I was pulling up at police headquarters. Only a few other people were there, mostly the curious rather than the press. At 1:15, the police brought in their suspect. There were no camera crews there, only a freelance photographer, and I bought his film for ABC.

Pooling

Assignment editors should make an effort to know the competition. Personally. While most of the time you will be trying to outfox them or get a better angle on a story, there will be times when cooperation will be essential and you will want to pool resources. On a breaking story that is going in different directions, for example, or when coverage is out of town and you really need more than one camera to get the important footage.

Pooling is the sharing of people, equipment, and/or facilities by two or more news organizations to create a team to produce coverage for the pool members. This is frequently done in coverage of the President, or in a smaller market it might be a situation like a trial where everyone had access to the same shots and just those. Also, many judges and some other public officials will insist on pool coverage at their events.

During the 1976 presidential campaign the three major commercial networks agreed to each cover one of the scheduled debates as a pool. ABC had the Philadelphia debate, and right in the middle, the audio died. As the story goes, it was a 25-cent capacitor that blew. For reasons that never satisfied anyone, the people and equipment assigned to the pool were inadequate to get them back on the air for a half-hour. The humiliation was not limited to ABC; the industry had failed. And being at ABC felt like second class. The bottom line is that if you are involved in a pool, send your best people and equipment. Raise the standard, don't lower it.

And speaking of equipment, the top assignment desks are prepared for whatever comes through the door, whether it be old family daguerreotypes, or something much more modern, like 8mm film; or any type of tape, from two-inch to mini-DV. Most stations won't have the equipment on premises to handle every medium, but they should know where to get it converted. It is up to the assignment desk to deliver the news in a medium that can be edited and broadcast.

Team Role

Ultimately, of course, the assignment desk works for the news director and the news show producers, though it is always better if the shared attitude is working *with* rather than *for*. Everyone needs to be on the same page when it comes to their definition of news—what is covered and how—and that's simply a matter of sharing views of the final product. The most successful news operations function like a team, with the assignment desk performing their tasks with an overt understanding of the editorial perspective and the production requirements of those who put the news on the air. Conversely, the producers who keep the assignment desk in the loop throughout the day get the most out of their reporters and crews.

I began my career on the overnight assignment desk at ABC Television News in New York. Most of my time was spent ripping wire copy from the eleven news and cable machines, answering phones, mimeographing and collating and stapling; and walking several blocks at three in the morning to get a hamburger for the editor. I knew immediately and never forgot that The Desk was the heart of the news operation. We were the people who first learned the news. We were the people who responded by committing large sums of money moving crews and equipment around the world at all hours of the day and night. It was where the assimilation-manipulation-dissemination process began, and never stopped.

It has been observed that the desk is sometimes a refuge more than a goal, attracting the less flashy news types. In fact, many earnest journalists choose the desk because they simply find field work too stressful, or they don't want to be on the road. It takes a certain personality to sit at a desk reading wires, talking on the phone constantly and wading through the traffic of moving people around all day, but the fact is that it can be very satisfying work.

9. Reporting

Reporting is the essence of journalism. It is the assimilation, manipulation and dissemination of information. Whether it is the anchor reading a twenty-second item or a correspondent reporting a two-minute package from the field, the work is to select the critical facts and deliver them in a clear and concise fashion. Most of this book is about various facets of reporting.

A reporter should know enough about a subject to speak about it off the cuff in an informing manner for twenty minutes. Since the average television news report is about a minute-thirty, this means that you need to seriously comprehend roughly twelve times the information that you're going to report. It's probably just a coincidence, but that's similar to the ratio of videotape shot to tape that makes the air, and it underscores the work of the journalist—to reduce a detailed event into a comprehensible news report. The bottom line is that the more you know, the greater your understanding of a situation, the better you can explain it, providing a context as well as the facts. That's the work of a journalist.

Every report should have has a beginning, a middle and an end. Unlike the printed word, television reporting doesn't allow the viewer to go back and re-read a paragraph that is unclear; most people don't tape newscasts let alone replay them. So a television reporter must write, produce and report a story that presents facts in a linear fashion that connects dots in the viewer's mind to create a comprehensive package of information.

The extra advantage—and added challenge—for a television journalist is the use of visuals to help to tell the story. The added task of the television reporter is to make the script and visuals work together, so that when the story is reported, it will be complete in the viewer's mind.

Television reporters are limited by time. A typical television news report might run about a minute-thirty, and including sound bites, be told in a total of less than 250 words. You can fit the entire script of a network news half-hour into the space of the front page of your newspaper, above the fold.

Television reporters also face strict deadlines. There are no presses to stop. Further, television newscasts are finite; you can't simply cut or ad pages as you can with a newspaper. That means most reporters given an assignment need to produce what's expected of them, or spike the story long before the anchor reads its lead-in.

Because many television news reports are told with images and sound bites, the good reporters are thinking about cover shots and potential interviews the moment they are assigned the story.

The top reporters will start to frame the story in their minds based on the possibility that they will have to go on live without shooting a single second of tape. Their car could break down, or a camera could malfunction and they wouldn't know it until they were back in the editing room. Starting from that baseline of a live standupper without any production support, they then collect the sound bites and b-roll on tape and begin to flesh out a tape package.

A critical starting point in reporting is understanding the viewers' knowledge base. The correspondent must report the new facts in a context that presumes a certain level of awareness on the part of the audience. For instance, reporting for a New York City station, you don't have to explain where is the Hudson River, but a network reporter might would have to locate it for the audience between New York and New Jersey.

Professional Distance

Perspective is an essential aspect of good reporting. Even if you know that the entire audience shares your personal outrage—or exhilaration—you must take particular care not to take a position. You are reporting, not cheerleading. It is not for you to make value judgments nor to shape minds with tinted copy. Even the weather caster who says we should pray for rain is getting closer to his audience than a professional perspective requires.

Welcoming home the local sports hero, you might be tempted to be overtly upbeat. But resist the temptation to get personally involved. Yes, it is important to reflect the excited atmosphere of the homecoming, but let the crowd show it. Your job is to report what is outside of yourself, untainted by personal feelings. If the sports hero turns out to have cheated, at least your own credibility will not be questioned.

It may seem that this point of non-involvement is being over-emphasized, but especially those people just starting in the business need to know that your professional integrity is your most important credential. If you lose the trust of your viewers, your ability to communicate is compromised. Like virginity, integrity is something that once lost can never be regained. That's why you don't want to be caught making a mistake. People sitting in their living rooms watching the television love to catch a reporter making a mistake. It's a jealousy thing, endemic in our culture as deTocqueville noted a century and a half ago, that Americans tend to want to pull down those above rather that raise themselves to a higher standard.

If you're on the air, you're a target. That is another reason why humility serves a good cause. If you're not arrogant, your errors don't mean as much. Especially if it was an accident in note-taking, or if you were lied to by a source. If you were making a sincere effort, that counts against an error. Laziness, on the other hand, as might be manifest through obvious misspellings or asking a dumb question in a live interview, earn scorn which is etched in long-term memories.

More serious, you don't ever want to get close to looking like you received benefits from your reporting. You can never show favoritism, even to well-known charities. Look at the scandals that have beset not only corporate America, but the Catholic Church, the American Red Cross and the United Way. By maintaining your personal distance from all social and civic organizations, you might receive some opprobrium for non-involvement, but people who respect the news will understand and respect you for not taking the easier, more "acceptable" choice of community participation. Your reporting is your contribution to the community, and an underlying reason why you want to do it right.

When a story is ostensibly one-sided—the town cheers the decision to build a new sewage treatment plant—and there is little or no apparent opposition, it is incumbent upon the reporter to provide some balance. If you can't find any significant opposition to discuss the matter, you might note in your script that certain issues have to be discussed before the planning commission, e.g., Will the bond issue passed to build the plant mean higher taxes? Will the plant be big enough to meet the needs of the community in ten years, when it's finally paid for? Is the plant a band-aid solution? Another route is to list the people or groups yet to be heard from on the issue, e.g., noting that environmentalists have opposed the sewage treatment plant because the residue threatens the aquifer. You don't have to be the community hair-shirt, but you should examine all the available information from a variety of perspectives.

There is no occasion when it is appropriate to show support or negativity. You don't know if a priest will be defrocked or the businessman of the year will be accused of dipping into the till. Even people who have had clean records for years can get into trouble. If you have been visibly supportive of them, your objectivity will be open to question. You can be pleased about the success of a local business leader, but let her supporters tell you how wonderful she is. Have the neighbors extol the virtues of the local shopping center. But make sure you listen carefully if all of the voices aren't a chorus. And listen to your gut. Remembering, you have the task—and the excuse—of reporting the facts.

There are times when as a reporter you might feel as though you are getting too drawn in to a story. For example, when a person goes missing and you feel natural empathy for the family. Be sure to maintain a professional distance. Even if they are obvious victims, in the moment, you can't be sure of all the facts right away. These people may have a history; they may even be responsible for the disappearance. This is said not to sound melodramatic but to share a concern about how easy it is to be deceived, to be taken in by less than honorable people.

If you feel yourself getting personally involved, back off and regain your perspective. The emotions—the thrill of victory and the agony of defeat—can be beguiling. Take a deep breath and remember that your report isn't more important than your reputation or career. It is merely a slice of time, a captured moment, significant in itself, but only a very small part. As T.S. Eliot said, "Except for the point, the still point, there would be no dance, and there is only the dance."

Competitive Positioning

On occasion you will find yourself competing with other reporters for the attention of a newsmaker. This can take the form of a formal press conference, or a rat pack chasing a busy or unwilling victim down a sidewalk. Sometimes it will just be one or two other people. In all of these situations, your approach can make a big difference in what you get out of the person.

Some reporters think that it is more important to ask the question than to elicit the answer. This syndrome is particularly visible during Presidential press conferences when it is clear on a number of the faces of reporters who jump up screaming for the President's attention that getting on the air is the essential act. In fact, most of the real news out of the White House comes through private sources.

The reporter who is more interested in the information than the exposure will hold back and let the others ask the obvious questions. This serves two functions. First, it doesn't reveal who you (or your information) are prematurely to the speaker. If the other reporters have identified themselves through their questions as hostile, the person may turn to you for relief. The other advantage is that you may phrase your question in such a way as to plug holes left by the previous questions. And then your questions not only evoke the most significant answers, but you also look good in asking them.

Good English

The English language, somewhat Americanized, is a primary tool of our journalistic craft, and should be respected. Diction and pronunciation are a part of reporting as well, and should be honed to an art. Reporters should be paragons of good usage.

The use of slang has its place, but generally reporters should speak the language simply, clearly and precisely. Good grammar is important, too, but not to the point that it is distracting.

Personal style is fine, again only so long as it doesn't become a distraction. And it should be an outgrowth of intelligent scripting and practiced delivery. Don't try to put on a style for its own sake. It comes across as phony, which it is. Basically, the most compelling and engaging styles have been those that were indeliberately developed but became a signature for a reporter's delivery.

First Person Singular

Many news operations call on reporters to say "I" or "me" in their scripts. Like the over-used "Live" super, it is intended to boost ratings, in this case by pushing the image of the reporter to the front of the story. "The fire chief told me that the blaze started in the basement." Actually, the fire chief told all of the six reporters on the scene where the fire started, so the use of "me" falsely implies that the reporter had the information exclusively. Even if the fire chief told the reporter alone, in most instances it is not such important information that it needs to be flagged as an exclusive.

The issue of using the first person is more than one of deceit or vanity. A good reporter is supposed to channel information from the source to the viewer, processing the raw data, extracting the salient information, and delivering it to the audience. By using "I" or "me," the flow of the information is stopped— albeit briefly—at the reporter. The viewer is forced to see the reporter as part of the news, and this interrupts the flow of the story. Unfortunately, a number of stations seek to boost their ratings by making news rather than covering it. Part of this scenario calls for making the reporters part of the story. But would you expect a waiter to sit down at your table before serving your food?

Geraldo Rivera, Howard Cosell and Mike Wallace all became bigger than the stories they covered, thus detracting in some instances from the integrity of their coverage. In some circumstances the journalist is forced to participate, but more often it is a news consultant who is pushing promotion of the reporter rather than the reportage.

The best reporters are transparent. That is, they act as a conduit for the information they report without distracting the viewer by making themselves part of the story. They are motivated by the desire to inform, rather than driven by an ego to be seen. Frank Gardner, one of the finest reporters in the country, was let go in part because he refused to insert himself in the stories he covered. He resisted saying "I" and "me" and putting himself on camera when it didn't advance the story. The best reporters are those who are invisible personally, while being recognized for their work.

After the Watergate affair, journalism and particularly television journalism, were basking in the glow of public appreciation. The excitement drew many otherwise-uninterested people to the limelight. Consultants encouraged the establishment of special investigative units. "Investigative reporter" became a calling second only to god. The term is redundant, or should be. Any reporter worth his salt is investigating every story he covers. That's what the job is about: gathering information from multiple perspectives, digesting it and then reporting it. Otherwise, staff announcers and voice coaches could read press releases and we'd call it news.

Some of these points may seem somewhat picky, but for on-air people, any mistakes will be picked up by some segment of the audience. If the talent's image isn't impeccable, they run the risk of losing some of their audience at a particularly critical time. It's like the girl who cried wolf. If a major story breaks, is the viewer going to watch the person who has made a lot of small mistakes or the person who hasn't? The station that has a reputation for consistently high quality journalism will be the one viewers turn to in a crisis.

10. Field Producer

The job of the field producer, mostly a network position, is to oversee the news coverage of an event from the time the assignment is made until the production has been on the air. He makes sure that all of the necessary people are on the scene, with all of the necessary equipment and facilities, in time to capture the story elements, package them for broadcast, and deliver them for air.

Often this means working with crews and correspondents from different domestic or foreign bureaus, and sometimes from affiliates or broadcast operations in other countries. He will occasionally find himself in places he's never been before, arranging transportation and editing and transmission facilities, after he has first found someone who can speak his own language. Much of the job is facilitating the work of the crew and correspondent, but in addition to handling the logistics of the coverage, he also oversees the editorial side, i.e., the script and how it integrates in the broadcast with leads-in and related coverage.

Usually at the network, the producers and correspondents know each other's jobs, and have the ability to fill in for the other. Frequently, correspondents are sent out without producers, and vice versa. Similarly, a field producer will conduct interviews and occasionally write scripts, for instance, when no correspondent is available and the story turns into a voice-over for the anchor. If there is a correspondent, the field producer—if he isn't required elsewhere on the story—will consult on the editorial content of the story, from questions for interviews to the choice of sound cuts and the final scripting.

11. Be Prepared

Most reporters frequently find themselves on their feet on the go. They are gunslingers or firefighters or the Minutemen. They go to the action, report on it and move on to the next story. This is not said in any way pejoratively, but to describe an active person who has to be ready to meet varying circumstances without a lot of warning. You can be called at any hour of the day or night and you have to be able to shift into high gear to get to your assignment with alacrity.

During my years as a field producer for ABC News, I carried a small (14"Wx6"Dx12"H) shoulder bag with me at all times. In that bag were a cassette recorder with extra tapes and batteries and phone connector, pens, a marker, note pads, change, aspirin, gum, mints, Chapstick, a current copy of the pocket OAG (Official Airlines Guide) and occasionally a small 35mm camera. Also, a compact in case the correspondent or an interviewee were too shiny. The change including plenty of dimes, back when that would buy you a phone call and the cellphone was an uncommon accessory. The coins are still a good idea for parking meters, toll booths and pay phones where cellphones don't work.

I chose to carry a shoulder bag instead of a briefcase because it left my hands free to take notes, hold a microphone or light, or to open doors. When covering breaking news, there are many times when an extra hand makes a world of difference. A shoulder bag slung over the back and out of the way meant that I could use my right hand to shift President Carter around to face the camera while recording his comments on the tape recorder held in my left.

Being that I was at the network, it also made sense for me to have my passport with me. On more than one occasion I was sent on the road without a chance to pack a bag, and once it was on an assignment out of the country. A passport is useful for identification, especially in today's security-conscious world.

If you drive to work, it makes sense to keep a small bag with fresh clothes and ditty bag in your trunk. You might also include some snack-type items, the kind that don't get stale, because one night you will find yourself in a motel or on a stake-out in the middle of nowhere with wet clothes and you won't have eaten in more hours than you'd care to count.

Also in the back of the car, you might want to keep a thermal blanket, water, flares and a flashlight and a transistor radio with extra batteries. A roll of duct tape and some sheet plastic isn't a bad idea, not for protection against terrorist attacks, but to provide shelter in inclement weather.

The issue of appearance is taken up later, but on the subject of being prepared, you need to remember that covering the news can be a messy business. Bad weather is the cause of a considerable amount of news, and if you're outdoors covering it, you don't want to worry about a blouse getting ruined. The fact is that general assignment reporting will take its toll on your wardrobe. Most reporters don't know day to day where their assignments will take them. They need to look appropriate in a board room, but also be able to walk through a crime scene without looking too out of place. If there is any advice to offer, it would be to wear clothes that wear well.

Being prepared often means making do. On the night of Jimmy Carter's Inauguration, I was working for *Good Morning America*. I had gone to bed mid-afternoon after a long night and morning of coverage when a call at 7:30pm awakened me. They needed me to produce the coverage of the Georgia Ball—one of four—at the Washington, D.C. armory. But first I had to cab from my hotel to the ABC Washington Bureau to pick up credentials.

Because it was Inauguration Day and the traffic was snarled with celebrants and motorcades, I couldn't find a cab so I walked the dozen blocks in the frigid January night. I got the credentials, and to my astonishment, there was an available cab in front of the bureau. Stunned and excited, I signaled it, opened the back door and jumped in.

Suddenly there was the sound of tearing cloth and I felt a cold swirl of air around my crotch. The tear went from the bottom of the zipper all the way to the belt loop in back. I did my best with a couple of safety pins I carried in my shoulder bag, and was glad of the long overcoat I was wearing. Until I arrived at the armory where the ball was being held; the temperature was over 80 degrees.

Doug Almond, an ever-resourceful cameraman, had the answer: gaffer's tape, now familiar to all Americans as duct tape, that silver filament tape that gets stuck to itself and is often difficult to tear where you want. I took a roll up to the men's room to engineer the repair. I put a strip lengthwise down the crotch and the seam held all night.

12. Taking Notes

It probably shouldn't need to be said, but every reporter worth her salt is always ready to take notes. Where she sits, where she sleeps, when she's riding the subway. Always at hand are at least one writing implement and something on which to take notes. I would go so far as to say that you should never leave the house without a pen or pencil that you can operate with one hand. This may seem obsessive, but the fact is sometimes you need to be able to write on the run, literally, and the fewer impediments to your note-taking, the more information you can gather and more quickly.

In the old days, reporters for some news services had to know shorthand. Today, most reporters not only don't know shorthand, but they leave note-taking to their tape recorders. Tape recorders are great for recording verbatims and timing sound cuts while you're preparing a script, but note-taking the old-fashioned way with a pen and notepad is a better practice for digesting the information you need to manipulate into a script.

Note-taking is a pre-editing process that can help you to formulate your thoughts in advance of putting them into final form. The fact of actually writing notes helps you to anchor thoughts and frame concepts. When taking notes, your mind has to function in a manner beyond just hearing the information; your brain has to translate ideas into muscle movement to form the letters, and your eyes record what you are writing. This creates a significantly richer foundation in your mind that will help with the final storytelling.

While you don't have to learn Gregg or Pittman to take copious notes, it certainly would be useful. Most reporters develop their own shorthand; more like short cuts, abbreviating the obvious, writing numerals instead of words, using initials instead of names and leaving out unnecessary words. A tip: whenever you are taking notes, whether at a sit-down interview or a press conference or describing a dam burst as you're running for high ground, write down the time. This will help you to keep order, especially in the hectic environment of a breaking news story. Also, you can often find a shot or sound cut more easily, especially if your videographer is recording real-time on the tape.

There is another reason to take notes, even if you also use a tape recorder. The machine may not be functioning, a fact that might not be apparent at the time. Unless your working on a feature story, you rarely have time to shoot an interview twice. And if the camera isn't recording, it's you, your memory, and your notes that will carry the coverage. You will look a lot more convincing telling your story without tape if you are able to access important information from your notes.

Finally, much of news coverage is on-the-fly. You often have to pick up a lot of brand new information very quickly, without knowing what will be important later. This is particularly true of a breaking story, in a new location with new players. It is wise to capture as many names and phone numbers as you can as you get from a story, because you don't know who, what, or where will be significant later.

A challenge for many reporters is remembering new names and putting them with the new faces. Repeat back to people their names as they give them to you—you always want to pronounce people's names correctly—and spell them aloud as you write them down, to avoid errors. You will appreciate this later when you are making a list of supers for your spot and don't have to go calling at the last minute for a correct spelling. There are a number of memory tricks you can try, but in addition to saying the name aloud and writing it down, you can also make a note about some unique aspect of the person's appearance, e.g., big ears, red jacket, next to tall cop.

13. Interviewing

The common reason for interviewing people is to get them to say on camera what might otherwise be included in a script, but which gains significance because it comes directly from a player in the story. Viewed this way, the purpose of an interview is not to elicit new information, but to generate a sound cut, i.e., in many instances, the purpose of taping an interview is to make a news report into better television.

That said, the visuals of a television interview aren't usually very dynamic, in this, a visual medium. Therefore, subtle visual nuances become more important, as does the content of the interview. Obviously this matters less if you are just going for a couple of short sound bites than if you have filling a ten-minute segment with one talking head.

But the substance of an interview is the almost always what is said, and while you have questions, and an expectation of some answers, neither you nor the interviewee is working from a script. The fact is that unlike the feature interviews with major public figures who are used to doing television, most news interviews are more complicated. For one thing, you have little control of what the interviewee will say or how.

Interviewing is an art, even if you're just going for an obvious sound bite. A good reporter is always thinking in terms of possible sound cuts for his piece as the words are being spoken, thinking ahead to the edit room and what copy will be needed in the script to set up a sound cut, or how the sound cut will flow into the next part of the script.

You can do some pulling-'n-pushing in the editing room, but if your interviewee is very good or not very good at all, you will find yourself with surprisingly few options. Which means that you must take advantage of the opportunity that presents itself during the taping to shape the final piece.

It might be said that in many cases, interviewing is less an art than it is an exercise in being present, knowing how to read the other person, to put people at ease, to elicit the information you seek in a way that will be comprehensible to the viewers.

The trick is no trick at all: deal with your interviewee honestly.

Know what you are talking about. Ask your questions directly, without any knowingness in your manner. Going in with a predisposition toward your interviewee is like asking questions from behind a mask. If you express genuine interest in the story, the interviewee will in most cases respond in kind. Or in a combative situation, he may be thrown off balance and reveal himself. You may not get the bank president to say "Yes I did it" when you ask if he knows who embezzled the $250,000, but his face or body language may speak more clearly than words.

Some reporters are adamant about not revealing the questions they intend to ask before the interview; it's almost as though they were playing some kind of game. It's not; outline the subjects you want to discuss. In most cases, the interviewee is going to know the gist of the questions anyway, and by putting laying out your questions you will provide some reassurance against the fear of surprises.

Some reporters worry that if they reveal their questions, the person might not consent to the interview. Sometimes this might is true, but there is another way to do it. Assure the person that you will go over the subject areas before the interview and if he decides then that he doesn't want to do it, so be it. But if you do get him to come to the interview, which is more likely if you reduce the potential for disaster, he is less likely to leave without answering at least some of your questions. And if he storms out, that can make for some informative pictures.

This is not to say that you should expect your interviewees to be combative; quite the contrary. While in some cases, sharp words or confusion and sputtering will tell the story, the majority of interviews are simply informational. Most people will be a little shy, and virtually all will be nervous.

Be patient. Don't be in a rush to jump in on the answer. Particularly in poignant interviews, the face should be given a chance to finish expressing what the words have said. As soon as a person is required to listen, the focus of attention shifts and the statement is cut off, sometimes prematurely. Take a beat before asking the next question, watching the person's eyes to let them know that you have taken in what they have said. You will see what happens in the editing room. Screen tape of an interview and watch the interviewees' eyes when they have finished speaking and begin to listen to you. You can see the shift.

Engaging the Interviewee

The most effective interviewers engage the interviewee. Even if it is someone who doesn't really want to be there, the more adept you are at relaxing her and committing her to the information process—to expand the awareness of the community on a particular subject—the more authentic will be her contribution. You should seek to enfranchise your interviewee, to impart to her the importance of her role in the report.

Put her at ease, make the camera and microphones secondary to the conversation; the less visible the equipment is, the easier this is to accomplish. Two lavaliers are much less distracting, for example, than you reaching back and forth with a hand-held mike. Tell her that you have plenty of tape, and that she shouldn't worry about stopping and restarting. Again, the purpose of the interview is to get the interviewee to say something significant in a concise and illuminating manner.

Obviously, the more comfortable your interviewee is, the easier will go the conversation. And that's what you want: a dialogue. Too often reporters will act self-importantly, and will offend the person, reducing her willingness to cooperate. Whether it is overt or subtle, the cooperation makes all the difference.

Regrettably, most interviews are already wired; that is, most reporters go in knowing the answers to their questions. But when you have the time, and if you ask the right questions, you can sometimes get people to say some very interesting things that were not expected. Everyone has a story, after all. Usually, what it takes to elicit an unexpected answer is to ask questions the interviewee didn't expect, and steering the conversation into areas for which she had not prepared. Indeed, interviews can become much more than just talking heads when a good reporter pushes the interviewee into unfamiliar territory.

Of course, this presumes that you are conducting an interview to find out more about the person, and are not just there to pick up a simple sound cut or two.

It is important to get even a guarded interviewee to speak honestly and clearly. This is not always easy if the person has something to hide, and especially with professional answerers like public relations flacks. But sometimes you can get a person to let his guard down by (1) being honest with him about the information that you seek, (2) looking him in the eyes when he answers rather that looking at your notes, and (3) by asking him questions that are deeper than what he expected.

For instance, I was producing an interview with a Bank of America executive whose answers sounded like they had been rehearsed or frequently delivered. It wasn't that he was being evasive, he just seemed overly familiar with the information. So I asked him, what was new about the circumstances he was seeing today, as opposed to twenty years ago. And suddenly he came alive and there was a new energy in his voice. He was forced to think, and he did so openly and visually.

You can get people to say the most fascinating things when you ask sincerely for their opinion. Enfranchising someone—expressing a real interest in his assessment of a situation—can open him right up. Some of the best sound cuts have come in response to questions like:

> "What do you see that is different now from when this happened previously?"
> "What is it going to mean?"
> "Why should people care about what's happening?"
> "What do you see as the most significant element of this situation?"
> "Where does that put us now?

But when you open things up, make sure that you stay within the scope of knowledge of the interviewee. This may sound obvious, but often a reporter will ask someone to comment on something, unaware that it is beyond his purview or knowledge. "Do you think the company is being run well?" is fine for the president but not wise if it is asked of the guard at the visitor's center. The guard will probably have his own opinion and may even be willing to voice it, but in most companies, he will not have an informed perspective.

Another direction you might take if you are having trouble getting someone to speak freely, is to change your posture and then ask in a more personal tone something like, "When you get home tonight, how will you characterize this interview to your husband?" You're not going to use your question or her answer, probably, but you are likely to move your interviewee off the dime and get her to realize the importance of that moment in the interview. Or at least that she isn't coming across effectively.

People who are unfamiliar with the interview process are often likely to produce convoluted answers. If you get an answer that is rambling or disjointed, you might invite your interviewee to restate her answer. With the information recently spoken, and thus closer to the front of their mind, people are able to re-assemble it more concisely. This should only be done when the person's inability to form a coherent answer is not part of the story. If you are interviewing a criminal about a crime, you don't want them to polish up their alibi.

Most times the circumstances will be less drastic and a second approach will be appropriate. Tell the person why you are offering her the opportunity to remake her statement. The reason why you want to explain is that some people, thinking they had answered the question, could become suspicious of your intentions. Or they might not think that you're very bright.

One qualification to the "rule" cited above about looking in a person's eyes. Some people get nervous with eye contact, and you may have to look at your notes to give them the "space" they need to think and speak. But for the most part, you will want to look at the subject until he has finished speaking. It is respectful, and it looks right. After he has answered your question, then look down at your notes if you need to, though in many cases, follow-up questions will flow from the answers and you will already have in mind other questions that need to be asked.

Speaking of looking down at your notes, even if you know what questions you want to ask, it is always a good plan to have at least some questions or ideas jotted down. It is also smart to write down the interviewee's name right at the top of the page. It is amazing how, particularly on a long shoot, you can draw a blank on a number, a fact, or even a person's name. It is something that happens to the best of reporters.

Be Comfortable

Putting your interviewee at ease about the context is done by showing them your peace of mind. It really is contagious. Some interviewers say nothing to their "victim" until just before the camera rolls, as if the interviewee were a prop. Talk to the person; let him hear your voice, cadence, tone. If you are calm, not looking for anything, unhurried but alive, you will raise the level of the communication, making it more productive.

You must not only act but feel yourself present. If you are doing the interview by rote, asking questions to which you presume you have already the answers, you are undercutting your interviewee. Letting your mind wander to your script or an upcoming weekend doesn't preclude your getting an appropriate answer, but it makes getting the optimum sound cut most unlikely. Just think what's it like talking to your boss when she's distracted.

Most people being interviewed are concerned about two things: how they look and how they sound. The first part can usually be taken care of with some suggestions on how to sit—"Be comfortable."—and by making an attentive and approving scan of the scene from the camera's view. The interviewee should be able to sit with her feet on the ground, with her eyes level with the camera lens.

Position the interviewee so that she is back far enough from the camera so that if she gestures or crosses her legs, the motion doesn't dominate the picture nor is it cut off by the frame. Sometimes a cameraman will go in tight on a person's face and if they suddenly move, they'll be out of frame. Inform your cameraman what might be expected, so that he knows whether to stay wide or to take a chance and go tight.

Swivel chairs are a problem; no one can resist swiveling. The interviewee should be facing the reporter, not the camera, but should be shot head-on within

30 degrees if at all possible. It is much easier for the audience to understand a person—verbally and not—when the face is open to them.

(For a concealed-identity interview, shoot from behind, or in silhouette.)

Massaging the Interview

Interviewees come in different attitudes—those who have information they want to deliver, and others. The others include people who are willing to speak but are nervous, sometimes to the point of silence. Also included are people who have information that they do not want to impart. That can be for a variety of reasons, some of them valid; like humility, dignity, or common decency. You will also no doubt run into people who think they can manipulate the process into serving their purposes. Never give up control of the interview.

It is important with all interviewees—from professional speakers like politicians to first-timers, e.g., witnesses to an accident—that you first develop a rapport with them. Before the camera rolls, try to make them comfortable simply conversing with you. With first-time interviewees, or with people you are interviewing for the first time, you should invest a couple of minutes in letting them discover that you are not dangerous. You want them to feel comfortable with you as a person; this will make the interview easier to manage. If you don't have a better opportunity, then take the time when you are sitting down with the interviewee and the cameraman is getting his lighting set and focus right.

Another task to be done while setting up is to confirm the spelling and pronunciation of the interviewee's name. Get a business card, or write everything down in your notebook, including an evening phone number, in case you need to check a fact after business hours.

For people who are unfamiliar with the interview process, you might offer some suggestions. For instance, that they answer in complete sentences, maybe incorporating your questions in their answers. Very few people remember to do this, but there is value in providing them with this framework because it helps them to think about the question before coming back with an answer. Another hint would be to ask them to think about what they have to say before they respond. Most accounts have a beginning, a middle and an end; they should start at the beginning.

The more relaxed you are about the interview, the more comfortable they will be. If you are feeling the stress of time pressure or anything else, that stress will be communicated, and it could be contagious. Humor is a good relaxer. You might joke with them that the first thing you'll ask them is to confirm that they are not doing the interview under duress. Often they will open up about feeling uncomfortable about the process, and you can then address specific concerns; if they are addressable and it would make a difference.

With some interviewees, it helps to explain what information you need from them. Put them in a mood to behave the same way that they see other people speak on television every night. Invite them to take their time, and think through the question before answering it. In some cases, however, people think better on their feet, without time to think about what they have to say. Whatever works; that is why it is worth the time to get to know the basics of how the interviewee comes together as a person.

Take away the confusion, and watch how quickly and dramatically a person's energy can change. It is readily perceptible on tape. In his book <u>The Silent Pulse</u>, George Leonard described a scientific experiment that examined how people listen. Using high-speed photography, researchers filmed two people, one speaking and one listening. Then they parsed the film into the smallest units of sound. For instance, the word "ask" had five separate sounds in it. And what they discovered was that during each of the five separate sounds, the speaker exhibited a different set of body movements. More significant was that the listener also exhibited five separate sets of body movements in perfect synch with the speaker. This under-scores how important it is to listen to the people you are interviewing. The more you entrain them in the conversation, the more likely you are to get the thoughtful, informed, discernable answers you seek.

What if you don't understand an answer? Ask for clarification. Don't let ego trip you up. If you don't understand it, you're going to have a hard time distilling it for your viewers. You might ask the same question differently to evoke another perspective. Or repeat a question later; the interviewee may have shifted his thoughts and be able to answer more coherently.

In this vein, ask the interviewee to speak in complete sentences, incorporating the salient points of the questions into the answers. "Do you think the colt will ever be able to race and when?" could be answered with a "Yeah. Six months." But if the answer is "I think the colt will be able to race in six months" you're going to have a lot more latitude in the editing room with both the sound and the set-up.

Professional Interviewees

With the expansion of news operations and coverage, many people have had experience with television news people. Many companies hold seminars for their press people and executives so that they know how to handle hostile questions from a Mike Wallace or a Geraldo Rivera or their emulators. Ironically, such training is not very valuable: it's usually the simple question and the simple answer taken out of context or mis-edited that puts yolk on the corporate seal.

Be wary of people who earn their keep by talking to the press. Especially those who try to take control of the interview. One trick is that they call you by your first name. ("Well, Frank, I'm glad you asked me that question, because you know me and you know those charges couldn't possibly be true.") The purpose is to show familiarity with you, which undercuts your impartiality in the minds of the viewers. If someone calls you by your first name, stop the interview, ask her not to use your name at all, and then ask the question over again. (An exception to the first-name rule is with minor children.)

Many times you will see in a practiced eye that he is thinking about the best political answer to your question. As long as he is able to keep a distance from you and can unload qualified statements to your audience, you've merely handed him the microphone. But if you can get underneath the veneer, and ask your questions with the weight of your viewers—their constituents—behind you, you can sometimes force a less varnished version of the truth.

Brow-beating a person is unprofessional and impolite. As a reporter, you represent the public and their right to know. Being a professional means you come prepared to conduct a dignified interview. It can be frustrating when your interviewee is holding back or being deceitful, but that doesn't give you permission to then ask your questions in any manner other than professionally, that is, fairly and evenly.

If someone isn't telling the truth, it usually comes across in their facial expression, tone of voice, and/or body language. If after trying evasion with you they simply refuse to answer, you can, under certain circumstances, explain to them what is the information that you seek, and ask how you might frame a question that would elicit that information. Most crooks still won't comply, but sometimes the interviewee was merely confused.

When you come up against someone who is being deliberately evasive, remain professionally courteous but press her. Ask her how she thinks the situation might be interpreted by the average viewer, and what might she say to help them understand. Point out mitigating factors and ask if she were in your seat might she not find her answer, er-hem, difficult to swallow. You never want to call someone a liar, but if the person is not telling the truth, your questions and her answers should reveal the fact.

Don't be rude, of course, but don't let your interviewee be rude to you either. The fact that you have sought the interview implies that they have something to say. Their agreement to do the interview says that they are willing for you to record what they have to say, and that puts the ball in your court. Thus you can ignore the demands that the powerful and/or insecure use in an attempt to control the situation, but always act professionally.

Try not to interrupt a guest during an interview. You can do so politely if they don't seem to understand your question or they get off on an irrelevancy or they try to filibuster. They should have heard from you in advance that you need short answers to provide the audience with more information. If you're taping, just ask the camerawoman or director to stop tape. If you are live, you have to be more judicious.

For instance, wait until the camera is on the guest, and show the director a subtle cut sign. By prior arrangement, that should mean cutting the guest's mike and coming to you. If the guest doesn't behave in a reasonable manner, find something to go to—like a commercial—and don't come back to the studio until you have regained control. This isn't about ego, it's about professional conduct of an interview and access to the airwaves. A surgeon wouldn't give up control of an operation to the patient.

A warning: don't be awed by titles. Whoever you are interviewing is "doing their thing" the same way you are. You are both equal human beings. Your position with the mayor should be the same as with a kindergartner: respectful and confident, attentive and discerning, dialogist and individual.

Advance Work

Reconfirm any appointments made more than three hours earlier. If only to say you're on your way, it gives them a chance to wind up other business and get ready for you. Sometimes, if this is their first experience with television, you will likely be asked if they can do anything for you, and there usually is.

For instance, you may ask to shoot in a board room or a laboratory. Perhaps they will need to clear those areas for you. Or if it's an old building and you're going to use a lot of lights, ask if the house electrician might be alerted. You may also ask that certain documents or graphics be available, .e.g., an annual report, a company logo on disk. The more they get involved in the process of providing the information, the better will be the communication.

And when you leave, make sure that the furniture is replaced, the tape is removed from the cornices, and the flowers are back on the table.

Polling

Polling is a abstract form of mass interviewing. The answers are pre-set, and a large number of people are being asked if they agree with those answers or not. As much as we enjoy reading poll results, the fact is that they tend to confuse popular ideas with true public consciousness, as they fail to register ideas outside of the mainstream. The fact that people are limited to saying yes or no to questions is deeply flawed to begin with, and especially when questions are improperly phrased.

For instance a poll during the Robert Bork nomination process asked people if they supported President Bush's choice, Robert Bork, for the Supreme Court. Regrettably, a sizeable number of people would answer yes, not because they knew or approved of Bork, but simply because he was the President's nominee. Consider, too, that there are a lot of people in our society who prefer to be considered—by others and themselves—mainstream, and this fact also skews results.

The problem with skewed results is that they are used to justify political positions, and that's hardly a healthy way to formulate policy.

One of the most scurrilous forms of "polling" is to invite viewers or website visitors to register their opinions with yes-no or multiple-choice responses to a series of questions. The results of such surveys are worse than meaningless since there is an implication of validity when the participants are self-chosen and unlimited in the number of times they can vote.

At the time of the 1980 Carter-Reagan debate—and it has become a familiar practice since—ABC invited viewers to "choose the winner" by phoning 900-numbers, one for Carter, the other for Reagan. It was a tragically glaring example of style-over-substance reporting. Not only did it invite manipulation by either or both candidates, but the results were further undermined by the fact that the calls cost 50¢ a piece.

A common form of polling that borders on reprehensible is the man-on-the-street interview, even when the views expressed by the interviewees reflect accurate polling data. In our society, the very fact that someone is on television gives them certain credibility, which is why man-on-the-street interviews run directly counter to good journalism. Especially since in most cases today, thoughtful, longer answers are sacrificed to pithy or entertaining remarks. Airing such interviews implies that the speakers are rational.

Remember, too, that even majority opinion is fluid and under-informed. Only a fifth of the colonists supported the Revolution.

Editing the Interview

When conducting an interview, it is often useful to record with an audio cassette as well. You can listen to the interview on the way back to the station and begin writing your script.

When editing your interview, you have several options for connecting two or more sound cuts. You can cover the jump with a cutaway listening shot or a wide two-shot. Or you might prefer to tie the cuts together with a dissolve or wipe. The point is that you want to have the sound cuts together to frame an idea, and whatever you use to smooth over the edit should be designed to help the audience view the two cuts as one, with as little distraction as possible.

There are varying opinions on the use of cutaways in editing interviews. For the longest time, some television news organizations refused to allow cutaways, unless they actually shot the interview with two cameras in real time. Which is certainly preferable, but few have the luxury of two or more cameras to shoot an interview.

Many professionals don't think that there's anything wrong with shooting reverse listening shots if they help to make a better flow. Some do it but complain that they feel like a performer rather than a journalist. The fact is that in many instances set-up shots and cutaways do look so staged—especially the intense, nodding shots—and they can cause more of a distraction from the content of the interview than would a dissolve or wipe.

When shooting cutaways—listening shots, two-shots, etc.—make sure that the camera is recording actual conversation. If you are conscious of the camera being on you, it will look stilted. The best route going into the edit room includes cutaways of both you and the interviewee actually listening and obviously interested. Engage your interviewee in what you are saying so that her listening set-up shot looks genuine, and when you're shooting a reverse, have the interviewee talking to you so that you are truly listening. The viewer can tell from your expression whether you are really listening. It is the same difference between the forced smiles of a photo op and real conversation.

If you're going to shoot note-taking or hands-in-the-lap shots, make sure that the tone of the edited conversation during the taking of those shots matches the tone of that part of the interview for which the shots will be used. A hand moving slowly across a notebook does not fit as a cutaway in a heated dialogue.

You can also use germane b-roll to cover multiple edits, with the same admonition to be careful that picture and sound don't conflict. The sound cuts, like any piece of scripted voice-over, should work with the video to present a comprehensive package of information. If you do cover part of the interview, you should make every effort to start with the person on camera for at least ten seconds before you take the voice under, so that the audience is clear about who is talking. Also, come back to end on that person speaking, when possible; it provides closure to the sound.

Protect your interviewee; don't ask stupid questions. "Will you miss your son?" to the mother of an accident victim is inviting a predictable and useless answer. Many people watch television in an attempt to substitute electronic pathos for the lack of feeling in their own lives. Journalists should not participate in the effort.

If you do find yourself with a predictable answer on tape, don't use it if it doesn't add to the telling of the story. Like asking a neighbor about the next-door mass murderer. "He was always such a nice boy," "Never heard a peep out of him," and "I always thought there was something odd about him" do nothing to contribute to the story, except to imply that there was little or no communication going on in that neighborhood.

Finally on editing, it is important to remember when cutting an interview, for a single sound cut or to underlay a minute of video, that the spoken words need to be easily understandable the first time through. If you have any trouble understanding what is being said or what is meant, you can be sure you're going to lose at least part of your audience. Especially since you conducted the interview and are listening to the sound in an editing room, with a professional ear. Your audience is probably listening with half-'n-ear while eating dinner or reading the paper.

14. The Technical Side

This book is oriented toward the editorial side of television news coverage because its lens is journalism, but there is a whole other side to television news, and that is the technical area—that which delivers the audio and video that support a script into homes and offices around the world. The technical side—recording, editing and broadcasting the sound and the picture—is a world of electronics and engineering.

Knowing the basics of the audio and video enables an editorial person to understand the parameters of what is possible with the available equipment under a variety of circumstances. For instance, when conducting a street interview with a small group, you need a handheld or a shotgun mike, not a lavalier. Another for instance, you make it a lot easier on your cameraman when you position your interviewee facing the sun.

I began shooting still photographs professionally in my seventeenth summer. A friend was the chief photographer for the *Daily Hampshire Gazette*, in Northampton, Massachusetts. He supplied me with a Hasselblad, and gave me access to his darkroom and supplies. More than fifty of my feature photographs were published in the paper over the summer, for which I was paid $4 a piece. I have been shooting stills ever since, but never took an interest in shooting moving pictures.

So while I understood about framing visuals and capturing shots, most of the technical knowledge that I acquired about television production came from watching and listening, and asking a lot of questions over the decade I worked in network and local news. I've also picked up a great deal more, staying current with the technology, through my independent broadcast producing over the subsequent 23 years.

The bottom line is that as good as the technology gets, and as easy as it makes it to record pictures and sound, you will still need a good storyteller looking through the eyepiece to get the right visuals. Someone who knows about panning and zooming, relationship shots, how to shoot for editing, and what plays well to the human eye. Similarly, you need an attentive person recording the audio. There's nothing worse than thinking you've got a brilliant sound cut, only to find that a plane flying overhead made the sound unintelligible.

I scatter throughout this book some of the significant technical points that I picked up on the job, but devote the succeeding few pages to discussing some of the elemental issues of the technical side of news gathering, as far as an editorial type should have to know them. This is not a complete volume of necessary information; it's more of a sampler.

Though most reporters don't need to deal with what happens inside the equipment, they should know at least the basics of how the camera captures pictures and the microphone picks up sounds. This is especially true in smaller markets where often the reporter is a one-man band—shooting, recording sound, reporting and editing it all together when he gets back to the station. But even in markets where someone else is doing the production, the more you know, the more control you will have over the elements being gathered to produce your report.

Most important is to know what are the capabilities of your production personnel and equipment. Appreciating your limitations, you can figure out what the optimum report might be—audio and video with all the bells and whistles— and what could be done in a crunch, e.g., if the tape failed; you could deliver a straight on-camera report. Knowing your options means that you'll almost always be able to come through in some way to present the news.

When I first got into the business in 1970, news was shot on 16mm film. The film had to be loaded into magazines, shot, unloaded, processed and edited. It was not only time-consuming but there were also numerous opportunities for things to go wrong. When tape came along, and the technology stabilized, the process of recording images and sound became faster and more certain. But it still happens that a mechanical glitch can occur, or for that matter, your videographer could sprain his ankle getting out of the car. And drop the camera onto the pavement. Always have in the back of your mind what you would do it there were no picture and sound.

Also, the more you understand the finer points of the technical side, the more you will be appreciated by your technical people. Occasionally you will run into people who, if you ask too many questions, will think that you're after their job. On the other hand, if you are lucky, you will work with production people who are glad to share their knowledge, because they know that it will help you to do your job, and all of you to produce a better final product.

Changing Technology

What television offers that other news media don't is the ability to show a story unfolding—history being written as it is being made. With satellites and microwave systems, it is now possible to cover a news story anywhere in the world—and beyond—and transmit that coverage to virtually every television set on the planet, to billions of people. Communications visionary Marshall McLuhan called it the Global Village. The technological changes have had a dramatic impact on how news is covered and broadcast.

In 1963, the installation of Pope Paul VI was filmed in Rome and then the film was flown by chartered plane to New York. It was picked up at the airport and put into a truck in which had been built a film processor. The film was developed on the ride back to the broadcast center, loaded onto projectors and broadcast to the nation, twelve hours after the event. Two decades later, the world watched the assassination attempt on Pope John Paul II only minutes after the shooting.

Technological changes this vast and rapid have exceeded the ability of some broadcasters to incorporate them into their news operations without sacrificing a degree of news judgment.

As of this writing in the winter of 2003, television is on the verge of shifting from tape to disk, although most stations will still be shooting tape for a number of years. From two-inch to one-inch to mini-DV, tape has shrunk in size and improved in quality. Being smaller has meant greater portability; it used to be that two or three people were required for the camera, tape deck and lights. Now one person can handle everything. It should be noted, however, that putting everything on the shoulders of one person can make for problems, and having at least two people gives you a better chance of coming back with everything you want, all properly lit and recorded.

The move from tape to disk, when it has been perfected, will be another time-saver since you won't have to roll through tape but can simply go directly to spots on the disk. It will also provide for more stable still shots, and other handling of video images, e.g., special effects like wipes and dissolves and transfers to other media.

Whatever equipment you are using, the basic process of capturing visuals is the same. Light bounces off of the objects being shot and images are transmitted electronically, either live back to the station via microwave, satellite or phone lines, or are recorded on tape for editing later. This tells you that in order to have a picture, you need enough light to be picked up by the camera, and on the subject. Light behind the subject without enough on the front of it will put the subject in silhouette. New technology makes it possible to shoot in extremely low-light conditions, and to raise pictures that were shot under poor conditions to broadcast-able levels.

Reporter Tips on Shooting

As useful as you as a reporter may find this information, be careful how you share it with a videographer. Even if you have information that could make her a better camerawoman, the likelihood is that she has not been waiting for you to instruct her, any more than you would expect her to help you write a better script.

This is unfortunate and ironic, since shooters tend to stay in a market longer than reporters, and thus have considerably more experience. Many reporters would benefit by listening to their camerawomen, but unfortunately, egos often get in the way of that experience-learned wisdom being shared. The exception is when the eager young reporter is more interested in the news than in his own image. More often, however, photographers have to suffer reporters whose egos are so big that they block the light.

In the practical every day of covering the news, the reporter does best who has the best relationship with the cameraman. The best relationship comes out of mutual respect. The reporter is given the assignment, and is expected to get the cameraman (and soundman) to record the television elements of the story. This is done by enfranchising the crew with all the authority they can use to accomplish your goals. A big reason why you will want a good relationship with your techs is that they often see or hear important elements out of your purview.

Explain to them the story you are going out to cover, what elements you think will help to tell the story, and how you think those elements might best be recorded, e.g., do you shoot the interview and then the b-roll or vice versa, and where might be the best spot for the standupper. Then ask what they think and how it might be done better. Accept as much of the input as you can, practically, and make sure they know that while you are ultimately responsible, you are relying on them to make it all work.

To make all your jobs easier, think about the jobs your camera and sound people must do. For instance, try not to conduct interviews outside in a strong breeze; even with a windscreen, the sound will suffer. On the affirmative side, when setting up an interview, think about what will be a good background for the shot, i.e., to reinforce the person's identity.

Shooting an interview in the Hershey chocolate boardroom, we positioned the company president in front of a wall on which hung a portrait of the founder, Milton S. Hershey II. The cameraman started tight on the portrait and then pulled back to show the president in a wide shot.

Positioning of course also applies to standuppers. Selecting the right backdrop can make the difference in the viewers' interpretation. A standup close to a child abuse story would have a significant impact, for example, if it were shot in front of a schoolyard; crowded or empty, by the way.

The wrong backdrop can also cause confusion. Standing in front of a massage parlor while delivering a script on the dangers of stress is going to create some interesting inferences amongst the viewers. (More on standuppers later.)

When you're shooting an on-the-go handheld interview, position yourself on the other side of the camera from the photographer. If she's using a right-eye viewfinder, you want to be on her right, her blind side. She can see on the left, and you can protect her on her right. If there is a second person in the crew, he should be on the other side of the photographer, protecting her from unexpected low branches or jostling.

Standing on the right side of the camera, you'll want to hold the microphone in your left. This way (1) you won't be reaching across yourself and will have more flexibility where you hold the mike, and (2) it will keep your right hand (usually the stronger one) free.

When driving, the photographer should sit on the passenger side, in the event she needs to jump out quickly.

Videographer Tips

Perhaps you are a reporter getting started in a small market and you also have to shoot your own pictures. You will have been taught how to operate the camera, at least the rudimentary aspects, enough to record images. Beyond the basics, it is important to understand how people see a picture so that you can present the visual information in the most effective way for them to receive.

Consider that most people see about three-thousands of a picture at which they are looking. While they may have an overall perception of shapes and colors, their focus is very limited. What I learned shooting stills, and what applies to motion pictures, may help you to frame your shots.

Look at the rectangle of the viewfinder or the screen and divide the frame into thirds, both vertically and horizontally. The four points of intersection define where the action should be taking place. Either the actual event, or the direction in which it is heading. For instance, you might frame a head shot with the person slight to the right of center, looking slightly to the left. In such a shot, the eye and mouth might be over the right intersections and the direction of their sight and speech might be focused on the left intersections.

Similarly, with an action shot, you might have a runner on the left intersecting points, and his motion would be directed at the right intersecting points. Whenever there is an action shot, it should be coming into the screen rather than leaving it.

When shooting with a reporter, the more you understand the story, the more likely you are to get the shots that will best tell that story. The more successful you are in capturing the elements that best tell the story, the more latitude you will earn and the more creativity you will be able to exercise. So it is in your best interests to ask questions, to learn as much as possible about what the reporter thinks the final piece will look like, and what shots she will need in the editing room.

Ultimately, it is the reporter's responsibility—her name is on the report, after all—for how the story comes out, so get her shots first and then supplement them with your own, when you have the time and opportunity. See which shots wind up in the piece, and that will give you an idea of how to better shoot the next story, at least with this reporter.

You will find that reporters vary in what they know and how they lead. Being in front of the camera can do strange things to people. Patience is often required, but on the other hand, you will sometimes have the pleasure of working with reporters who give you the story outline and more or less free rein, and then you can truly enjoy practicing your craft.

You can help the reporter in providing perspective, underscoring points in her script or filling in some holes. Pans, zooms and tilts can illustrate the relationship of protagonists, or elements in a situation. Panning from someone's back porch all cluttered with children's playthings to a bubbling toxic waste dump fifty feet away, for example, makes a number of points—about the pollution danger and the quality of the parenting. Or tilting from the farmer's soggy corn to rain-filled clouds provides a gloomy forecast.

When shooting scenes, consider that the audience is completely unfamiliar with what is being presented, and it is your job to provide perspective. If someone is giving a speech, you will want to show the whole room, both facing the speaker and from the side or behind to show the audience. You may want medium shots as well, especially if there is going to be a lot of voice-over that needs to be covered.

If you are covering a news conference or a speech, you will likely need some cutaway shots of people listening. Try to shoot them from a distance so that the people you are shooting aren't conscious of the camera and become a distraction. Cutaways need to be as bland as possible so they don't disrupt the flow of the sound cuts.

Whenever you are shooting people close enough so that they are aware of the camera, it often causes a transformation in their demeanor, posture and expression. Most people get self-conscious, and if you are paying attention to before and after shots, you can see quite clearly when they realized they were on camera. This is most obvious when people give you an SEG. SEG is an acronym I picked up when I was learning still photography and brought back shots of a person offering a shit-eating-grin. It is the posed smile—the Say Cheese! Picture—often seen during official smiling sessions (photo ops) when heads of state stage a peaceful facade in front of the press photographers…before they go behind closed doors to disagree.

When shooting an interview, try to leave room for a super. Only in extended interviews should you go in very tight, for effect, and risk not providing the space for a lower-third. Also when shooting an interview, usually at the beginning, you will want to get some establishing shots, i.e., wide and two-shots and maybe some close-ups of the person's hands in her lap.

On general news stories, most of the shots you need will be obvious, especially if you outline the story in your mind, or in a discussion with the reporter before-hand. But it is best to get a variety of shots, in case the story takes an unexpected turn, mixing wide and tight shots, and adding medium shots when you have time.

Each static shot should run at least ten seconds, which gives you some margin at either end for jiggle if you're turning on and off the camera. Pans and zooms should have a couple of seconds of static on each end. If you have the time and you know the relational shots are going to be important to the piece, shoot several, at different speeds.

If there is one rule about shooting, it is that you want to provide the editor with as many options as possible. That means bringing in a tape that allows as much flexibility as possible in telling the story with pictures. It means shooting as much as you can, time permitting, to allow the reporter to cover as many angles as possible without your pictures supplanting his script.

If you are also the editor, which is common in many markets, make sure that you don't cut shots too short. Remember, by having been on the scene and by viewing your footage in the editing room, you have a familiarity with the pictures that the audience doesn't have. Pictures that aren't terribly clear or that have a number of important elements in them need more time to be seen; the more complicated the content, the more time your audience will need to view your shots.

Try to look at and listen to your final cut as though for the first time, the way your viewers will. Objectively consider whether or not your selected sequence of images and sounds, that you have witnessed several times now, and in their original context, is practical and comfortable to follow for a person who is brand new to the story. That's the goal.

Recording Sound

If you are shooting your own pictures, you are likely recording your own sound as well. The first rule of audio is that whatever you intend to put on the air has to be understandable the first time it is played. And if you really want to be picky, you need to be able to understand that audio the first time without seeing the person who is speaking. Actually, that shouldn't be too tough most of the time, when you are recording sound in controlled situations. Outside in a hurricane, during a rowdy demonstration, picking up sound at a distance off of a sound system when the speaker has a cleft palate—that's when you're pushing the envelope.

If you have trouble understanding audio in the editing room, your viewer is liable to miss it entirely. This can be very frustrating when you're cutting a sound bite and you hear exactly what you want, but only after you play it three or four times. Apply this criterion strictly: if you are selecting a cut from an interview you conducted yourself and it isn't clear the first time you play the tape back, alarm bells should go off.

One trick to help your viewers better understand someone who is going to speak on camera, perhaps not very intelligibly, is to show that person speaking before you have him deliver the sound cut. Using such an establishing shot creates a degree of familiarity with the person before the viewer has to understand the words coming from his mouth.

Another suggestion: give the person time to speak. Any sound cut shorter than ten seconds, especially the first time that person speaks, is going to strain the viewers' ability to contextualize the new voice. Obvious exceptions include hearing a person speaking a second or third time, and chants, screams and other brief exclamations. Considering the attention span and subliminal expectations of the average viewer, eighteen seconds seems to be the optimum length for a basic sound cut.

This goes against the grain for a lot of today's news directors who seem to like staccato editing with short sound cuts. They object to "talking heads" on principle, and will rant and rave about their reporters not having the brains to realize that television is a visual medium. Sometimes they have a point, but usually they have been reading too much paid research or listening to consultants, neither of which sources usually consider journalism to be an important factor in television news. If you don't need the job, or already have another one lined up, you might remind that news director that people like Ted Koppel, Barbara Walters and Mike Wallace have found considerable success in using talking heads.

Sometimes, if the sound is particularly crucial to your story, you can run sub-titles below it. Sometimes. In the late Seventies, Harry Reasoner conducted a long-distance interview with Leon Spinks, the day after the boxer had beaten Muhammad Ali. A camera was set up in Harry's office, and another was set up on Spinks in a hotel room in Las Vegas. The two talked with each other by telephone. The tape from Las Vegas was then to be satellited to New York, where I would edit the pieces together.

I listened in on a telephone extension so that I could take notes on both sides of the conversation. I became very worried because I could not understand but every few words that Spinks said. After the short conversation, which Reasoner somehow understood without difficulty, I spoke with Av Westin, the executive producer of the *ABC Evening News*, and expressed my concerns about Spink's intelligibility. Westin said it would be all right when people could watch Spinks' lips move. That made sense.

The alternative was to put sub-titles under Spinks, but that would have elicited attacks from people who would suggest we were slandering Spinks because he was black. It was not an unreasonable concern on our part, even in those days when political correctness had not gone as far overboard as it did. But with Westin's mollification in my mind, I headed for the tape room.

Westin was right, it was easier, but it was still difficult to understand what the boxer was saying. As it turned out, there was enough video that was marginal that we could play without sub-titles, but surely a good percentage of the audience didn't understand half of what Spinks said, inferring most of what they did from Reasoner's questions and responses.

Microphones

When you are in the field recording the sound that you will be using in your piece, give it the attention it deserves. Used properly, sound can present both facts and feeling. A mike on the top of a camera recording ambient sound can add significantly to the feeling of the visuals. Many top crews will record room tone after an interview in a seemingly quite room, and when used under set-up shots or voice-over bridges, it can enhance the overall quality of the report.

Even when you are recording a simple interview, where the sound should be easy to control, make sure that you take the time to set up correctly. Pushing a microphone in the general direction of a person's mouth may be enough in some situations, but you would be surprised how often the quality of the audio can be muddled unless the mike is properly positioned and held still. Also, a windscreen can make the difference between intelligible or not.

The larger the market, the more options you will have to use different types of microphones for different recording situations.

Lavaliers are the small clip-on microphones usually attached to a collar or shirt front, usually used in studios and in other controlled situations, like sit-down interviews. Interviewees unfamiliar with television frequently make the mistake of brushing the lav with their hands or arms, or creating noise by rustling their clothing. Watch out, too, for necklaces and neckties, which can clatter, rustle, or scratch at exactly the wrong moment. You can save time, tape and effort by (1) placing the microphone out of the way as much as possible, and (2) by instructing the person to avoid touching the microphone. If you see the person brush the microphone, wait until she has finished her answer and then check your tape to make sure the answer is usable.

A hand-held microphone looks like a large round lollipop with a thick stem. Hand-helds are useful in standuppers or in an unstructured location interview where the reporter needs to control who is speaking, e.g., collecting eyewitness accounts from a group of bystanders. Make sure that you are on the same page with whoever is recording the sound as far as where to position the microphone, e.g., directly in front of or below the person's mouth, and how far away.

A shotgun mike looks like a baton; it is usually protected by a foam windscreen that surrounds it. Shotguns—which come in sizes that range from eight inches to a couple of feet—are used in directional work, pointed at the source of the sound. Shotguns are very useful in crowd scenes, like walking news conferences and for recording a standupper or an interview when the reporter needs to keep his hands free.

A table microphone is the kind you see sitting on a desk and isn't used in news much today, except at times to record group interviews, though many such shoots will be conducted with an overhead boom mike.

A boom microphone is used in studios, lowered from above the speaker(s). The boom is a long pole with a swivel control on the end that allows the mike to be held above the camera shot, and pointed directly toward the speaker.

A parabolic is a long-distance directional microphone that looks like a microwave dish. It is often used at sporting events to pick up the sound of the athletes on the field.

Reflection and Imagination

As mentioned above, when I started in television news, virtually all coverage was done on 16mm film. Videotape arrived in the early Seventies, and film was mostly gone by the eighties in most middle-size markets. There was an advantage to using film, which was the same as its drawback, and that was the time it took to process and edit. Usually you'd have to wait at least three-quarters of an hour before the film came out of the *soup*. That gave you time to think and write. Now with tape, you walk in through the front door and directly into the editing room.

Electronic editing of videotape is as different from the linear editing of film as writing with a computer is to using a typewriter. You can do it faster, with myriad effects options, and never suffer the problems of cutting the film in the wrong place or not pulling up the audio track 24 frames in advance of the pictures.

The sword of technical instantaneity is double-edged. Just because the technology provides the capability to go live anywhere-anytime and to "enjoy" instant editing doesn't mean that it has to be employed, at least not all the time. Some practitioners take advantage of the speed, and set up coverage without enough time to digest all of the information intrinsic in the story. It makes for rushed presentations, choppy reports and unnecessary mistakes.

Coming full circle, it's important to remember that the first element in television news are the facts. The pictures and sound, as stupendous as they may be—even commanding—are nothing without the attention of the journalist. And taking it a step a little beyond the commonplace, consider that what sets human beings—and especially journalists—apart from the rest of the creatures are the powers of reflection and imagination. They're even more important than reality.

II—Producing the News

A man who dares to waste one hour of time has not discovered the value of life.

—Charles Darwin

The second stage of the news process is the manipulation. The word has negative connotations in other situations, but in the news operations, it means the hands-on crafting of the script, pictures and sound to create mind-edible bites of news. The entire news department is involved, with the producers deciding what should be in the broadcast. They are supported by the reporters who produce their individual packages, the photographers shooting the visuals for those packages and voice-overs, the editors picking the shots and the news editor and writers picking the salient facts to go into the readers and voice-overs.

Since the preparation of the broadcast will go on for six to eight hours, much of the news that will wind up going on the air is happening, or has yet to occur. What news events are already complete can be written up and footage edited with the knowledge that some of the pieces will be pushed out by late-breaking and more important news. And on some days, stories that are written before noon will lead the broadcast, depending on events, but even if they don't make air, the writing and editing process warms up the minds and fingers.

All the while, the assignment desk is monitoring developments of on-going stories, keeping an eye on forecasted events, and watching the wires for the unforeseen, knowing that literally anything is possible. Planes crash, politicians are scandalized, tornadoes touch down in trailer parks. They happen regardless of the time left before the broadcast starts, and all too often the fickle gods of the news Olympus seem to take particular pleasure in toying with broadcast journalists.

The Elvis Presley Story

Perhaps the most compelling aspect of being a journalist is that you cover new stories—people and events—all the time. You watch history unfold before you, and chronicle it to your viewers. While that can be interesting at the local level, working for the networks dramatically broadens the arena both in terms of geography and cultures. It offers an extraordinary opportunity to broaden your perspectives.

It was 3:20 when the phone in my Chicago hotel room rang for the third time that morning. It was the ABC Television News Assignment Desk: Get to the airport, meet the John Braddock crew and correspondent Greg Dobbs, fly to Denver, charter to Eagle and drive to Vail. Former President Gerald Ford was going to meet with two of President Carter's advisors and give his support to the relinquishing of the Panama Canal.

It was during the 1977 strike by NABET, the engineers union, which in Chicago also included the editorial personnel. I had been sent out from New York to produce, along with Laura Palmer who was to manage assignments for the Midwest. The first call to me, as I informed them, should have been directed to Laura as they were calling about assigning coverage of the Ford story. The second call to me a few minutes later was to find out at what hotel they might reach Laura since they couldn't find her.

Why the coverage was being initiated at 2:14AM (the time of the first call) was never clear, though it was another proof that what goes on at the network level is not always top flight. That the third call didn't come until forty minutes before the plane was to leave O'Hare was, generously speaking, an oversight.

I threw on pants and shoes, grabbed the rest of the clothes I'd been wearing the day before along with my shoulder bag, and ran. I finished dressing in the elevator, jumped into a cab and handed the driver a twenty dollar bill. "This is the tip if we can get to O'Hare in twenty minutes." We did, and I ran down the concourse to the furthest gate, arriving huffing and puffing at the plane with less than two minutes to spare. There I found Greg and the crew sitting quietly in the front of the first class section sipping Bloody Mary's in a nearly empty plane.

Arriving in Denver, there was time for a bite of breakfast before the clouds broke and the charter was able to leave for Eagle. But weather still forced the pilot to take a longer route, so that when we landed, we barely had time to load the gear into the car that was waiting by the lonely airstrip. Dobbs, known on several continents for his driving, got in behind the wheel and took off.

When we got to Vail, the helicopter carrying the emissaries from President Carter was just coming into view. Dobbs flew through the sleepy summer scene of Vail and pulled up in front of the Ford chalet only minutes before the officials arrived. As you discover so many times when you rush, there had been no need. Our troops, along with a number of other journalists, stood around in front of the ex-President's house for two hours before there was anything to shoot.

Ford and the officials emerged with their flaccid smiles and perfunctory comments, and all was duly recorded. Then it was back in the car for the ride back to Eagle and the charter back to Denver. At the ABC affiliate, the film was put into the lab and Dobbs started to write his script.

In those days, ABC fed its evening newscast three times, at 6:00, 6:30 and 7:00. This meant that the Ford story had to be fed to New York by 3:45 local, 5:45 in the East. Dobbs, a former producer himself and ever the professional, roughed out his script, went over the sound cuts with me, and had his track completed in short order. The piece itself was easily put together in plenty of time to make the feed to New York.

Then came the news that Elvis Presley was dead. Dobbs and the crew would have time for a sumptuous dinner in Denver before flying back to Chicago that evening, but I had to rush back to the airport to fly to Memphis to help produce the Presley coverage.

When I arrived in Memphis shortly after midnight, I cabbed to the affiliate to meet with Bill Knowles, a senior producer from the Washington bureau, plus various producers, reporters and technical staff who had flown in from New York, New Orleans and Atlanta. We planned the next day's coverage and headed off to our various hotels.

Presley's death seemed to throw much of the city into a state of confusion. To further complicate matters, Memphis was jammed to overflowing with a Shriners' convention. Thirty-thousand of the red-fez bedecked conventioneers had virtually every hotel room in the city.

Knowles had gotten me a place to stay at the Hyatt; it was a ground floor room normally used for small meetings, furnished with a fold-away bed. It wasn't until five that morning that I discovered that the room abutted a small artificial pond, frequented at that hour by very real and squawking ducks.

The next day was Wednesday; in the middle of August, the temperature and humidity climbed for 100. The crowds that gathered in front of the gates of Graceland, the Presley mansion, spilled into the street, causing snarls in the traffic and on many faces. Most of those standing in front of the gates were women in their twenties and thirties, many in curlers, some holding young children. By midday, the soaking heat was breathtaking.

The people at the gates were unsheltered under the sun, and were packed so tightly together that some who fainted were held up in place by the crowd. When the crowd shifted slightly, those people who had passed out fell to the pavement. The sound of bodies hitting the cement, children crying and horns blaring echoed like a faux Presley death rattle. Medics set up an emergency recovery area just inside the gates of Graceland. At any one time, twenty or so of the crowd would be lying on the grass under the large elm trees.

Late that afternoon, people were allowed to walk single file up the long drive to the mansion to pay their final respects. They were silently ushered into the foyer, where Presley lay in an open coffin. The morticians had probably done their best, but it looked like they had been faced with an impossible task. Presley's face was ashen and bloated. What with his condition—reportedly induced by drugs overdoses—and the puffery of the coffin lining, it looked as though he had been stuffed into the box. And to complete the scene, the foyer was indecorously filled with Presley aides.

It was befitting the scene of moral squalor in which Presley finished out his life—days filled with drugs and guns—that these aides looked little better than extras in a *Godfather* movie. Several had guns, all wore the special Presley pendants. The pendants featured a lightning zig-zag design of the letters "T-L-C" which stood for, ironically, tender loving care. According to local lore, the importance of the aides was measured by the quality of their pendants, i.e., the more diamonds they wore, the closer it meant they were to The King.

Coverage went smoothly that evening, and I was taken to one of the city's finest down-home restaurants by the local anchorwoman. The food and ambience were marvelous and became the reason for later not wanting the whole city to slip into the Mississippi River. After dinner, I had to change hotels, as my duck blind at the Hyatt had already been committed to another. So I found myself in the Admiral Benbow, catching a few hours of sleep between serenades by Shriners marching up and down the halls playing bagpipes.

It was about four o'clock that Thursday morning, the day Presley was to be buried, that a man drove his car into the crowd still standing in front of Graceland, killing four young girls. Bill Knowles was roused by the affiliate staff and pulled together what pictures there were, fed them to New York for *Good Morning America*, and went back to bed for a few hours before he had to coordinate the funeral coverage for the evening show.

(At the ABC morning conference call a few hours later, the *GMA* news producer, who was used to playing second fiddle to the evening broadcast, complained that he had been short-changed because the Memphis team had not been covering the mansion at four in the morning. He was hooted down. Most staffers were already upset that in the midst of the NABET strike so many ABC troops had been sent to cover the story in the first place.)

As meticulous as he always was, Knowles had already established assignments for everyone before he went to bed, placing crews at Graceland and at the cemetery. I was to stay at Graceland until the cortege departed, and so I arrived at the scene a couple of hours before the funeral procession was to begin. I located the crew and positioned them advantageously inside the mansion gates. Then I went across the four-lane street to the shopping center on the other side to make a call to Knowles.

The day before, I had ingratiated myself with the people who operated a flower shop in the shopping center. They were very busy, naturally, creating floral arrangements—in the shape of a guitar and the like—but they were willing to let a producer from ABC who was covering The King's funeral to use their phone.

After I called in to report the set-up, I walked back across the parking lot to the street to return to the crew. The crowd on the shopping center side of the street was already twelve deep and tightly packed. Dressed in a coat and tie, I would have stood out anyway, even if I hadn't had the large laminated "Working Press" card hanging by a chain in front of my chest.

When I broke through the crowd to the street, I looked for an opening in the traffic, which had slowed to a crawl from rubber-necking, so I could cross back to the mansion. As I walked along the street waiting for my chance, I was suddenly yelled at by a policeman who told me I couldn't cross. I held up my credentials and told the policeman who I was. Didn't matter, I was told, I couldn't cross there.

I had been walking back and forth, crossing through the traffic there for two days, but I didn't have the energy to argue. I walked along looking for a place to get back into the crowd, that I might traverse the shopping center parking lot and cross at the light several hundred yards away. Apparently the policeman thought I was disobeying him and he yelled for another cop to grab me.

The original cop—Patrolman J. E. Johnstone, Badge Number 673, if memory serves—put a vice grip on my arm and led me over to a police captain. I protested mildly that there must be some mistake, but the cop, despite an argument from his superior, insisted on taking me in. He brought me to a patrol car and ordered me to put my hands on the roof and spread my legs. The car had been sitting in the sun so the roof was extremely hot; I had to balance on my fingertips to keep from being burned. The patrolman nudged my ankles further apart with his foot—just like in the movies—and gave me a full body frisk. Then he hand-cuffed my hands behind my back and put me in the back seat of the patrol car.

If you've never been handcuffed behind your back—and it was certainly a first for me—you discover that you really can't sit up comfortably. (Try putting your wrists together behind you.) So slumped over in the back seat of the patrol car, I was driven to police headquarters. On the way, we passed the cemetery where Presley was to be buried in a few hours; I saw the second ABC crew sitting on the curb, waiting. At least the patrol car was air-conditioned.

The patrolman and his partner—apparently they needed two cops to bring me in—explained en route that I was to be charged with disorderly conduct. I muttered to myself, "Oh, not attempted jaywalking."

They informed me that if I could post $50 bond, I would be allowed to go free.

When we arrived at police headquarters, the patrolman burbled his way through his written report—I had to help him with some spelling—and then he took me to the booking sergeant. Because I lived outside of Memphis, the sergeant said, the bond would be $250.

I thought I saw a smug look on the patrolman's face, but then I reached into my sock and pulled out two one hundred dollar bills that I "wore" when I was out of town, and another fifty dollars from my pocket. I was given my release, but told that I would have to return to Memphis in two weeks for a hearing or forfeit the money. From the police station, I called the ABC Operations Manager in New York to tell him what happened. The ABC legal department immediately set about notifying the top law firm in Memphis. My attitude at that point was that it was worth $250 never to have to return.

When the paperwork was completed, I cabbed back to the station. When I told Knowles and the WHBQ assignment manager Kathie Wolff what had happened, they at first didn't believe me. But about a half-hour later Kathy came up to me and told me to report to the police commissioner's office immediately.

The commissioner was very gracious in his apology, and he then sent me to night court in the company of the department's legal officer. Following a couple of traffic violations and several prostitution cases, my case was called up and the judge quickly acceded to the department's request that the charges against me be dropped.

I fled the court, stopping briefly on the way back to the station to pick up a bottle of fine scotch and a dozen roses for Kathie Wolff. An hour later I was on a flight back to Chicago. The check for $250 from the City of Memphis was in the mail the next day.

15. Show Producer

The sign above my desk at WPRI in Providence in 1975 read "Duh Producah," and if anything it was a reminder that a person in my position could take very little for granted. Even though I made the decisions about what went into the early and late evening broadcasts, I had only marginal control. I was 24 at the time and sometimes my youthful ego needed to have its sails trimmed.

The truth is that producing a live television newscast is about the most thrilling work I could imagine. You can make all the right decisions while you are sitting at your desk formatting the program, but when you are sitting in the control room and something goes wrong, you are the go-to person. You have to know your options, and their consequences, and you often need to be able to make decisions in a matter of a second or two—literally—in order to reverse a deteriorating situation.

Producing a newscast is something like piloting an aircraft, which is described as hours of boredom (flying) and minutes of terror (landing). Putting a newscast together and getting it on the air, you have six or seven hours of slogging followed by an hour of on-the-edge-of-your-seat rapt attention. As the minutes are marked off the clock, you cross off each item on your line-up, and you relax a little. But not too much, knowing that there are fewer things that can go wrong, but also less time to make repairs.

The job of producing involves news judgement, awareness of your people and their strengths and weaknesses, and the ability to juggle ideas and circumstances so that at the end of the broadcast, you've told your audience what they need to know in a way that they could effectively assimilate it. You also want your news staff to feel as though they have accomplished something important, and to be imbued with a desire to do their job even better tomorrow.

While the producer is titularly in charge of the production, the success of the broadcast is dependent upon everyone working together. From the first alert to a news story by the assignment desk to the moment the director rolls tape on the finished packaged, virtually the entire news department is involved. Collaboration and cooperation are essential. It is a team effort or it fails, and the person overseeing it all is the producer.

A key function of a producer is to understand the needs of the individuals who are working with him. Av Westin said that a major part of his job was to be the staff psychiatrist. You don't have to go overboard, but it is useful to understand the motivations of the people around you. Does a reporter care more about being on air than covering the story? Does the director get huffy if you slot in a by-play between the weather and sports people?

Knowing the needs and capabilities of your technical crew is also important. If you have a slow tape editor or a studio camera operator with a tic, it's best to have them assigned to tasks where they won't get the broadcast into trouble. In the past, when the news department got the dirty end of the station's stick, this wasn't easy, as most of the less competent personnel were assigned to the news. But now things have changed, and a news director can usually ask for the top people to support her.

The producer has the overall responsibility for making the primary decisions and handling the changes that are a part of every broadcast. The producer essentially frames the program and the news staff works to implement the format. Reporters screen and log their footage, choosing and timing sound bites. Editors screen for the best visuals. Videographers shoot last minute inserts and standuppers. Scripts are written, checked with the producer and tracked. Sound cuts and b-roll are assembled. Supers are ordered, checked and corrected. Reporters argue for more time. Graphics are designed. File footage is located. Voice-overs are scripted and cut. Lead-ins and outros are coordinated. The weather and sports people are off preparing their segments. Interviewees are confirmed. Remotes are rechecked. The director is alerted to any unusual elements.

Until the last minute before going to the control room, the producer is watching the wires for breaking news or late developments that will require rewriting a script or re-editing a spot. As the deadline ticks forward, every time the phone rings, the producer knows his line-up is in jeopardy.

Journalistically, the role of a television news producer—whether for the local cut-in for *The Today Show* or a ninety minute local-network newscast in the early evening—is to know what information the viewers need to be well-roundedly informed. You must look at all of the stories that occurred in the past twenty-four hours, determinate which of them should be reported to the audience, in what order, format and duration. The more information you have in your head already about the stories and the audience, the more effective you will be in producing your digest of the past day's news.

The first thing a producer must do is read in, that is be familiar with what has run in the newspaper, on other broadcast media, and the wires during twenty-four hours since the last broadcast. You can't count on your viewers to have gotten news from another source, any more than you can count on them having watched your last broadcast, though many people who watch the news watch the same newscast every day. It is not unreasonable to consider every program a new day as a factor when you are squeezed in making a story selection, which means that the oldest of equally significant stories are going to go away.

When reading in, make a list of the important and otherwise attractive stories. You might break the list down into four sections: local, national, international and other. You might also list your packages, sound cuts and voice-overs separately. When it comes time to making a line up, you will know which stories you will definitely run and how much time each needs. Then you can select which other stories—among otherwise equals—will play with your primary selections.

On most days, you can list all of your stories in order of importance. It is a good place to start. In print journalism, a reporter will green-line a particular paragraph, or several, denoting that these can be edited out for space. Un-green-lined writing that would be cut for space contains material that would have to be rewritten because it is essential to the story or intertwined with other paragraphs. Similarly with your list of stories, you can usually pick from the top and hack from the bottom.

When it comes time to lock in the story selection for broadcast, you create a line-up (also called a rundown or a format), which is a list of the stories, reporters, video sources, spot times and running times. Some producers wait until late in the day to do their first line-up, but usually when you get one out three hours before air it gives the staff—both editorial and technical—an idea of what you are anticipating.

Some paranoid producer-types think they have to hold everything in their heads until the last minute, afraid of showing indecision or changing their minds. That treats the process as a game, when, in fact, everyone should be working together. An early line-up can alert the technical side to special needs, and can indicate to reporters how much time you are thinking about for their spots.

All newscasts should lead with the most important story, or the headlines of the top stories. This enables a viewer to check-in and know, more or less, if he is current with events. The reason why the headlines approach can be valuable is that sometimes there simply isn't a dominant lead, only a handful of less important stories, of varying significance to your audience. If your lead story isn't important to some of your viewers, probably one or some of the other headline stories will be, and they will stay tuned.

Think of how the audience hears the news. Try to understand how they assimilate the information your deliver. Putting your stories out in a coherent fashion enables them to more easily follow the flow of information, both from story to story and within each story.

This is an issue of pacing. You need to organize your show so that the viewer has a chance to absorb the information you are putting out. Pacing includes spacing your tape pieces. Videotape takes a lot more of the viewer's attention than does an on-camera reader. Putting a couple of readers between tape packages gives the viewer's mind a rest from constantly changing visual information. It also gives her time to digest the content.

Think of how uncomfortable it would be to watch a news program with all the tape packages butted together without copy stories in between. To get an idea, you have but to tune into a local sports segment, where so many sportscasters think they are judged by the quantity of tapes they run. They produce video overload. The same is a problem in a newscast when every small fire, auto accident and ribbon-cutting has tape over the copy.

Using too many graphics can be as jarring as a series of split-second edits, or filling a screen with different windows, changing text, and a crawl. And by airing graphics that don't dovetail or that conflict with the copy is like airing the wrong tape. While the viewer is trying to understand the visual, the copy is spooling off uselessly beyond his attention.

By the same token, not giving a story enough time also leaves the viewer in confusion. Allocating :15 for a story that needs :20 is going to bewilder a portion of the audience, who will carry that confused state of mind into the next story.

Finally, good, consistent writing is a tremendous aid to your viewers; it creates a dialogue, with the viewers sub-consciously registering the show's punctuation. It enhances comprehension and allows for more content and faster pacing. People become familiar with your style of presentation, and they expect information to be delivered in a particular way. For instance, they know that the anchorman's voice drops as he is nearing the end of a story or the close of a segment.

The more a newscast makes sense to your audience, the more likely they are to return. You will get into a rhythm that the audience will find comfortable. They will know where you place emphasis, when they need to apply extra attention. They will also develop a sense of trust, that what they hear on your newscast, they can repeat as fact. Whether it be a nightly routine or a breaking news story, they will turn to you when they need to know.

16. Story Selection

When selecting stories for a newscast, there are two criteria discussed earlier that may assist. First is picking stories that affect as well as interest a substantial segment of the market. Many business stories or government decisions may not be of immediate interest to the audience, but may have long-term impact of which the audience should be aware. That's the case even if the story is complicated and needs more time to explain.

For instance, in 2003 the state of California faced a budget deficit that was estimated at $35 billion. There were significant ramifications for just about everyone in the state, and the better informed the public was, the more likely their government officials would be to act responsibly, instead of just politically. Regrettably, most stations reported the size of the budget and the political fighting over it without providing the in-depth reporting that would have enfranchised the citizens to help in the decision-making.

Then there are other stories like smoke from a forest fire or a major tie-up on the interstate that should be reported, not for their long-term impact, but because of the public is personally aware that something has happened. Even though the effects of these events may be transitory and minor, to air the stories shows you are aware of what is going on in front of the public, and offers explanations for the acrid air or late spouses. To not air these stories could cause inferences that you weren't on top of what was happening, or couldn't manage the coverage, or didn't think the stories important. Reporting what is on everyone's minds can help to strengthen your voice in the community.

A third criterion for story selection is that reporting should help to resolve the (top five) major issues facing the community by focusing attention on them. This means that in addition to covering events of the day, it is important to extend the audience's scope. That is, reaching beyond reactive coverage regarding the day's events and unearthing information that helps people to better understand and manage their community's affairs. This doesn't mean shoot-'em-up investigative reports, but digging more deeply into a story of why some schools fail to teach their students effectively, or why some children get fat, or why a particular intersection is the site of many more accidents, or how can the city reduce its overhead with a minimum reduction in services.

These are guidelines for coverage, of course; there are no rules. Having a nose for news helps, as does experience watching stories develop, and learning how to journalistically separate the wheat from the chaff. There might be a news conference announcing a new building project. Later there will be a photo of the mayor turning over the first spade of dirt. At some point, the doors will open. And further down the road there will be an opportunity to look back and see how the project has done. Some of the early stories will make packages on the day they occur, depending on the events competing for coverage that day. Some will be voice-overs, some readers and some may not get reported at all.

Often, events of the day are hooks for think pieces. For instance, a mugging in a poor part of town might not be news because it happens ten times a night every night, and more on weekends with a full moon. But a particularly senseless or brutal attack might be the peg for an in-depth report on reasons why crime is prevalent in the area, and what's being done—or not—to deal with the problem.

And not just deal with the problem, but advance understanding of the issues involved. Most of what the networks produce in their news magazines are stories dripping in pathos. They evoke anger or despair, often over the failure of government and/or society to resolve certain issues. Regrettably, they don't take the critical next step of informing people where solutions might lie, often because they don't want to offend someone. For example, the primary factor in ghetto crime is a continuing generational cycle of ignorance, obstinance and brutality.

But if you say that, you'll be accused of racism, and few news operations are willing to risk offending a part of their audience.

Choosing which stories to cover and which to report is an on-going process based on the information needs of the community, what other events are competing for precious broadcast time, and what resources are available to tell the story. Some choices are obvious, some are not. Sometimes a producer is tempted to over-cover, as when some large and tragic event like a shuttle explosion occurs. While the temptation may be to go vertical—that is, devote the entire newscast (or most of it) to stories about the disaster—it is important not to exclude some of the other major stories of the day, even if they are merely recapped with a series of readers at the end of the newscast.

Another factor determining story selection is what other stories are being reported. For instance, you might have two foreign stories and need a third to flesh out the segment. The third story may not be quite as important as some other domestic stories, but it will create the necessary pacing for the segment. Or you might have a segment that is heavy with readers and choose to substitute out one reader for a less important story that has some fascinating footage.

The ultimate job of the producer is to make sure that the audience has all of the information that they need, according to the particular lights of the community; then what's merely useful; and finally what's simply interesting. You will never have all the time you need to report everything, so you have to choose primarily from the first list before going to the second and the third. It's a juggling act, and story selection is choosing which balls are in the air. It is the most important editorial job of producing.

In a sardonic salute to the dilemma, Bill Seamans, then news editor for the *ABC Evening News*, made up a casualty list of types of disasters and the number of people who would have to be killed to make news. For instance, 300 would have to drown in a Bangladesh ferry sinking, because it happened so frequently at lower death rates that it would be disproportionately (from New York) reported as news. More than 100 would have to die in a Japanese Bullet Train accident. Fifty Korean children—orphans, preferably—in a school bus plunging into a ravine. Twenty-five Swiss in a bus caught in an avalanche. And so on. It was morbid, certainly, and vaguely funny, and ironically, he kept the list posted next to the executive producer as a reminder that news decisions concern people.

17. Formatting the Broadcast

The order of stories provides important information in itself. Most viewers presume that stories are reported in order of importance. That's the nature of our culture; latest, fastest, most, biggest, first. Also remember that some viewers may only be able to watch the first few minutes of a newscast and would like to know the top stories. So the first step in formatting a newscast is to make a list of stories on the basis of newsworthiness. When stories have relative news value, you might group them by subject or geography.

While an essential aspect of the formatting process is the order in which stories are reported, you shouldn't be a slave to a pre-defined rule of order. It is important to maintain a flow between stories. You might want to run them in the order of importance, but on most days, that would mean changing subjects frequently. For instance, say your first, third and sixth most important stories are out of Washington, while your second and fifth are foreign and the fourth is economic. It would be clumsy, at best, and probably confusing to report them in strict order of importance. It would make more sense to group them together with similar, important stories.

The best way to mitigate the issue of order by importance is to lead an hour newscast with four to six headlines. This informs the audience of the most important stories at the top, and then enables you to report the stories out of order, so to speak.

Don't force connections or create them; your audience appreciates that there are many different stories and more often that not, they are unrelated. It's a big world, after all, and a diverse nation, on many levels. "Also overseas tonight", "Closer to home", "In other business news" are popular but mindless. If there is a natural connection, your audience will get it. Also, support visuals can make connections between stories more obvious.

The flip side of the connection "problem" is the benefit of bridges. Some stories play conveniently one into another. For instance, you have a report on Congress passing important environmental legislation. You have another report on the White House pushing for oil drilling on the North Slope. That's not complicated. Or your medical correspondent is going to report that the FDA says it will ban a certain line of skin creams. You also have a report from a town whose primary income comes from a plant that manufactures those skin creams. You might not even need an anchor bridge between that pair.

Less obvious might be a court ruling against Microsoft and a drop in the Dow. If tech stocks are generally hot and the NASDAQ rises, you might report the connection, but want to explain that Microsoft is on the Big Board.

Another way to transition between stories in the middle of a segment is shift anchors. The simple change in the person reading breaks the presumed editorial thread quite effectively.

Finally, of course, you can use commercials to separate your stories. Commercials are very practical for blocking segments, and can actually be valuable in a number of ways. Besides making an obvious break between stories, commercials can be used to mark the clock and position bumpers; this will be discussed in more detail in a later chapter. Commercials can also give you time to regroup if things go wrong. If your show falls apart, you can jump into a commercial break earlier than planned, and the two minutes can give you the time to finish a final edit, re-order a line-up, or load a bank piece.

A final thought on commercials. The spots that air in your news program say something about your audience, maybe. At least your sales team and the advertisers choosing to run their spots in the news believe so. If you are thought to have an upscale audience, then you might have commercials for Lexus and Charles Schwab, whereas if you were talking to a less affluent, less educated crowd, you might be selling time for Kia's and McDonald's. Geritol would seek to reach older viewers while Pepsi would go for younger viewers.

Of course, it may be that the company or agency is erring by buying the time they do, but it's often a clue to the perception of your newscast and who is watching it. The reason why a news director would care is that the audience may respond in kind. That is, if they see a program that is loaded with commercials that don't speak to them, they may feel a sense of disconnect. If your commercials don't reflect the viewership to whom you as the producer are programming, you might invite the sales manager to seek more appropriate advertisers.

18. Allocating Time

In addition to selecting the stories to be reported, and determining the order in which they will be presented, a third critical element in the producing of a newscast is the allocation of time. Allocating time depends on (1) how many stories there are that need to be reported, (2) how much is required to explain what needs to be reported, and (3) what's left. At some point, if you find yourself with extra time—a rare occurrence—you can either give more time to the stories you've already selected or add more stories to the line-up.

There is no rule about how long a story should run; that depends on the facts and the degree of context that is needed to tell it. Whether you are offering a reporter's account or a delivering a reader, the point of telling the story is to communicate the facts that make it newsworthy. Sometimes those facts require a considerable amount of background information. Others require none at all.

Using the who-what-where-when-how-and-why guideline, you can check most of your coverage points. You can then add copy to flesh out the important issues, or insert new material that takes the story in another direction; if you have the time and it fits in with the rest of what you are reporting. Whatever you decide, remember that when you get to the end of the story, the viewer shouldn't be asking "So what?" Make sure that is tacit in the report.

Unless you're reading headlines, most stories—even with a paucity of facts—should be allocated at least fifteen seconds. The viewers need time to adjust their thinking when you change subjects. They haven't been reading the wires all day and don't have your line-up in front of them. In most cases, a certain degree of spooling goes on in their brains, where they receiving new information while they're processing an earlier batch. Think about how you record and playback in your own mind when someone says something to you out of context or changes the subject; or when you're listening to someone, become distracted, and then have to replay in your mind what was said to you.

This approach also applies to the use of sound bites. Very few cuts—sound bites and/or voice-overs—should run less than ten seconds; the best length is about eighteen seconds. This gives the audience a chance to understand what is happening and to get used to the different sights and sounds. It's not that they can't follow at a faster clip, but it's more comfortable to watch a less frenetic program—longer readers, longer sound bites, fewer video edits—and the comprehension and retention levels are significantly higher.

In the standard newscast, reporter packages also must meet the criteria of providing all of the essential facts to cover the story, but they shouldn't dawdle. Most reports on even complicated news events can be summarized in a minute-and-a-half. After all, television news is a headline service so it stands to reason that you are providing the highlights of each event, and need to keep the delivery of stories tight.

There are certainly exceptions. On some longer newscasts—e.g., when you have ninety minutes or more of local evening news—you're likely to have lengthy reports that provide considerable background and detail. These reports, which may run five or six minutes, are usually aired at the back of an hour so that the audience has had a chance to get filled up on the day's latest news.

There are several reasons to keep reports to a minute-thirty or less, most of the time. First, the shorter the package the more room there is for a larger complement of stories. Second, the audience has been trained to consume their stories in relatively bite-size pieces. A third factor to consider is that most people watching the news are also doing something else, like preparing or eating dinner during the early show or getting ready to turn in during the late newscast, which means that their attention span is limited.

This is not a rule, of course. Many reports on local news today run in the range of forty-five seconds, but often during sweeps, stations will air spicy features that run several minutes, twice a night, for a week, for a month. If you find yourself with a story that needs a lot of time—especially if it is complex and takes different directions—you might think about splitting it into two separate correspondent reports. Or let the anchor report some of the facts in the lead-in. A voice-over leading in using historical footage, for example, or a sound cut that sets up the rest of the story might work. Also, more elements might be reported in an anchor outro.

Don't get carried away with myriad elements. Some stories are too complex to fully report in an evening news broadcast. If you have a place in the broadcast for a on-set guest, you might have that person explain the finer details.

In most cases, as important as a story may seem tonight, it will usually seem less so the next day. And one of the reasons why you don't want to go overboard with your coverage is that the more time that you devote to a story, the more importance you give it with your audience. If you get caught up in the moment and overplay events, you can lose credibility with your viewers. Remember, it is easier to expand on your coverage the next night, if that is warranted, than to say, oops, folks, it wasn't that big of a deal.

When the Son of Sam capture broke in New York City in the summer of 1977, Roone Arledge ordered four separate reports for the network's evening broadcast. There was some discussion at the time that this might be too much for a network broadcast, but once the wheels were in motion, there was little resistance. The next day, however, most agreed that the coverage of the arrest of the New York City killer, as heinous as he was, had been excessive.

A 15-Minute Half Hour

When thinking about the allocation of time in a newscast, it becomes much more simplified when you do the basic math. In a half-hour local news program with 7:30 minutes of commercials (and billboards), for example, if you have 3:00 set aside for sports and 2:30 for weather, as is common for the late local news in many markets, you find yourself with 17:00 to play with. Pull out time for your opening and goodnight, leads to sports and weather, bumpers leading into three commercial breaks, and a brite to close the show, you're down to under fifteen minutes. That's not a lot of time to cover the world, national and local scenes. No wonder so many stations ignore foreign stories.

Many local stations will have one reporter to give them one new report for the late news. Then they might have four packages from the early evening news that have been updated, or not. Maybe a couple that featured live standuppers now have the on-camera on tape. Plus it would not be uncommon to have a half-dozen voice-overs and maybe three sound bites, culled from the early news and the network. If the packages average 1:35 with leads-in and the voice-overs and sound bites :20 each, you've consumed about eleven minutes covering a dozen stories, more or less. That leaves you with four minutes, and that's what makes allocating time such a tough job.

Finally this consideration when it comes to time in a newscast: you need to be flexible in the control room. If a report has been mis-timed, if there are technical glitches, if the commercial doesn't roll when it should, you could find yourself with ten minutes of news and only 9:30 in which to air it. That is why it is a good idea to have a (small) handful of stories—readers, usually—that you can discard if you get into a crunch.

On the *ABC Evening News*, Av Westin had a PPT section before the last commercial break. In it were three or four People, Places, or Things stories running about twenty seconds each that provided some flexibility in the show, in the likely event that one report or another which might not have been completed by the start of the program, would run long. There were very few nights that all of the PPT stories aired.

(One day in 1976, I had reported to the *Good Morning America* news producer that the time of a Frank Reynolds spot on Ronald Reagan's campaign was 1:58. While the spot was running, the phone from the Washington control room rang, with show producer wondering how long the piece actually ran. One-fifty-eight, I responded. From the front row, the ever-calm associate director looked up and said, "It's already run 2:10." "How 'bout 2:58?" I told the producer, who didn't find my comment amusing.)

Of course, problems can occur in the other direction. A 1:30 report that you were counting on might be derailed, by events or technology, and suddenly you find yourself with more time on your hands than you have program. That's one reason to go into the control room with extra copy stories in hand; they may be on your clipboard, and not even on the format. You can also run credits on a night you ordinarily wouldn't, and there's always the bank, which is discussed later.

19. The Look of the News

The Look of a news operation should extend from its business cards to its closing credits, and include the opening effects, supers, graphics, camera framing, as well as the appearance of reporters and anchors. A consistency in The Look helps to connect everything and to solidify an overall image.

There is a line between retail branding and station identification, and it's not terribly fine. For example, having all your on-air people wear bright yellow sailing jackets or large orange logos on their clothes is plain and obvious advertising. Whereas a humble logo on a microphone clip is a good idea, because it helps the interviewee remember to whom he is speaking; nothing large and jazzy; just the channel number, maybe stylized, is enough.

As far as the reporters are concerned, you really want your people to show themselves as individuals, albeit in accordance with a style established by the station. Simplicity, clean lines and dignity are good starting points. There are markets so rural that a necktie would look out of place, but in most cases, it's appropriate. Reporters in the field should be spiffed up enough to feel comfortable visiting a corporate board room.

(Of course, you may be called away from that board room to cover a mountain top rescue that has you scaling the heights on your hands and knees, so it's always a good idea to have spare clothes in the trunk of your car. Covering the news can be a messy business, literally, and few stations cover the cost of ruined clothing.)

The Look should also be reflected in how your videographers capture their images. Standuppers and interviews should be framed in a consistent manner, unless special circumstances dictate otherwise. The anchors should be framed in the same way every newscast. There should be a standard policy on zooms and pans, not restrictive but instructive, so that your station is recognized for having the most illuminating visuals, and the most comfortable—accessible, under-standable—editing.

Graphics should share the identity with the set and the appearance of the on-camera personnel. Again, the simplest designs and the cleanest lines present messages in the shortest time with the least possibility for confusion.

How people are addressed on-camera, live throws, sign-offs and general pacing should all be standardized, again to accomplish the task with the most clarity, facility and dignity. This doesn't not mean vanilla-izing personal style. Anyone can strut their own "stuff," within appropriate bounds, as long as they share the same journalistic mission, sense of humility about using the public airwaves, and high standards of quality.

By trying to present a uniformed appearance throughout your newscasts, one that demonstrates respect for the news and the audience, you create an aura that extends throughout your productions. Done properly, it not only identifies your work—entire newscasts and individual reports—but it is also engaging. When a major story breaks, it will be your station that people turn to learn the facts because they have a relationship with you.

20. The Set

Many news operations choose to broadcast with their working news room as the backdrop. Conceptually, this might make sense, but, in fact, there are numerous drawbacks. First, anything in the background can be a distraction, from people typing or talking on the phone to screen-savers on computer monitors. Someone just walking through the newsroom can catch a viewer's eye.

You might also consider that when an audience is watching a newscast and in the background two people are talking, or someone is on the phone, there is often the question in the back of the viewer's mind—at least subliminally—as to what those people might be discussing that is more important than the newscast.

Another problem is that newsrooms can look particularly vacant by the time an evening or late evening newscast hits the air, which might be inferred by some viewers to mean that the news operation has shut down; hardly a positive image. Also unappetizing is a sloppy newsroom, which seems endemic after a long day of news-gathering.

Stationing anchors or reporters in front of a window facing out onto Main Street also invites distraction, and it doesn't take much to divert a viewer's attention from the story being read. Considering how tightly newscasts are formatted and written, to distract a viewer for just a few seconds can make the difference between understanding a story—hearing a qualifier or a negative, for example—and missing it entirely.

The ideal news set is clean, almost sterile, with all elements directing attention to the anchors. They're the source of news, after all; that's why people are watching the newscast. Also realize that the less you see of the anchors, the less opportunity there is for distraction from their natural shifting about. So you would want to put them behind a desk, rather than have them standing behind a podium. A simple set which can be cross-shot and allows for the easy insertion of graphics makes the most sense.

21. Supers

When you shoot good tape, you don't want to obscure it with unnecessary clutter, like extraneous supers. The only supers that should appear over tape are those that advance understanding of what's being shown. Only use such supers as are necessary for identifying the location or time or person, for example. This is contrary to the policy of many stations today, which wallpaper virtually every clip with"Tonight" or "Live," which in most cases is superfluous. An intelligent viewer will view such supers as merely an annoying form of self-promotion.

Especially when the supers take up a third or more of the screen, often with a graphic station logo imbedded in them. Their use implies that your newscast is so weakly regarded that you have to remind viewers what station they're watching. A quality television news operation, on the other hand, attracts deliberate viewers who choose your program because it is the best written, produced, directed and reported. You don't want to cover your tape nor hype your call letters.

Supers should complement the video. Simple, clean, concise. Use as few words as possible. When identifying people on the screen, be sparse in the description. For instance, if you are talking with an eyewitness, you rarely need to use that as a second line, and you certainly don't need "Saw Victim Abducted." Similarly, use "Brother" if it's not apparent and relevant instead of "Victim's Brother" unless there's a question; the latter adds gratuitously to the pathos.

The reason for this stern caution about excess in use of supers is that every time you add an element to your presentation, you immediately take the viewers' attention from what they were looking at, either a person or b-roll. That diversion breaks the train of comprehension, so it better be worth it, e.g., a point of clarification. That's also why you want to try to insert the super a couple of seconds after a scene change, so the audience has a chance to register the video before their eyes are drawn to the super.

Also, when you use supers, whether to identify someone or some place in a news report or as a credit at the end of a broadcast, make sure the viewer has enough time to read it. This is more important when it is part of a news report, of course, but the general rule is that if it is worth putting on the air, make sure the audience has enough time to view it to digest the information. One way to know if a super has been up long enough is to read it aloud slowly, take a beat and then lose it.

There are situations when you will want to super a person more than once. For example, you have an extended report on a dispute about a new sewer line and in the first thirty seconds you run a sound cut of the county administrator outlining his position. He shows up a second time in the last thirty seconds of what is a three-minute package, and unless he is a focus of the report, you will probably need to re-identify him. You can introduce the second cut orally with "County Administrator Smith" but you may also want to super him again.

Full screen supers can take considerable time to be assimilated, so when you use them, leave them up long enough to be read by a slow viewer. And with crawls (horizontal) and rolls (vertical) leave extra time for the viewers to read, as they are more difficult to follow than static supers. It is advisable to start a crawl with alerting copy, e.g., "This weather advisory...", before running the news information, so people can acclimate to the new visual.

Identification of anchors and reporters should be limited. For anchors, once at the top of the half-hour program; in an hour program, once at the top of each half-hour. More than that looks silly; especially since most people are tuned into the station because of the anchors. For reporters, once supered is enough; either on-camera or voice over "reporting". The identification is for information purposes, not promotion.

It probably needn't be said, but readability of supers can be an issue. Some fonts read better than others, and kerning—leaving enough space between letters—can increase the distance from the screen that supers can be read. Choosing the font and kerning for the supers should be done in conjunction with the rest of the station's look, but your goal is to make sure that what you put on the screen informs effectively and efficiently.

22. Graphics

Graphics can be instrumental in both connecting a viewer to a subject and elucidating it. They can be used over the anchor's shoulder to supplement a reader or an intro, or they can be used internally in a report, either on their own, or in place of or in conjunction with video. They can also be used full-screen in an anchor voice-over or report.

Graphics sometimes work more effectively than video; for instance, when complex elements in a story might be better told with a static image than one that's moving and inherently distracting.

Graphics can be more effective in communicating ideas because they can be custom-designed to fit the unique circumstances of a particular story, which can't always be done using available video. You can also create powerful images using still frames from video—file or new—and putting text over them, or maybe arrows. Graphics are often more effective in diagraming, e.g., a business flow chart.

Anchor graphics can be very valuable in providing your broadcast with a look; especially when their design has a relationship with the set. One approach to creating that look is to use a selection of generic graphics and add supers that add enough specificity to identify the story.

The value of generic graphics is that they can immediately inform the audience about the subject of the story, e.g., medicine, business/economics, crime, Congress, education, et cetera. A caduceus with a stethoscope might say that the story is about medicine. Add the super "Flu Shots" underneath or "Nursing Homes", and you've immediately got your audience on the right subject. A gavel over prison bars with the super "Hijacker Sentenced" will similarly catch up the viewer. A few dozen generic graphics with a keyword or two underneath can probably illustrate most every story you will ever report.

With the clip art libraries available these days, you can be guaranteed of finding virtually any image, icon, or picture you might need. Any news operation would benefit from having a staffer or two who was familiar with such libraries, knew how to track down obscure visuals, and also how to "clip" them and produce them for air.

It would be more advisable to create a news library of visuals, not only of the generic type frequently used on the air, but also those that help tell repeating or on-going local stories. A collection of maps, for instance, that showed the local area would also be useful from time to time. Add to it shots of local public figures—civic, business, political, sports, etc.—to have available for use at a moment's notice. When someone makes news and is likely to do so again, you might pull a frame from their video and put it in your library. Also include corporate logos and shots of signs of local businesses. [Some schools offer formal training in media library sciences.]

As useful as graphics can be, you should be careful which ones you select. Some generic graphics carry implications that might lead the viewer in the wrong direction. Also, using file shots of individuals might be inappropriate at times, especially smiling faces when something bad has happened to them. We are regularly treated to shots of smiling people when they have been arrested, indicted, or killed, and though the practice is so common we don't even think about it any-more, we probably should.

Finally this suggestion. You don't always have to use a visual. As easy as they are to come by—from tape or file photos or clip art—you don't have to support every story with a graphic. There are times when the anchor reading the story without graphic support can have the most impact. Some stories are simply better told without them, e.g., the occasional brite where a graphic would give away the punch line, or a somber story that needs no highlight.

23. Bumpers

Bumpers are the segments between the news and commercials. Originally, bumpers were designed to give the director time to roll his commercials; it took ten seconds for the tape to lock. The director would roll the tape towards the end of the anchor copy, then go to a bumper before taking the commercial. In those days, the bumper was often simply an image from a spot from the next segment with the words"coming up."

The *ABC Evening News* featured an opening billboard that included graphics representing four headline stories and six "clicker" headlines of correspondent reports and commentary. At each commercial break, the director would take a shot of the billboard, with the next report highlighted. It was effective not only in telling people what was to come, but also in reinforcing what they had already seen.

The main use of bumpers today is as a venue to play titillating video from upcoming stories to keep the viewers from changing channels. The bumpers can last twenty seconds or more, depending on the excitement value of the visuals. The result is that often more than a minute of an hour program is consumed showing a few video clips two or three times. It is not uncommon for a producer to select a piece of highly entertaining (though often insignificant) video to close his program, and then will air it in five bumpers. By the time the end of the show rolls around, the viewers—if they've found the bumper video compelling—are likely to be inured to the "entertainment" value.

It's understandable that bumpers would be seen as an opportunity to keep viewers interest by promising irresistible pictures on the other side of the break, but the fact is that today's technology does not require a ten-second pre-roll. In fact, commercials can be rolled virtually instantaneously. Does that mean that bumpers should go? No.

The concept of a buffer between the anchored newscast and the sponsors' messages is a sound one. Perhaps rather than bumper—the function it performed in the old days—it might instead be called buffer, in that the video teases give viewer a chance to transition from paying serious attention to none, theoretically. But at many stations the time could be put to better use.

Viewers would be well-served, for example, if the buffer were filled with weather, stocks, or sports information in the same position (at the same time) every night. By airing the same bumpers every night at the same time—e.g., weather before the first break, stocks before the second, et cetera—you give your audience a sense of continuity and scheduling that better engages them. They know to look for the information they seek at a particular time, which fosters greater loyalty to your broadcast.

You might also consider putting a clock in the lower-right corner of every bumper (or just for the last five seconds) going into the commercial, as part of The Look of serving the public that they can set their watch by your newscast. Make sure that the time is right.

When you air four bumpers in a half-hour newscast, if you fill the time with teases, you're squandering precious seconds that might be better utilized reporting another story. If you program for an intelligent, news-hungry, consumer-minded audience, you deliver more of your product and more efficiently—and respectfully—to your audience if you fill your buffers with useful information.

If you do use bumpers for content, make sure that you leave them on the screen long enough for a slow reader to read everything. While your regular viewers may be used to your style and come to expect the information in a particular format, new viewers need more time. A rule of thumb from Charlie Heinz, one of ABC's finest news directors because he concerned himself with the viewers' perception, is that you should take the shot, and then read the entire screen aloud to the control room.

24. Credits

When you get your first credit, it can be very exciting. At least for the first couple of programs. Then the work seems like so much more. Still, everyone likes credits, even if they've stopped looking for them.

Some people place a greater importance on credits than others. For instance, the network anchors whose newscasts have their names in the title, plus have themselves credited as Managing Editor. But for the "laborers in the vineyard," as Murrow referred to them, credits can mean recognition of being part of a team of serious-minded journalists. (I also enjoyed the fact that people would come up to my mother in the Stop-'n-Shop in Northampton, Massachusetts, and tell her they'd seen my name on television.)

Many newscasts limit the number of credits that they'll roll, sometimes just rolling until they run into end of the program time. That is, the credits are used as fill, as a tail bumper. Other stations show the top credits every night; in some places there are contract requirements for certain positions, like director, to be credited for each broadcast. So be it; these credits would precede the copyright screen in the close.

With a large news organization, it can take some time to roll the credits of everyone responsible for the news coverage, but it should be done anyway at least once a week, probably on Fridays. There is usually a sizeable support side of staffers in the newsroom, in the studio and out in the field, who should be recognized for their part in the presentation.

When you do run credits, allow enough time so that they can be read. It is oxymoronic to air anything that can't be assimilated. This applies especially to the names of the people who are contributing to the broadcast.

It's not really necessary to give credits to the anchors. Their faces are on the air for several minutes every newscast; that should be enough. Also, since reporters get their names supered when they are on the air, unless they are contributing to the news in other ways, e.g., writing or producing, they probably don't need another credit either. Another school of thought is that you list the entire reportorial staff in the weekly credits, to identify them as a group, which makes some sense.

As part of that last (copyright) visual, you should also put up your URL, together with an invitation to viewers to stay up to the moment at your website.

25. The Bank

Bank stories are generally features, and most usually have a limited shelf-life. Some bank pieces are pegged to particular events, e.g., an upcoming trial, or to a date, e.g., an anniversary story. Other stories are more generic, and can be aired with or without a direct hook. The former bank stories are slated to go on particular days, while the generic can be used on a light news day, or when you are more understaffed than usual.

Most likely you will find yourself running a bank piece because a story you were counting on for your broadcast never gelled, or there was a technical problem that prevented its airing. It could also be that a major story that is expected to break late in the afternoon suddenly doesn't break; e.g., the labor negotiations continue past a deadline, the plane carrying the sports hero is delayed, or the press conference is called off by the politician you thought was going to resign.

A camera malfunction can suddenly chop a hole into your line-up that is not so easy to fill. If, as can happen at a small station, you don't discover until 4:00 that a tape containing a reporter's package and two voice-overs has no control track, you are in a lot better shape to handle the curve if you have a half-dozen features ready to go. Or maybe the transmitter at a live remote suddenly goes on the fritz; a bank provides some cushion.

It is important not only to have the bank spots, but also the scripts—including lead-in and -out, within close grasp. Usually when you discover you need to tap into the bank, there is little time and much confusion. Often someone knows where the tape is, but the copy could be in dozen different places, none of them doing you any good.

Running a bank story can sometimes free up a reporter, cameraman, and/or editor to work on a special assignment, or simply to have the time to harvest recently-aired footage for the library. While most news operations are run on a tight budget, there are opportunities on slow news days to put stories in the bank. You should always have in the back of your mind, when you have a reporter or camerawoman with some free time, to pick up sound cuts and visuals to support future pieces. They don't have to be packages shot in their entirety; you can collect the elements over a matter of weeks. For instance, if there is a expert on obesity coming to town for a medical forum and you have a reporter free, you might send her over for an interview, maybe for a sound cut about the forum for that night, and one on obesity for future use.

Shifting Focus

It may take some re-training, but it is vital to fulfilling the true news function that you shift the consciousness of the coverage to a more comprehensive approach. You might cut back on your daily shooting, if you can, and sacrifice some of the shots of twisted metal and charred timbers to pick up sound bites of school and health officials for a future report. It may not be exciting visually, but if you're asking the right questions you'll evoke some engaging answers. And the public will recognize and respect the effort.

There could also be more time freed up for shooting bank pieces if standup-pers were shot early and crews not stuck waiting for the ubiquitous "live" shot. Crew time could also be saved using file footage where appropriate instead of shooting new footage that doesn't advance the story. And finally, crews could be better used if stories were simply told as readers without b-roll. Gratuitous video is a distraction; viz, a local station reporting the arrest of a juvenile for vandalism and car theft aired pictures of a line of cars—not the ones that were hit; just some parked cars—and tight shots of door locks.

The creation of bank shots or b-roll library can be a valuable tool, both in reducing the amount of daily shooting that is required, and having shots available when there isn't time to send someone out to get them for a breaking story. It takes some time and effort to produce and maintain a library, but the benefits are many. In eighteen months of producing business/economics coverage for ABC, I amassed a library of over 100 tapes which contained shots on such a variety of subjects that we could produce voice-over video on virtually any subject in our purview. When Dan Cordtz was asked an hour before show time to come up with a piece on a late-breaking business or economics story, we regularly managed to provided a visual report by pulling shots from the bank and adding simple graphics.

Be careful about investing too much time and effort in bank pieces or features, as they can be outdated by the calendar, and/or events. And make sure they are still viable before you slap them into the player to fill a sudden chasm in your broadcast. Don't just read the script; screen the spot. The script may read fine, but the picture might show snow and this is August. Some bank pieces may age grace-fully. Others die on the vine. Others can be the victim of circumstances.

To wit, what happened to a report Bob Sirkin and I did in March of 1979 for the *ABC Evening News*. It was about the tenth anniversary of the attack on My Lai, and we had labored mightily on the report, tracking down William Calley at his in-laws' jewelry store in Georgia, interviewing philosopher Michael Walzer in Boston, pulling in the horrific shots of the village that Ron Haberle had taken, and obtaining new film from Vietnamese sources of a memorial being built on the site.

It didn't matter; the story never ran. On the day the report was to air, Israel had just invaded Lebanon, the Senate was voting on the Panama Canal Treaty, and the body of former Italian Prime Minister Aldo Moro was found in the trunk of a car.

The lesson is…build a bank, but try to keep its contents fresh. Some pieces are truly evergreen but others begin to smell of mothballs. You never know when you will need to make a withdrawal, and currency will always be an issue.

Part of the altered mindset should include considering all the tape you shoot for its potential future use, either as library (file) footage or perhaps for a future story or a bank piece. For example, file footage might be useful as a voice-over to flesh out future coverage, e.g., crime scene footage might be aired when the perp goes on trial.

Make sure that whenever you use file footage, that it is identified on the air properly, and that any differences between then and now are handled in the script and/or with supers. If, for instance, you are discussing a story where there are buildings in the file footage that have since been demolished, you would want to address the point. If someone has aged dramatically, you might need to tell your audience that they are looking at the same person. Sometimes a change in the seasons requires an explanation, if certain landmarks aren't visible or as clear.

Whether bank pieces or library footage, what you have filed away can be useful, not only for explaining a story but also for illuminating the depth of your coverage.

III—Broadcasting the News

When I am working on a problem I never think about beauty. I only think about how to solve the problem. But when I have finished, if the solution is not beautiful, I know it is wrong.

—Buckminster Fuller

Section Three of *Don't Mess with the Press* explains the nuts and bolts of an actual newscast. This is when you walk into the control room after a day of covering and producing, and you broadcast your work. You have assembled your packages and voice-overs, graphics and scripts. Your anchors are at their desk. The control room crew is ready to roll tape. You look down at your line-up and wonder…at the end of the next hour, how much of it will make it on the air in order?

In truth, anything can happen. In the spring of 1975, I was working at WPRI in Providence, Rhode Island as the producer of the six and eleven o'clock news. It was ten seconds before late news, and I was sitting at the console in the control room. The director on my left pressed a button to roll the videotape. We were about to begin our late broadcast in a special way. Instead of the normal start with graphic titles, we were cold-opening with a clip from the *CBS Evening News*.

In the report that had aired earlier on the network, correspondent Richard Threlkeld described the beginning of an orphan airlift out of Vietnam. We were beginning our newscast with a poignant ten seconds of his report that described the children arriving in Oakland. Threlkeld finished the ten-second segment saying, "And tomorrow, for the first time in their lives, these children will wake up in the morning in a country that is not at war."

It was an exciting moment, as the tape rolled and locked in the preview monitor. I felt that opening our late news in this unusual way, we would draw people into the true horror of the war, even as our country was extricating our own participants. I counted myself very lucky to have the creative latitude to offer alternatives to the standard fare to our news audience.

Andy Fisher was the news director, his first management post after leaving a reporter's position at WCBS television in New York. He and I had worked together for WCBS, and he had brought me up to Providence to produce the weeknight newscasts. It was my first shot at such work. I was 24 years old.

"Track it," said director/TD Ron Moses to the audio man on my right. The audio man slid forward the control for the tape machine. When the sweep second hand passed the 59 mark, Ron punched the button that put the tape on line, exactly as I had envisioned. A second passed, and another. The chill of ice water filled my veins.

"Where's the sound?" Ron demanded. By then the audio guy's hands were scrambling like so many crabs across his board, opening every channel he could.

"Where's the audio?" I demanded, as the seconds of excruciating silence mounted.

"It's not there," the audio man cried back.

"What do I do?" Ron asked me urgently.

I looked at the monitors. Doug White, the anchorman, was looking up with arched brows. He should have been hearing the sound in the studio and wasn't.

"Play the opening."

Ron hit another button. "Standby tape two," he told the audio man.

"Doug on the phone," I ordered.

Through his headset, Ron instructed the studio camerawoman to tell the anchorman to pick up his phone to the control room.

"We're going to opening. Out of it, apologize for the glitch. Go to your script."

Ron punched up the opening. We had a few seconds to catch up. When the normal tape opening ended, Ron punched up Doug on camera, and we rejoined the format. Ever the professional, Doug did the "good evening", explained what people had seen but not heard, and led into the rest of the Threlkeld tape, as planned. Once it was rolling—with audio, thank goodness—I got out of my chair, opened the door to the tape operation, and shouted over the din of the equipment, "What happened?"

"Whaddya mean, 'what happened'?" asked the tape guy, a fine fellow, and usually on his mark.

"Where was the sound at the top?"

"I erased it," he said matter-of-factly. He paused. "Didn't you want it erased?"

Nope. I looked around in vain for a wall to hit, but this being a new facility, everything was glass, and the doorposts didn't seem nearly strong enough to absorb my frustration. On more than one occasion in my brief tenure at the station, I had opened with a studio voice-over of tape, and the tape guy had correctly erased the sound to prevent an inadvertent slip-up by the audio man. It was difficult to fault him for his initiative.

Of course at that point there was nothing that could be done; there is no west coast update of the TV-12 News. But in that moment, I knew and I etched indelibly into the deepest part of my professional soul that ultimately it was my responsibility as the producer that everyone get everything right. There could be no presumptions that anyone—camera crew, reporter, tape editor—was going to do their part unless I told them what I saw as the final product and their role in it.

Regardless of circumstances, no matter who comes through or doesn't, the fact is that the producer is responsible for what is broadcast. The more experience, intelligence, dedication, and flexibility brought into the control room, the more likely the result will be satisfactory or better. Outlined in the following pages is much of what you need to know to produce a successful broadcast.

26. The Audience

When presenting the news, you need to understand not only the story, but to whom you are telling it. You need to tailor your presentation to your particular audience, based on what they know and how they listen. Consider the range of viewers who get their news from Fox and PBS; your viewers are somewhere in between.

Newscasts do not air in a vacuum; they are written, produced and reported by the same people every night. If you are consistent in your presentation—delivery, formatting and pacing—you're probably talking to the same audience, since most viewers tend to watch the same newscast night after night. They have an understanding of the newscast, a relationship with those who put it together, and expectations (often subliminal) of how it will be presented.

The higher the quality of the presentation, the higher the quality of the audience you'll attract. Produce a tight, informative, seamless broadcast with all of the news that needs to be reported, and you will earn a loyal, top-demographics audience every night.

27. Tone

Quality television news calls for the tone of your newscast to be as clear as possible, with no suggestions about your feelings toward the content. Let your script speak to the audience without an emotional undertone. Whether you are covering a tragedy or a triumph, it is your job to inform, not to sway opinion. Even when the story should touch every viewer, let the facts do the touching, not your characterization through intonation.

If you're looking for a voice, imagine who's sitting at the dinner table watching you. Don't think in terms of vast numbers, but of one or a few people who are listening deliberately to what you have to say. Picture the successful small businessman husband of your general manager. You would instinctively respect the man for having some intelligence, to be successful and to have married your boss. You wouldn't talk down to him. On the contrary, you'd make every effort to provide him with the important information in a way that he would understand it the first time. You wouldn't dare sound impatient or condescending.

The job of a reporter—in the field or behind the anchor desk—is to be respectful of both the task and the audience, the facts and the coverage. He should sound professional and informed, and be able to inform without sounding pedantic or patronizing. He should not befriend the audience. He should maintain an appropriate distance, just as would a doctor or a lawyer.

(If a station is pitching a mass audience that connects viscerally, it probably makes sense to promote your anchors smiling beneficently. But if you are presenting quality television news, which will primarily target a higher end audience, the smiling anchors are going to raise more questions than provide a sense of paternalistic familiarity. Thoughtful viewers would wonder why they are smiling. Haven't they read the news? Maybe they're smiling all the way to the bank.)

The best journalist is a clean vehicle, a clear vessel, a conveyor of a story. He should separate himself from the event, so that the viewers can watch and listen to the news and not be distracted by the coverage itself. Frank Gardner, a former colleague at WCBS television, in New York was let go because he refused to play himself up in a way he felt could get in the way of reporting the story.

One story in particular comes to mind. Frank was scheduled on an early shift because he was one of the uncelebrated reporters. When French aerialist Phillipe Petit tightrope-walked between the two towers of the World Trade Center in New York City early one morning, Frank was sent to cover. He did an excellent job, as usual, writing and reporting a rich account of the aerial feat, and he did so without making himself a part of the story.

The importance of neutrality is also, perhaps particularly, true for people covering sports; they shouldn't become cheerleaders for the local teams. Not everyone roots for the home team. Some people keep their allegiances for teams from where they have relocated. Other viewers are just visiting. And some simply don't like the home team, maybe because they don't like the jerseys. In any event, it is inappropriate, unnecessary and even counter-productive to promote a team. Even when it is an American team competing in an international arena. A sports-caster who maintains her objectivity is likely to be more appealing and effective—both to the objective viewers, as well as those who would like to see her support their team; which she must never grant.

Counting Bodies

It is true that journalists can seem a little hard-boiled. You have to shut off some part of you when the pictures come back from Tenerife showing the results of two loaded 747's having collided. The challenge to remain objective becomes even more acute when the tragedies become personal, to wit, you hear from the survivor of the crash who lost her entire family. In those times, it is critical that you not get involved in the story, and not display sympathy for the victims. Individuals pull themselves from out of the deepest pits of despair and need. It is not for journalists to help them out, but to distill their struggles for others to understand.

Another reason not to show personal involvement is that stories can twist and turn, and you don't want to be positioned somewhere in the middle of the curve. Even when a story seems obvious, you never want to climb on board it emotionally. Think about the problem in these terms.

With all of our progress in managing disasters, it still takes time to count the bodies. It sounds gruesome, but it is a fact of a reporter's life. In some cases like fires, where a lot of people are critically injured, the death toll can start at horrific and then climb higher. As happened during the coverage of a night club fire in West Warwick, Rhode Island, on February 20, 2003.

The West Warwick tragedy happened only a few days after a night club trampling in Chicago; it had been induced by security guards macing two scrapping women. But the West Warwick fire started in a building without sprinklers; it didn't need them, according to code. Two hundred people were in the facility that was said to have a capacity for 300.

But it had no capacity for a fire, which was proved when pyrotechnics were set off to complement the heavy metal band playing that night. The place caught fire, and though none of the exits was blocked, most people fled toward the one main door through which they had entered.

The body count remained around 50 fatalities and 160 injured until late-afternoon (Eastern) of the following day, and then it went up through the 60's, jumped to the 80's and right on into the 90's toward triple digits. The number of injured also climbed to 180. The change in numbers is why it is important not to report even obvious horrors with any kind of emotional overlay. If it's tragic at 50 deaths, you're going to sound insipid at 80.

Even when the story is of the nature to bring a community together, let the facts of the news coverage instigate that; don't you become a participant. First, because you can lose your credibility for being too close to the story. And second, it's impossible to remain objective about what's going on with that story, and also the relative value of other stories.

In watching this story develop, I thought about my friend Doug White, the leading anchor in Providence, the state capital, fifteen miles away. Doug lives with his family in Warwick. I thought about the personal pain he must be feeling, and the professional countenance he would give to the coverage.

I had the pleasure of working with Doug White for three months in 1975 at the CBS affiliate in Providence. The time frame coincided with the ratings sweep period. On the eleven o'clock news, which Doug anchored, we added four points and the competition lost three. Shortly thereafter Doug moved over to the NBC affiliate and has since dominated the market as a quality journalist.

28. Appearance

Communication is much more clear when the focus of the viewer is on the content, not the deliverer. The reporter or anchor must have the same focus to look alive and attractive and not be a distraction.

Because television is a visual medium, on-camera people have to be aware of their appearance, but that doesn't mean be consumed by it. If you spend an inordinate amount of time thinking about how you look or sound, you are going to be distracted from your primary purpose of gathering and reporting information.

The basic rule is: Dress neatly and comfortably and wear your hair in a way that it doesn't require much attention, even in heavy weather.

Find clothes that feel good on you. They should follow your contours, and not chafe anywhere. Do they give you the flexibility to move around, to stoop below a camera lens or jump over a low barricade? Can you plunk yourself down on the curb next to someone without worrying about getting your seat dirty?

If you don't know what looks best on you, there are experts in the area of color and style. But it shouldn't be difficult for someone working in a visual arena to recognize what looks best on you, all by yourself. Buy colors that don't jump out at you. You and your clothes should become a blended image. You are wearing them, not the other way around. Fashion should be one of the last criteria; consider that some viewers would resent you for being fashionable, which is why relative invisibility is a good thing.

(Though some people look good wearing the color scarlet, on camera it can be less than flattering. For technical reasons, scarlet and some other shades appear to bleed when seen on television. Barbara Walters loved the color and continued to wear it even though it was pointed out to her that it added ten pounds to her appearance. A great many politicians also choose scarlet, perhaps because it makes then stand out, which it does, for better or for worse. People who would like to appear heavier on the air should eat more.)

Striped shirts, pin stripes in general, tweeds, and some plaids can all look a lot different in the mirror of a dressing room and on the television set of a viewer. It's not that you will look bad, necessarily, if you wear the "wrong" clothes, but they can look weird sometimes and cause a distraction from your script.

It should be unnecessary to say that you should wear comfortable shoes—the kind that can take a gentle lope on cobblestones. News doesn't always set itself off in front of cameras; some times it has to be chased. Those reporters wearing high heels or glossy leather soles are not going to keep up with the pack in those increasingly-popular chase scenes. Remember, too that practical footware doesn't have to be part of the shot, if that's worrisome for you.

More Appearance Tips

How you stand or sit on camera also affects your communication with the audience. If you are rigid, the audience will wonder what you're afraid of. If you slouch, they will wonder what you take seriously, if not your own carriage. If you pose in any way, they will wonder what you are trying to say, or to hide. Stand open to the camera, or at a slight angle that makes uses of the background. Standing sideways and talking over the shoulder is self-defeating. It is an instinctual response to maintain a distance from a person who isn't facing your directly.

—Never have you hands in your pocket when you're on camera, particularly in a standupper. It shows uncertainty, and sometimes fear. Holding a notebook and/or microphone usually looks professional. In most cases, standuppers should be framed from just above the waist to about four inches above the head, unless the background is significant and needs to be seen throughout. That gives you some latitude in your appearance.

—In the matter of sound, one rues the women reporters and anchors today who speak in voices more stentorian than John Houseman's. As with the visual side, anything put on is a mask and necessarily raises flags with the viewers about the truth within the reporter. Yes, some speech coaching is useful for stutterers and people who are not used to breathing deeply. If you need help, there is often someone in the local college speech department who can help you with delivery. But stick with your own voice.

—Some people starting out in broadcasting will find that they have to swallow a lot, particularly in the middle of an important reading. When it happens again, see if you are reading with your head down. Try to position yourself so that you are speaking up to the microphone; at least be level with it. This way the saliva doesn't flow to the front of your mouth and force you to swallow.

—It is the nature of camera lights to make a face shiny, and in our society that connotes fear, defensiveness and untrustworthiness. This being the case, one can hardly object to basic pancake make-up to cut the shine on someone's face. But any make-up, at least philosophically, is a mask. Novices should do with the barest minimum, if any, and heavy users should cut down. There's less maintenance, cost and concern.

Visceral Appearance

Finally, a discussion some of you may find beyond your ken. Read on, anyway; you may find that it has relevance later. It has to do with how you are perceived on a non-cognitive level. Because how you are perceived by the viewer is more than a suit and a voice. The camera transmits more than a picture. The audience inevitably experiences a visceral reaction to a reporter, to the tone and the general appearance; they get a general feeling about you.

It is not something that can be hidden. Even though on the surface you may look good, if you are in conflict inside the audience will know it. Not consciously perhaps, but they will react. Their response will be toward what's going on inside of you, and to the fact that you are not being honest with them by sending two messages: the external calm and the internal chaos.

For instance, if you are distracted and your full attention is not on what you're doing, your viewers are going to sense it and be wary of you. You can see an analogous situation in many rock videos in which the rock stars merely mouth the words, rather than singing with feeling, the way it is on the CD. The result is that when matched with the recorded audio, the star winds up lip-synching with himself, and even though the timing of the lip movement may be on, the energy is different. It lacks congruence.

In theater there is a term called suspension of disbelief. It means that the audience will go along with the premises put forth on stage, to the degree that the actors are consistent with their own story. The audience suspends their own reality and accepts the one on stage. Of course the audience can resume its own reality at any time. With good television journalists, the reality is not exchanged but shared.

If the reporter is deliberately putting on an act—deep voices, too much make-up, over-done hair, etc.—some in the audience will wonder what else is false. This also applies to indeliberate acts, like reporting by rote, or reading a tired script. Whatever the reason that you are not all there, the quality of the communication is compromised.

There should be a certain dignity in a news operation. While the images of the reporters in movies like *Front Page* and *Year of Living Dangerously* were somewhere between unruly and stupid, real-life journalists should appreciate that they have a special status to stand outside the fray and to observe, and for that privilege, they should show respect for the people and the scenes that play out before them.

In some professions, the distinction between personal and work lives doesn't mean a great deal, but in journalism, how you conduct yourself off-camera can impinge upon how you are accepted by the audience. Living one's life with dignity can make a real difference on air. Not only because you won't make the gossip column, but because the respect you hold for yourself will come across on the television.

29. On Camera

Back in 1971, Walter Cronkite opened the *CBS Evening News* with a 2:45 report on mercury in tuna fish. For whatever reason, they had no b-roll, so Cronkite delivered the story straight to camera, with a graphic over his shoulder. It was compelling, because the story was important and Cronkite delivered it cleanly, as was his style. And that's the way it should be, because for a true journalist the story is why he's there. And when it comes right down to it, in the absence of any support visuals, television news is someone talking to camera, either an anchor or a reporter. Television is a visual medium, of course, but when you don't have relevant footage to support the copy, then you're left with your mug on the screen and that should be enough.

The very idea of a 2:45 reader today would send the average television news consultant into apoplexy. Their breed prefers to have shots change every few seconds. They believe viewers need to be mesmerized by a constant stream of mind-snatching visuals, and they're probably correct in presuming that many viewers from the MTV school of television would click away unless they were entranced by staccato shot changes.

There is another school of television, however, that believes that when television journalism is at its best it is the story that captures the audience. You may not get the largest number of viewers with such an approach, but you will get those most interested in being informed, which, after all, is your charter. You don't need to draw them in with an incessant stream of special effects. When the information is important, when the writing is concise, and when the delivery is thoughtful, the audience will stay tuned to hear the story from someone sitting behind a desk reading it. Consider that until the tape gets back to the station or you get an uplink, that is the way all major breaking stories are first imparted to the public.

Of course, nowadays most newscasts are formatted to avoid on-camera appearances of more than twenty seconds. The producer will scrounge for even distantly-related b-roll or file footage to break up the on-camera. And while b-roll can be effective in helping to tell a story, it can also be a distraction from the copy. If you are programming for an intelligent audience, instead of regarding them as mere ratings eyeballs, show them respect. Don't feel that you have to entrain them. Give them the news in a straightforward manner. When visuals help to tell and understand the story, use them, but stay on-camera if that's the clearest way of reporting the information.

If you have strong supporting visuals, by all means, use them. Whether they are iconic graphics sitting humbly over the anchor's shoulder or compelling tape you run as voice-over, people are watching television, not listening to the radio.

Today's audience is used to a mix of on-camera and voice-over. The tendency to provide b-roll has gone over-board, however, with the greater availability of video. Use it intelligently, not as wallpaper.

It may boil down to this. In the worst case, visually speaking, you can produce a correspondent on-camera report in front of a camera in the newsroom. If you have a little more time, you can set up a location standupper, or pull out some appurtenant b-roll or file footage, or generate some enhancing graphics. But don't be afraid to go with your reporter straight. That's what reporters are hired to do...tell the story.

Where an on-camera report is delivered from makes a difference, of course. Newsroom shots can work if there isn't the time to put the reporter in a more significant location, but be careful that the background activity isn't a distraction. You can also put her on the set in the "guest" chair with the anchors, but this should be restricted to only the most important stories. There should be a certain cachet to reporting from the anchor desk, as in when a story is breaking and the reportage would benefit from a by-play with the anchor.

Finally on the subject of reporting on camera, as mentioned earlier but it's an important if unpopular point, a serious journalist will make every effort to strike the use of first person singular from his on-air lexicon. Don't use "I" or "me" unless you simply can't avoid it. Also avoid the use the royal "we" in reference to your news operation. Say that "TV-12 News has learned..." or "...told TV-12 News". That will not only demonstrate humility, but also endear you to the team who help make your report possible. Using "I" or "me" makes you part of the story, and if you are part of the story, someone else should be reporting it.

30. The Standupper

In the days when television news and journalism were more or less synonymous, standuppers were used when no other pictures were available. Today, b-roll is ubiquitous. There are very few stories for which an ardent producer can't scare up some b-roll, either fresh or from the library. And while it's true that most standuppers aren't as compelling, visually, as some strong b-roll, there are times when none is available. For instance, if you are covering a secret grand jury proceeding. Or it might be that you are covering a breaking story and there hasn't been time to shoot pictures or pull file footage.

With computer graphics capabilities and tape libraries, you can usually generate something in the way of support visuals. If you have been covering that grand jury for a while, you may have daily shots of the witnesses entering and exiting the hearing room. You might have file footage of the grand jury's target. You might also hire a sketch artist to produce an artist's conception. But make sure that you don't use pictures for their own sake. You don't want to distract your audience when the facts of your report might come across more forcefully just watching you deliver them to camera.

(Promotion-conscious news directors sometimes want their reporters on camera even if there are better visuals. They believe that this will increase the reporter's recognition factor and will garner a more loyal audience and higher ratings. That's why so many reports start with a live on-camera whose only function is to lead into a tape package. Also, there are some reporters who are so anxious to have themselves seen on camera that they will opt for a standupper when b-roll would better tell the story. Appreciating both of these concerns, the first criterion should remain journalism.)

In addition to resolving the problems of lack of visuals and lateness of hour, standuppers can be very useful in other ways. A standupper can be used to deliver information from in front of a particular scene when other pictures are inappropriate for reasons of time, accessability, or repetition. "This dam behind us…" might make a good standupper if you've used all of your tight shots of the dam, or if the dam is likely to break before you can get any closer. Also as a transition between two locations or ideas, a standupper can change the direction of a story. If you've just finished interviewing the Hatfields, you might shoot a standup bridge in front of the McCoy's house to prepare the viewers for a new point of view.

More often than not, the location of a standupper will be related to the story. A reporter standing in front of a court house if the story is about a trial going on inside. Or in front of a hospital for a medical story, or a police station, a busy intersection, etc. What you are standing in front of is a set, and the picture sends its own messages to the viewers. What's important is to make sure that that message doesn't distract or distort. For instance, standing in front of the jail when someone has been indicted might imply that the person is guilty.

Producing business/economics coverage for ABC meant that there was a natural paucity of relevant visuals. When talking about the Leading Economic Indicators or the Consumer Price Index, we were necessarily forced to use generic graphics and b-roll. Indeed, we pioneered the use of graphics back in the days of gels and rear-screen projection, but we always limited the graphics to a supporting role. Also, we developed a library of over a hundred cassettes of file footage to cover narration where it helped to tell the story.

These elements were valuable in making clear certain issues that didn't inherently offer their own images. For instance, in talking about a change in the Consumer Price Index, we could pull shots of produce and overlay an arrow showing an up or down price change. With leading economic indicators, we had shots of appliances—white-ware, it was called—and car lots and cattle on the hoof. When talking about Medicare, we had tape from nursing homes. These shots were more than wallpaper; they helped people understand the relevance of the statistics that might not have come through as effectively as from a straight standupper.

When push came to shove, however, especially on late-breaking stories, we could always put correspondent Dan Cordtz in front of a camera and let him report. A tight, well-scripted minute, properly delivered could convey the facts without excuses.

Another way we dealt with the picture-poor nature of the subject was to get creative with standuppers. For instance, in reporting on the ripple effects of the approaching Chrysler bankruptcy in 1979, Dan delivered a single sentence in three separate standuppers at three different locations: in front of an auto parts supplier in Mt. Clemens, Michigan, at Chrysler headquarters near Detroit, and at the Capitol in Washington. The sentence told how the parts supplier depended on Chrysler and Chrysler depended on a Congress for a bailout. Dan was framed the same in each shot, and delivered the full sentence with the same intonation at each location. The backgrounds were so significantly different from each other while Dan remained the same that we were able to cut from one to the next in mid-sentence.

In another instance, Dan was reporting on lay-offs at three different recession-hit companies in Decatur, Illinois. In front of each location, he would turn from a right profile to straight to the camera and then deliver about ten seconds on the plant and the number of layoffs. At the end of the delivery, he would pivot another ninety degrees to left profile. When the standuppers were put together—turn in, talk, turn out; turn in, talk, turnout; turn in, talk, turn out—the standupper in front of the three separate companies showed the connection.

In another report on the auto industry, Dan was on-camera in a high tight shot, saying that at the end of the Second World War, the President of the Bank of Japan had recommended that his country stay out of automobile manufacturing. As Dan continued to speak, noting that Japanese industry had rejected the advice, the cameraman slowly widened out. With Dan citing figures on Japanese auto imports, the shot pulled back to show him in the midst of a huge parking area filled with thousands of Datsuns recently unloaded from Japanese freighters.

Most times, the location of a standupper is determined by the circumstances, but it is worth repeating to be alert to the danger of the script competing with the visuals. For instance, standing on a levy with a flood in the background, the pictures behind the reporter are going to seize the attention of the viewer, with the script being drowned out, so to speak, by the visuals. It might be wise to start on the flood shots and pull back at an appropriate time to reveal the reporter.

In most cases, the background should be fairly static, so as not to draw the viewers' attention away from your words. A familiar background like the White House or city hall has certain significance; the meat of the piece will be in the copy. When finding a spot, make sure that the angle is such that elements in the background fit with where the reporter is positioned. Inattentiveness can lead to telephone poles rising from the top of a reporter's head, or a bridge span exiting an ear.

Walking standuppers have their place, when demonstrating a relationship between two background points, but in most cases a pan from one to the other works better. This is because while most reporters can walk and talk at the same time, their movements create an unnecessary distraction. At the very least, it makes the picture of the reporter more important than it should be, adding visual cues that engage the viewer when he should be listening instead. An exception: a walking standupper works very well in a think piece, where you have a lot of copy, and you don't want to distract the viewer with extraneous video. In that event, pick a spot where the background remains constant, e.g., walking down a sidewalk or by a sea wall.

Most standuppers should be straightforward, delivered directly and squarely to camera without any glitz. Hand gestures are a distraction. Pointing, or making references to "behind me" will also draw the viewer away from the script.

Many reporters will record their standup copy into a cassette recorder and play it back through an earpiece invisible to the camera. This can be a particularly effective way of delivering a longer piece that would be difficult to memorize. Record your script with the intonation and directness you want to present to the audience. Since it is in your own words and your own voice, you are able to embody more of the energy and tone coming through you, than you would if you were reading off of cue cards, or reciting from memory. Make sure to keep your face angled slightly away from the camera with the wire hidden.

If you are going live, you may prefer to use notes instead of a script. This is particularly true if you have a series of points to make. The audience will be quite comfortable if you refer to your notebook to report your items.

If you know your information you shouldn't have any trouble. Ultimately, you should be able to throw away your script and simply tell the story. This proviso when you are listening to your voice come back: use the recording as a guide, not like TelePrompter. Don't just parrot yourself back to the camera because discerning viewers can tell when you are merely delivering your lines. Speak with a fresh voice that expresses your real interest in the subject you are reporting.

Sometimes a standupper will wrap around a live interview. In this case especially, you will want to have cues for the cameraman to widen out to include the guest, and to tighten up at the end of the interview. While you can offer some obvious lines like "with us now is…" and "thank you…", you might also have simple hand signals. Make sure that the cameraman will be looking for them at the appropriate time, and not through the lens.

Cues would also be useful when you are shooting a standupper without a guest. For instance, you might want the cameraman to zoom past you or pan away to a different shot during your standupper. Verbal cues are usually good enough prompts, and you can expect him to follow your lead if you turn your head or body while you are speaking, but again, hand signals beneath the shot frame can also be useful.

Speaking of hands, unless you need both of them free—and not for gesturing—you might consider the advantages of using a handheld microphone instead of a lavalier. First of all, you control the audio. If you have to suddenly sneeze, for example, you can slip the mike behind you. If you are conducting an interview and the person is talking too long, you can pull the mike away. Also, it gives you something to do with one hand while you're holding your notes, perhaps, in the other. On a more ethereal level, it gives the audience a sense of completion because they see how the sound is getting to them.

Standupper Tips

—If you are shooting a standupper in an urban area, you may find yourself hassled by people on the street who want to be in your shot. Some of them are simply enjoying the excitement; others want to mess with your work. And there are certainly plenty of crazy people on the streets who don't need a reason to make your life difficult. One trick that sometimes works, depending on the crowd, is to ask the more obstreperous in the crowd—the leaders—some questions, as though you were interviewing them for your report. Or offer to tape them after your standupper. That will frequently silence them while you do your standupper. And sometimes you just have to find another location.

—Whenever you do a standupper, even if its just a 15-second close, don't leave the scene without making a protection copy. Even though the technical side of the industry has improved dramatically, even though no film is going to be lost in the lab, there is always the possibility of a head clog or bad tape. Yes, you can be zapped twice, but the odds are greatly reduced if you have a back-up take.

—Slate each standupper, i.e., Take One, Take Six, etc. It makes it much easier to find the right version when you're in a hurry to put your piece together after an unexpectedly confusing day. If you forget to slate at the beginning, wait a few beats after your closing copy, and then tail-slate it, i.e., "That was Take 14".

—Many reporters provide editing notes on their tape when they are sending it in and heading out themselves to another location. This is practical, but requires some care. Make sure the picture could not possible be confused with a standupper; e.g., turn your back to camera.

—It is standard procedure in many news operations to recite a "three-two-one" countdown before you begin reading your script, except when you do a standup open. The countdown should be delivered at the same pace as the script. This allows the editor to pause the playback machine just after the "one", cuing up the standup for the edit. The reason not to do a countdown before a standup open is that if the spot is rolled late or is to be dissolved to, the director would rather go to a picture of a reporter waiting silently than to watch his lips mouthing "three-two-one".

—One of the most critical rules about standuppers—in fact, for any time you are recording either audio or video—is that you should treat the situation as though you were actually live on the air. "The mike is always hot" is an old and frequently forgotten saw. Most viewers have, at one time or another, seen rude gestures, mouthed invectives and a variety of other regrettable displays on the air, all as the result of the camera or microphone being "off." It is not limited to live shots, either. Whether it is a director who punches up the wrong camera to find the anchor picking his nose, or the harried editor who slaps in the wrong take of the standupper, the results can be embarrassing. Just as people who value life treat every gun as loaded, so should every camera and microphone be thought of as potentially hot.

31. Writing

Every night, tens of millions of news viewers are witness to "the cold-blooded murder of the English tongue." (*My Fair Lady*) And not just language in terms of words, definitions and ideas, but sometimes the very notion of communication. In fact, taken as a whole, American television news is an assault on both correct pronunciation and context.

This is in part due to the fact that many television types jumped on the technology bandwagon without understanding the difference between vehicle and the content, style over substance. With live remotes all over town and tape coverage of every story regardless of how small, viewers today are barraged with glitz and flash. Lost in the electronic maelstrom, many times, is the news.

What is most important about television news is not the pictures or being exclusive, though these are important factors. Above and beyond everything else is the content, the information that is the *raison d'être* of the report. That information is communicated through a script, generally written against a fast-approaching deadline amidst a flurry of other frenetic if significant activities that involve the writer. Whether a reporter, anchor, or newswriter, she is a storyteller, handcuffed by the need to stick to the facts and to present them to a unique audience.

*   *   *   *   *   *   *

One of the sharpest veteran observers of the television news biz is Don Fitzpatrick, a consultant who is well known throughout the industry for his *Shoptalk* daily e-newsletter on television news. He and I met on a beach in Mexico. He was dragging his beach gear in a CBS New film bag. We became friends over a couple of beers and many war stories. One of the ways we connected was when Don was talking about the declining quality of reporters. "They don't know," he said, "that every story needs"—and here's where I broke in and we said together—"a beginning, a middle and an end."

Writing seems to be a dying art, and that's particularly obvious in television news, where you are handicapped by the need to write simply enough so that your viewers get what you're saying in the moment. In broadcast news, you have one shot at the viewer. He has got to understand it the first time it goes by. There is no time for confusion; no way to go back to reread the story from the top.

So in broadcast writing, the sequence of information must be linear. Plus, there has to be a logical progression from fact to fact; broadcast journalism requires the viewer to contextualize each bit of information as it goes by. You deliver the facts in an order that compiles immediately and then go on to add more details to the story.

Another challenge with television news is to write in conjunction with pictures. Whether you are writing a lead-in or -out, or a voice-over, your words have to dance with the visuals so that they complement rather than compete with each other. The viewer must assimilate both the verbal and the visual, simultaneously.

And there is so little time. You're up against the clock, dealing with sources that may or may not be on your schedule. Maybe you've got a piece or two of wire copy and you're told "Give me twenty seconds on the latest in the Middle East. We've got more pictures of rioting today." In all too many instances, you won't see the video until it's on the air, with your copy being read under it. Obviously, any relationship between your words and the pictures then is going to be pure happenstance. The facts may correlate, but rarely does the cadence or change in thoughts match the edits of the video. At the very least, you can expect a change in shots right in the middle of a sentence or phrase.

Good visuals can tell a story, but if the salient information is in the copy and the viewer is distracted by the pictures, the point can be lost. Ideally, when you write to video, your words will flow with the pictures, so that ideas change just after an edit. It requires more time and collaboration with the editor, but the difference in viewer comprehension can be significant. A news report is far easier to assimilate when the narration is written to the pictures.

Some stories don't need a lot of words, e.g., the destruction of the World Trade Center towers, but most stories are about less blatant ideas, and your words are going to transmit the facts. On the flip side are stories that are so complicated that they almost defy a television news explanation. A breakthrough in the study of quarks and photons would be well beyond the scope of even the most diligent television news writers. Few have the background knowledge to understand what is being discussed, let alone can relate it within the time/space limitations of general newscast reporting. Occasionally you have to punt.

But most stories are not beyond the ken of either journalist or audience, and it is for the newswriter to make the connection. A useful device for journalists to employ in explaining a complicated story is the use of a local metaphor. The distance between the Libyan and Egyptian front lines, for example, might be compared to the distance between the high school and the shopping center. The federal budget might be related to a family budget; is three-quarters of your household income already allocated in "entitlements" before you write your first check? Would you spend 20% of every dollar earned every year on home security?

There is also what is referred to as the micro-macro approach: take a piece of the whole, describe it and extrapolate. Say the local auto parts plant is laying off half its work force. To get a good description of the event, you could explore the situation of a typical worker being laid off, and then report that 500 people are facing similar concerns.

The converse is macro-micro, taking the big story and bringing it down to a size that interests and affects the local viewer. Perhaps you are an industrious reporter trying to illustrate the effects of the trade deficit and the over-valued dollar. You might relate the figures to the local candy store. For example, the wholesale cost of buying Belgian chocolates has dropped 40%; are they passing on the savings to their customers?

A caution: This style of writing—up-close-'n-personal—became popularized in the Seventies, and it never let go. It may draw in the viewer because the story is made particularly human, but when used too frequently, this approach is also simplistic and lazy.

Another challenge facing news writers is that many stories have beginnings and middles but have not been resolved. The Iranian hostage crisis dragged on for more than a year, as did the search for the anthrax mailer. Not only were the stories unresolved during that period, but there was no information to suggest when they might conclude. Some stories don't have endings. Others, like the Palatine, Illinois murders, might be closed nearly a decade later. In the meantime, you have to find a way to end a story that hasn't ended.

If you were covering the Reagan assassination attempt at the time the President went into surgery, you might have passed on the latest from the doctors: "We don't know yet." An alternative ending might have been to give the viewers a status report, i.e., "This is what we know at the moment." Or you could inform your audience as to when new information will be available, e.g., "Doctors will have more to say in two hours."

("Only time will tell" may be the classic sign-off. It is meaningless, of course, earns appropriate ridicule from anyone still paying attention.)

Most stories do have their own conclusions, or have reached some plateau. With some on-going stories, you may have created a theme in your writing, one that will have it's own conclusion regardless of the status of the event, as in on-going trial coverage: "Court resumes tomorrow." It's not brilliant, but you're in the middle of a trial.

*   *   *   *   *   *   *

If you get a script (or even write it yourself) or see a spot that has some good elements in it but it just doesn't seem to work, try altering the script by moving sentences around. First, take in all the information and then retell the story to yourself. See if most of the elements don't already exist in the script. ABC producer John Kippycash got a reporter package on the problem of birds nesting near the new Narita Airport outside of Tokyo. The piece as written was virtually unintelligible, but then Kippy chopped up the piece in his mind and reassembled the film. He used all of the pieces and required no additional copy or pictures. The new package was actually quite good.

Selecting the Facts

When people pick up a newspaper, if the headlines don't grab their attention, the stories go unread. In broadcasting, you have about three seconds to engage the viewer. She may not leave the couch, but she may pick up her paper if the story doesn't capture her attention, or she might punch the remote. This doesn't mean you should write grabber first sentences for every story. What it means is that you need to say what's important right up front, and then maintain a smooth flow of facts that will be enough in themselves to hold your viewers' attention. If you do it well, you will develop a loyal audience that will get comfortable with your fact-selecting, vocabulary and pacing. And even if you slip occasionally, they will hang with you; at least for a little while.

As a newswriter, you need to tell a complete story in about twenty seconds. Often, especially on a story that isn't on-going or familiar, you need to relate all of the essential facts in a manner that they flow from the introduction through the body into the close. You want to tell the who, what, where and when in the first sentence, in a way that the information will stick. Then you want to add the how and the why—the second level of details—which provide a context for the information. When you are done, the reader should also understand the so-what of the story. Too often, with abbreviated writing, the viewer is left wondering why They told me this *stuff*.

In truth, most important and too often neglected in the telling of the news is the reason why the viewer should care about a particular event or person. If the viewer doesn't understand why you are reporting something, the something will be forgotten. This may seem an obvious criterion, but many reporters will cover a story they barely understand themselves, and just parrot back a press release and what they hear from their colleagues. This occurs frequently when a general assignment reporter will cover a specialty story, e.g., something scientific, economics, the courts, the arts, et cetera, a field that has its own unique history, principles and lexicon.

When unsure of the significance of a story, a good question to ask yourself is, "How does it affect my audience?" If you wonder whether or not you have a handle on the story, ask yourself the three or five most important questions about the story. Did you answer them in your script? When you get home at night, will your wife raise an issue about your story that should have been dealt with in your report?

You'll rarely have enough time to report every element—or even every important element—of a story in the time you have allotted, but you don't want to miss the obvious. This is why it is so important to understand the details well-beyond what you are reporting. The more that you know about a story that you don't have time to report, the better you will be able to select the kernels that will make up your story. Remember, reporting is both commission and omission; what you say and what you don't. In the mind of the informed viewer, what you choose to report is what defines you as a journalist.

Writing to Be Read

Television news writing is also a challenge in that, like radio, you have to write your stories so that they can be read aloud. Logically, you are discouraged from writing long, complicated sentences; you want to write in bite-size thoughts. Also, you don't want to string out one thought over several sentences.

This is true especially if you are writing for someone else. In that case you need to take time to listen to the reader's speaking style and pace. Some readers, for example, prefer short phrases to full sentences. It does no good to write purple prose if the anchor can't read it well. And since the anchor is your "client" you need to customize your writing to facilitate his delivery. You will best serve that person when you are familiar with how he reads, literally, i.e., how his eyes scan the page, and how his brain informs his lips. Roland Smith, the late evening news anchor at WCBS, preferred short sentences, even phrases. That's the way he read, and the way his favorite writers wrote for him.

Accuracy[3]

What are the three most important criteria of a television news report, asks the old saw? Accuracy. Accuracy. Accuracy. The truth is impeccable and fierce. You either know something or you don't, and compromising your professional integrity—for whatever reason—is like cheating on your spouse. Even if the spouse never finds out, you will always know of your failure.

Shortly after the 1978 near-disaster at the Three Mile Island nuclear facility, ABC broadcast a report on what went wrong inside the plant. They used a graphic depicting a boiling water reactor (BWR). But the TMI reactor was a pressured water reactor (PWR). (In a BWR the reactor boils the water and the steam turns the power turbines. In a PWR, the water is heated by the reactor and then the heat is exchanged to a second water system which runs the turbines.) The "reason" for using the BWR drawing was that the single-line water system was easier to understand than the dual-line system. A very dangerous practice and the phones rang off the hook that night with viewers who took exception to the error.

Getting it right is more important than getting it on. Whether you're reporting on the installation of a new stop sign in West Dewdrop, or on missing Pentagon billions, you must go with what you know to be fact and couch the rest appropriately. When information significant to your report is unavailable, it should be so noted.

With Feeling

There is more than just reporting the facts. In addition to telling the basic facts of the story and in a logical order, you also want to create a feeling for the story by adding details that help to define the atmosphere. For instance, if the labor negotiations are conducted in a small room under hot lights, then that description might explain why the two sides look so angry. Sometimes you can get a participant to offer the description in a sound bite; sometimes you have to find five seconds to supply the details in your script. Remember that a viewer is absorbing the information both cerebrally and viscerally. Atmosphere helps the assimilation process.

Without Feeling

Just as you might try to cram an extra five seconds into your copy to better tell a story, so you have to be know where you can make cuts. Yes, a story should have a beginning, middle and end, but sometimes you don't have time for all of it. You have to be ready until the show is off the air to make cuts that will limit the number of facts being imparted without mangling the story.

Live broadcasting, by its very nature, lends itself to surprises. If a tape rolls late or if the meteorologist pleads successfully for an extra twenty seconds, the producer may ask that twenty seconds be taken out of a piece. The reporter or writer who best knows the script will know if, how and from where, the time can be best cut.

Step one is to divorce yourself from the script. Ownership can get in the way of speedy decisions. It's not "your baby" once it lands on the producer's desk, it is merely a body part.

The issue of time is a fundamental of television, of course, and sometimes it becomes absurd. During the waning days of *AM America*, the pre-cursor to *Good Morning America*, I spent several weeks in the ABC News Washington Bureau writing the 7:25 and 8:25 cutaways. These were the five-minute segments which the network aired, mostly for smaller markets, and which the larger markets replaced with their own local news.

Suddenly a frantic producer appeared at my desk, needing a lead-in for a report that was to roll in less than two minutes.

"What's the piece? Where's the script?" I asked.

"No time for a script," the producer stammered as I rolled a copy book into the typewriter, "It's an Angelico spot out of V-U-E about lobbyists pushing for price supports for sugar."

"How long?" I asked about the time of the lead-in copy.

"Ten!" said the producer on the verge of panic.

Without a lot of cognitive thought driving them, my hands flew across the keyboard and within twenty seconds, the copy was on its way to the studio. It said something like "Will consumers face continued high prices for sugar and sugar products? The debate continues, as we hear in this report from Richard Angelico of New Orleans station W-V-U-E."

Not a Pulitzer, but functional under the circumstances. And what made it possible was a broad knowledge of current events, familiarity with the circumstances of the newscasts, and knowing how to type. Also, experience with the news writing animal. When you have written over 2,000 "tape-rolls," you don't always have to think.

Entertainment Writing

Competition has impelled many news operations to go for hype. In some cases it means front-loading a sentence, e.g., "The world is going to collide with the sun during late September. This according to Irwin Mendahl, who for the past fifteen years has been selling crayons and dispensing free advice on the corner of Alvarado and Third." Putting attributions at the end of a quote or idea—especially when the credentials of the speaker are questionable—fights with the inherent linear nature of television, forcing the viewer to reconsider the quote after judging the credibility of the source.

A subtler form of the same style-over-substance consciousness is the insertion of the words "today" and "tonight" into virtually every story. Ostensibly, it gives immediacy to the report, telling the viewer that the station is all over the news just for them. But it is frequently done to excess, interrupting the flow of the copy with relatively-insignificant or extraneous information.

Another plague is the forced transitions, a favorite of consultants and the scene of some of the most extraordinary journalistic carnage in the industry. (Hyperbole is another.) Transitions are the copy that link stories in a broadcast. They can be the first line of the next story, or completely separate copy.

A news radio anchorman finished a story on a new bank opening its doors and then said, "Speaking of money, at the economic summit today...." Another anchor on the same station transited from a story on the state lottery with "More money in the news" to the announcement of a $5,000 reward in a murder investigation.

There are a number of ways that stories can be linked. If there are no inherent editorial connections, as discussed in the section on formatting, you might group the international news in one segment, perhaps combined with the national stories. This instead of taking the viewer from the local bank to the Bonn Summit to a local fire and then to news from Thailand. You can also link stories of the same subject, e.g., stocks, banks, inflation.

Some obvious transition lines when there are no obvious connections are "In other news...," "From Washington (or overseas) tonight...," and "Back home in Dewdrop...." "By the way, Lance..." as a transition between stories (and anchors) is chatty and brainless; there is no real connection and the viewers know it. Don't insult them.

If there is no logical transition, don't force it. Just stop talking. In a report, change pictures and/or sound. Between anchors, the one who is finished looks away from the camera to her colleague.

And when you are done, when there are no more stories (in a segment) to which you might want to transition, you can always, at most stations, go to a commercial. Indeed, sometimes a commercial is the only place to go, as when you have finished a segment with an obituary. Dissolve to black, take the detergent.

In an effort to reach a greater audience, particularly those who would be informed but gravitate toward an entertainment approach, many news outlets have yukked up their reporting. Rather than reporting that the Coalition troops are advancing on the Iraqi capital, they might say, "If you're Saddam Hussein, you better not be listening to this in Baghdad." Or, less egregious, instead of saying a hurricane is bearing down on Miami, they will lead with "Time to batten down the hatches in Southern Florida."

This chatty style may not seem terribly harmful, and it does engage viewers who might have trouble focusing on straight news. The problems with this approach are several. First, it wastes time since it's longer to tell stories this way. Second, it invites confusion because it delivers the conclusion at the beginning and then backs through the facts. And third, if you're a purist and looking for a reason to be disturbed, the fact is that stylizing cheapens the news and disrespects the audience. It says that the listeners must be entertained, that they have a short attention span, and a limited capacity for information, both regarding the number of stories and the details that might otherwise have been communicated.

Writing Style

There are many technical issues in writing news, and many of them are resolved in guides. The AP Stylebook, for example, is especially good for beginners, and many veterans have found it a useful guide to read through every few years or so. In it, you can study all the basics: how to handle acronyms, numbers, abbreviations, titles, pronouncers, initials and much more.

Much of what you will find in the AP and other stylebooks is common sense that has been standardized by usage. It dramatically eliminates confusion for even the rip-'n-readers, those brave (or insane) people who read their copy for the first time when they are on the air.

WCBS anchor Jim Jensen not only read his copy fresh, but he edited as he read. Jerry Liddell, his news editor, would have writers use colloquialisms in their copy which he knew Jensen would change. Words like "bucks" instead of dollars, "nabbed" instead of caught. And Jensen would move from prompter to script and back "correcting" as he went along, prompting smiles of respect on the faces of Liddell and his writers who were watching the program in the newsroom. Very few anchors could come close to Jensen's talent.

There were a number of tips I picked up as a freelance writer at WCBS. One was to make each sentence a paragraph, i.e., indent it, which made reading the copy a lot easier. Another, a function of the Teleprompter system, was that all copy was written between two vertical margins on the right-hand side of the copy book. This served to track the copy under the Teleprompter camera. The lines were 22 spaces apart, and it turned out that each line of copy, on average, timed out at one second. So by counting lines, you could quickly calculate the length of the copy.

Some issues of style are a matter of station or personal policy. The use of first names instead of last, for example; you don't call a five-year-old "Mister", but how do you address an 82-year-old neighborhood uncle whom everyone calls by his first name? And with titles, can you say Bush without a "President" or "Mister" in front of it? What about ex-Presidents? When in doubt, be polite.

Finally on the matter of style, personal style is fine, again only so long as it doesn't become a distraction. And it should be an outgrowth of intelligent scripting and practiced delivery; don't try to put on a style for its own sake. It comes across as phony. Basically, the most compelling and engaging styles have been those that were indeliberately developed but over time became a signature for a reporter's delivery.

Pronunciation

A major pitfall for copy readers is pronunciation. Any word and most names that could possibly be mispronounced should have a pronouncer adjoining them in parentheses. Don't take the simple ones for granted.

The story cited earlier of the hurried scripting of the lead-in for the spot on *AM America* made it to the studio on time, but the anchor mispronounced the reporter's name. Granted, it wasn't an ABC correspondent—it was an affiliate reporter—but it never crossed my mind that she wouldn't know his name. And there wasn't time to write a pronouncer for it anyway. But the story makes the point that stentorian voices of staff announcers and the polished delivery of anchors don't mean that they know everything.

The wire services are very good at printing pronouncers, and you can usually find what you need in a reference work—dictionary, Who's Who, etc.—or on-line, or through a quick phone call. Preventing a mispronunciation is part of the job of a newswriter. But sometimes, as in the case cited above, there isn't time.

(Many years ago, a network anchor, accompanied by a producer who should have known better, shipped back a spot from Hong Kong pronouncing the word homogeneous as huh-MAH-jih-nis, like the milk. By the time the film arrived in New York, the anchor had moved on to another Asian city. It was decided that most in the audience wouldn't know the difference anyway, so the spot ran.)

More Writing Tips

—A few anchors remain sticklers for grammar. Grammar is important, but stilted construction is not only difficult to say, it is difficult to understand. "This is the sort of English," Winston Churchill was said to have said, "up with which I will not put."

—The use of slang has its place, but generally reporters should speak the language simply, clearly and precisely. The English language, somewhat Americanized, is one of the vital tools of our journalistic craft, and should be respected. Diction and pronunciation are a part of reporting as well, and should be honed to an art. Of course, if you are working for a Spanish-language station....

—Be careful in the use of pronouns. If there can be any doubt about who "he" is, repeat the name or title instead.

—Avoid passive construction, e.g., "The freighter struck the trestle" is easier to read and hear than is "The trestle was struck by the freighter."

—Colloquialisms should be strenuously avoided. Regionalisms are one thing, but saying "S-F" when you mean San Francisco merely sounds cheap. The use of initials—e.g., MTA, MARTA, CTA, BART—which are common parlance locally are going to be confusing to an out-of-town viewer. Obviously there has to be some flexibility on this issue, since you can't presume that there are a lot of visitors watching, and they are not your primary audience. Just try to keep the facts clear for everyone; for instance, shots of a tram with the letters on it can do the trick.

—Know whereof you speak. Many words are simply used incorrectly. This should come as no surprise; once we're out of school, how many people are going to correct us? One prevalent example of misuse is "to infer" and "to imply." The former means to presume; the latter means to indicate. You might remember it that the "f" in infer reminds you the word means to take from.

—Another popular mistake with reporters is the use of "literally", instead of "virtually" and "figuratively". "Literally" refers to reality; what is literal is fact. "Virtually" means almost all. "Figuratively" is offering a metaphor. A news radio reporter in San Francisco said that there were "literally" millions of people demonstrating on Market Street; there were, in fact, several hundred demonstrators. He might have said that virtually all of Market Street was blocked off, since all but a few hundred yards were closed to traffic. And he could have said, "Figuratively speaking, Market Street was awash with humanity."

—Be aware of alliterations.

—Guide inflection with simple, logical punctuation.

—Commandment: read your copy out loud before it leaves your desk.

Finally on the subject of writing, and getting all of the facts straight, take your job seriously. A few weeks into the 2001 anthrax scare, a local reporter pronounced the word "antrax" several times. It's one thing to botch a foreign name or scientific term, but after weeks of the word being at the top of the news, it's hard to understand how someone could mispronounce it; and be allowed to by colleagues. If you hear someone mispronounce or misuse a word on the air, you have a professional obligation to provide the correct information because the whole station's image is besmirched by the mistake.

Parallel Construction

In television news, the clock is not forgiving. Either you are ready for air or you are not. There is no way to *Stop the Presses*. Most of television news is eleventh hour, which means that the majority of all news reports are conceived, shot, written and edited on the day of air. This situation requires then that the reporter know how to make air under the most difficult circumstances.

On normal days, in the worst case, you can always go on with a simple standupper. With more time, you can add graphics, or shoot an interview and some b-roll. And with a lot of advance warning, as in the case of a documentary for instance, you can pretty much design your report with all the bells and whistles your budget and facilities can support.

The first step in any report is to be able to tell the story. You first want to play it out in your mind, then put pen to paper and finally assemble the visuals and sound cuts that will support your telling of the story on the air. Know your limitations, though, and don't let anything get in the way of making air.

It was during the summer of '77 when the Chicago news producers joined their technical colleagues in NABET for a disastrous (for the union) five-month strike against ABC. I was one of three editorial types in the bureau normally staffed by fifteen. Since the Chicago bureau was responsible for the network news coverage of the entire Midwest from the Rockies to the Appalachians and South to Texas, there was a lot of traveling.

One morning, I found myself on a chartered plane to Dayton, Ohio with a reporter and a film crew to cover a firemen's strike. We had less than two hours on the ground in Dayton but we were still able to shoot in four locations and conduct two interviews before flying on to Cincinnati to process the film, assemble a spot, and feed it to New York.

Due to technical and scheduling restrictions at the affiliate the latest we could feed was 5:20, and we didn't reach the station until 3:45. The film was put in the processor, and while the reporter sat down to write her script, I went to screen the tape that the station had shot earlier in the day; we anticipated incorporating some of their footage into the network spot. At 4:30, the film came out of the processor and was screened. I and the reporter already had a good idea of what we wanted, and quickly selected the sound bites we would use.

Next we roughed out a script so that I could pull shots of the appropriate lengths and description to match her script. At 5:00 I returned to find that she had written two pieces of copy that ran twenty seconds where, per our discussion, I'd cut only ten seconds of picture. And she was sitting in front of the typewriter staring at the script while she was filing her nails. Realizing that we were in serious danger of not making the 5:20 feed, I ordered her to make several specific cuts in her script.

"But I'll loose my parallel construction," complained the young woman, a former English teacher.

"If you aren't in the announce booth with your script written the way the film will be fed," I said evenly, "I'll tell New York to provide their own voice-over."

The reporter, a bit put out, nevertheless did make the proper cuts and read her narration to New York, live, on the second take. She finished speaking at 5:19:40, twenty seconds before we would have lost the line to New York.

On the way back to the airport, I, the seasoned veteran of 26, attempted to reconnect with the somewhat arch reporter. "You know," I said gently, "sometimes you have to make compromises to get on the air."

"I was in New York ten days ago," she responded petulantly, "and [Executive Producer] Av Westin told me that a reporter has the final say over the script."

"Yes," I replied clippedly, "And the producer has the final say over whether that script gets out of the goddamn station!"

It felt good at the time, though it sounds awfully young today. But at the end of the day, the business of television news is to deliver information. It would be nice if you had a week and unlimited resources for every 1:30 story, but it doesn't happen that way. After all, news—by definition—is current, and if everything else fails and you can only get on with a standupper, then do it. But get it right and get it on.

32. Delivery

The perfect delivery resonates with confidence tempered by humility. You want to know what you're talking about—and sound it—but you don't want to sound superior. As you look into the center of the camera lens and speak into the microphone, you want to come across as knowledgeable, professional and perhaps a touch honored to be allowed into your viewer's living room.

(For all of that confidence, it should be noted, butterflies are normal, even appropriate, since upon your shoulders is the obligation to bring important information to your audience. Many talented professionals have to deal with nerves every time the tally light lights. For most, the butterflies disappear moments after they begin speaking.)

Always presume that your audience is smarter than the general public. If you are looking for a touchstone—a way to define the intelligence of your audience and how to speak with them—you might consider that you are talking to a well-informed person who doesn't happen to be up on the particular story you are telling.

Understand that condescension is far more impactful on a visceral than cognitive level, and it's not something you can mask. If you ever find yourself feeling condescending toward the viewers, you can be sure that you have already offended a whole slew of them, without many of them even knowing why.

If you do find yourself feeling superior, take a break. Get quiet with yourself and realize that they may not have all of the information that you do—that's why they're watching, after all—and they may not be nearly as smart as you, but they control the remote. Plus, it is your job to inform, not just report. So find your more generous self, and then speak the words.

That said, as compassionate and as humble as you want to feel toward your audience, you should also make every effort to keep your voice free of emotion. There are stories that will grab you in the gut, and you will want to share that energy with your viewers. Don't. There will be stories that you find stultifyingly boring, but before you write your script—and certainly before you deliver it— enliven your attitude. Remember, most of your communication with your viewers will be non-verbal, and if you're bored or angry or flaky, it will come across far more powerfully than will your words.

A number of years ago, a Harvard study of the communication from an anchor reading copy to a viewer determined that 55% of a viewer's impression came from the anchor's body language and facial expression. Another 37% was generated by the tone of voice and other elements in the shot. Only 8% of the communication was conveyed through the actual words.

Those numbers may not be the same today, but the concept holds. And while it doesn't say much about the written word, the script is what prompts and carries the delivery of those words through body language and intonation. Which means that it is vital, if the information is to be transmitted in a non-subjective manner, that you approach the news objectively. You are a vehicle of communication, and the more you can remove your self and attitudes from the news, the better will be your delivery of information.

Also, the fact that most of the information delivered by an anchor comes from his facial expressions and body language means you don't have to spend a great deal of time on producing additional visual images, although they can certainly help to correct, qualify and balance the anchor's presentation. But while you can benefit from background graphics and tape voice-overs, understand that they aren't essential. Anchors and most reporters are adequate in appearance to be on screen for a couple of minutes at a time without forcing a change of channels. Which is to say, stay away from electronic wallpaper. Don't feel that every shot, or even every other story needs to have a visual to support it. The rule is that if it provides more information than distraction, then you're moving in the right direction.

In finding the right voice to talk with your audience, you have to presume to deal with a certain mindset. First of all there is an ethos endemic to the community. People have specific beliefs about themselves and their neighbors. The community may be so insular that the shared attitudes are not lightly questioned or examined. Rural areas are likely to be hard-nosed conservative, for example, and some are populated with hyper-religious people, though not in their own eyes, since everyone around them holds the same beliefs.

A second point is the attitude the public has toward television reporters. Once they were heroes, but mostly now they are not. The industry has been degraded as the degree of journalism has slipped, dramatically and consistently, since Walter Cronkite left the anchor desk, and with the quality have fallen the ratings. Fewer than half the number of viewers are watching the network newscasts as were twenty years ago in 1981. Local news has also lost considerable luster, as many stations have shed content for style, dumbing down to reach a broader audience.

What this means to the anchor and reporter is that the more objective, the better informed, and the more self-aware that you present yourself to the audience—cognitively and viscerally; smoothly and professionally—the better you will practice your craft with the right viewers. If you find yourself working in a shop where these qualities aren't respected, where you're asked to put on a personality, you might be happier at another station.

33. Anchors

"Good evening, everyone." That well-coifed stentorian opening is familiar to many Americans. Many anchors find it irresistible. But it's both presumptuous and gratuitous. Anchors are important people by the very fact of their position. They have been hired to keep the community informed. It is on their shoulders that the very intellectual health of our democratic republic lies. But no anchor is speaking to everyone.

While confidence is a fine and important quality in an anchor, humility is also vital. Anchors who know their stuff, do it well, and still show respect for the news and for their audience generally attract a substantial and loyal following of higher-end viewers. To be anchoring a newscast—from a network desk in New York or a local desk in Boise—is an honor. The better they do their job, the better informed is the public to make intelligent decisions about public officials and issues that will chart our future.

The job of the anchor is to maintain a home base for the news. During the course of the newscast, there will be news from around the world and across the country; and the state and the city, if it is a local program. It is vital for the effective delivery of a world of news that everything be brought back to the home base. The anchor dispatches our attention—to places and ideas—and then returns it. At the end of the newscast, when she says goodnight, we are back in our own homes.

Anchors are called such for a reason. They are the familiar moorings for the audience. They are there at their desk every night, or should be. With satellite technology making transmissions possible from all over the globe, anchors have been going on the road to cover major stories. The purpose is promotional, to show them on the scene of major events. The implication is that they circulate with the decision-makers and can get the inside poop, and perhaps that's true, to an extent.

But the larger truth is that if they stayed home and used their staff and the telephone they could get as much information from home base. Another reason for staying home is that as important as a story might be, it is only one piece of the news. By going to the story instead of anchoring from their own desk, they give the story added importance. The question often arises, is the story so important that the network should be sending out the anchor along with an entourage, or are they moving all those people around for promotional and competitive reasons?

When a network anchor travels, it costs hundreds of thousands of extra dollars, because they are moving much of the newscast with him. This is money that could be better spent on hiring more and better staffers, expanding news coverage and obtaining more footage from more sources. Another drawback is that by moving all those extra people, there is a need to use them on location to justify the expense, which results in coverage that is often extraneous, or at least of secondary importance.

Selecting Anchors

The choice of the anchors is obviously important; usually it's what defines the margin of profit or loss. A man and a woman together offer the best diversity—in appearance, tone and attitude. A male-female team will appeal to a larger audience, and offend fewer people than two people of the same gender. Usually.

Partnership and amicability are valuable but professionalism is vital. It is far more important that both individuals understand current events, know how to report them clearly—and ad-lib when necessary—than it is that they seem like friends.

Ideally, the anchor team would have varying and complementary interests. One might be more interested in national and international news and the other like local news better. Perhaps one would be well-schooled in the sciences and the other in the arts; one would be focused on education and the other would enjoy discussing business. Together they would have a lot of the world covered. They would also know upon whom to call for the most current and trustworthy information. They would know the people, personally or by reputation, who might be called upon for elucidation. They would be well-rounded, independent thinkers who see their mission as sharing knowledge to cultivate wisdom.

Anchors should be college graduates—probably, though some of the great ones were not—who have majored in something other than journalism. Maybe history or political science. They don't need graduate school; better if they've spent time reporting from the streets. They need to know how to write, for themselves and for others and how to interview. It is especially important that they know how to think on their seat. Unexpected technical problems can leave them without the standard tools of the trade, and they should be able to pick up the pieces and continue the broadcast without looking lost.

"Happy Talk"

When anchoring began, there was little by-play if any between the anchors. "Good night, Chet. Good night, David." was most of it. Then came the "Happy Talk" format of the Seventies, which had the anchors and sports and weather people chatting back and forth, ostensibly to warm up the program, and make us all feel familiar. That tended to get over-played to the point where a considerable number of stations promote their anchors as our friends.

(All this feel-good pap has led us ever farther away from journalism; to the degree that some management is now telling their news staff to report only the news the viewers want to see; which explains why there is so little foreign coverage, except for war. Or reports on the arts. Or indeed, anything that requires any reflection on the part of the audience.)

There are some traditionalists who push in the other direction, not only eschewing all the chatter, but going so far as to question the need for anchors to toss back and forth to reporters and each other. They object to the effusive "Thank you very much for that fine report, Lance…Channel Seven's Lance Allot live in the newsroom."

Not only is it excessive, and smells like self-promotion, but it's really a waste of time. As far as handing off to your co-anchor, he's got the script. He knows it's his turn. So does the director, who will take another camera shot, or pan or widen out, to put him on the air. Many stations program tosses to increase name-awareness, but it's not very honest, not necessary, and tends to add unnecessarily to the general clutter.

Sharing Time

It helps to increase understanding of the news if you format a consistent pattern of delivery from the anchors. With two anchors, you will usually want to split the time fairly evenly, but you don't want them switching back and forth after every other story. Instead, one should handle a block of stories that defines itself in some way, e.g., domestic, international, a segment on medicine and science, et cetera, and then the other takes a turn.

If you use headlines, the anchor who reads the headline should handle the story when it comes up in the line-up. Having this policy tempts fate when a show gets turned upside down due to technical problems, but it offers a good rule of thumb for enabling the viewer to track the whole newscast, as well as the individual reports.

If your first segment is stacked with unconnected news stories, try to group at least two or three stories together so you don't open your broadcast with a ping-pong match. There is no reason why one anchor can't read a selection of unconnected news items, after all. The fact is that the fewer exchanges in the middle of a segment, the easier it is for the viewer to follow. Also, the anchor who leads into a correspondent report should also come out on the back end. Coming out of a commercial break, it doesn't matter.

Tips on Anchoring

Some on-camera problems are due to bad writing, but sometimes it's a matter of the reading. A common problem for some on-air people is that they don't know how to bail out of an errant mouth; when the eyes and the tongue seem to be on different pages. Being human, there are occasions when you might use the wrong word or mispronounce the right one. Inexperienced talent will try to cover up a verbal glitch with a phrase like "or rather…" or "that is to say…" to transit them (they hope) to the right pronunciation. Usually they continue to fumble, when the solution—and it always works—is to stop talking, or at least slow down.

Problems also can arise when talent gets lost in a script or when the Teleprompter dies. Confusion sets in as you try to connect with the script on your desk that has been functioning mostly as a prop. To make for less embarrassment and a smoother transition, you would be wise to refer to the script frequently, and not become dependent on the Prompter.

And remember, when you stumble, you stumble. If the pages get mixed up and you have to sort them out, big deal. You may have a director screaming her head off in the control room, but the studio is sound-proofed. You haven't done anything naughty; you're not going to be punished. So relax, and do what needs to be done. You might tell the audience what's going on if it takes you more than a couple of seconds. And when you return, regain eye contact through the lens. Subconsciously, it acknowledges that you've been away and are now back. In truth, being shown human in this way helps to bind you to the audience in a healthy way.

There may also be occasions when you are live and have to deal with a technical error, e.g., a remote mike is dead. Again, it is a matter of using common sense and being grounded. Don't panic; if the answer isn't obvious and you don't have an earpiece wired to the control room, excuse yourself to the camera and look to the floor manager or camera operator for directions from the control room. Or pick up the phone, that always generates an answer.

One way to avoid problems is to make sure that when an anchor goes on the air, her script has not only her own copy, but also that of everyone else on the show. Every reporter should provide a copy of his script, along with super information and timings to identify sound bites. If an audio channel goes out, the anchor can pick up the slack and the piece won't be lost. This is also true for the weather and sports people; they should include a copy of their script in the anchor copy.

Whatever happens, stay calm, be graceful and you will maintain the essential contact with your viewers. Never blame or complain about staff or facilities.

The perfect news anchors want to raise the bar. To develop a smarter audience that is not only hungry for news, but has a cultivated appetite for context and perspective. These journalists will occasionally use less familiar words, though in a context where their meaning can be easily inferred. They will go with readers that might take thirty seconds or longer, because that's how much information is in the story. They will present themselves and their work with dignity. They will respect their audience.

The best anchors have been those who have demonstrated intellect, dignity, humility, confidence, integrity and a sense of humor. People like Walter Cronkite and Harry Reasoner; there haven't been many like them. Many others, while sporting journalistic credentials and yards of experience, have shown a propensity to let their egos get in the way of their reporting.

A newspaper editor friend observed, "They command seven- and eight-figure compensation packages, more like sports and entertainment stars, which is really what they are like. They have a staff to insulate them and travel with an entourage. They enjoy limos and power lunches and circulate visibly in the higher social circles. The rarefied air goes to their heads, and they lose touch with life as it affects the other 98% of society. This," he suggests, "is why their ratings have been declining for twenty years."

The Barbara Walters Story

I went to Bonn for the 1978 G-7 Economic Summit as Barbara Walters' news producer. It hadn't been a trip I expected to take, having shot stories in San Juan, St. Louis, Washington, and New York the week before. Plus, a three-part special on *The Subterranean Economy* I had produced with Dan Cordtz was airing that week on the evening news; it was the first time that the story of the epidemic of American tax cheating was presented on commercial television.

So I found myself flying to London on the Concorde with Barbara and her researcher on the first leg of our trip to the German capital. In the first four days in Germany, we did two major interviews with German Chancellor Helmut Schmidt—one for the *World News Tonight* and the other for *Issues and Answers* (the ABC Sunday talk show later replaced by *This Week*)—in addition to several "flavor" pieces. For all the complaints about the woman, she certainly worked hard when she was on location.

On the last day of the summit with nothing planned, Barbara and I happened to be walking through the ABC office when we heard a squawk on the walkie-talkie that someone named "Owens" needed a ride to the Palais Schaumberg, the site of the talks.

"That's Henry Owens!" Barbara said, recognizing the name of the official U.S. Ambassador to the Summit. "We'll take him!"

We ran out of the building, found Owens, and pushed him unceremoniously into Barbara's Mercedes limousine. We tried our best to act nonchalant, as Owens showed his diplomatic credentials at the security checkpoint, and we were ushered onto the Palais grounds.

We were the only journalists there, except for ZDF, the German television network, which had two studio cameras in position outside the Palais to provide live coverage of the heads of state leaving the final session.

Not wanting to be recognized and thrown out, Barbara and I shuffled unobtrusively about the grounds, staying near the fringes of the groups of aides and security people who were milling around the entrance of the Palais. After two hours, the aides stopped their milling and looked up expectantly. Jody Powell, President Carter's press secretary, recognized Barbara and walked over to us. He seemed bemused and unconcerned with our presence.

Barbara asked if it would be possible to get the President to speak with her for a moment as he was leaving. Powell said he thought it would be possible, just as long as we didn't hold up the proceedings.

In a few minutes, the heads of state began to leave. Suddenly I looked up and there was President Carter, standing on the steps a few feet away, almost unnoticed. Quickly we slid over to the President, both of us inconspicuously taking out micro-cassette recorders.

I stood behind Barbara and the President, and trying not to seem obvious, with a hand on each of their backs, gently shifted them so they were face on to the closer of the ZDF cameras.

The interview was brief, with the President stating his satisfaction with the way the talks had gone, and then it was over. Barbara got into one of the Carter staff cars for the trip to the closing ceremonies. I took Barbara's car and driver and rushed back to the press headquarters. By walkie-talkie, I told senior ABC producer Bob Siegenthaler what had happened, and asked him to get a copy of the ZDF coverage.

When I got back to the editing facility, it was a simple matter of hooking a few cables between the micro-cassette recorder and the videotape editing machine, and in minutes the synching of the interview—audio from micro-cassette, video from German television—was complete.

It was only thirty-seven seconds and not earth-shattering news. However, John Chancellor had done a major interview with Carter that morning, and it was supposed to have been the last exclusive from the talks. We went on the air with a quick bite that said all that most viewers would care about, while NBC with much appropriate pomp, spent several minutes covering the same facts.

This final note. The *I&A* interview with Helmut Schmidt was shot in the Kempinski Hotel in West Berlin, in the suite where President John F. Kennedy stayed when he gave his historic "Ich bin ein Berliner"speech to cheering West Berliners. The Soviets controlled the area around West Berlin, and didn't allow West Germany to fly planes over their territory, which left Schmidt flying on U.S. Air Force aircraft. We flew in and out of Templehof Airport in a very comfortable USAF 727, served graciously by an Air Force sergeant.

It was an extraordinary time, some of the most exciting weeks in my life. I did some of my best work, under a variety of challenging circumstances. Most of it wasn't even on my radar before it arrived, but all was engaged and exhilarating. You don't make opportunities like that; you just make yourself ready to take advantage of them.

34. Weather

Weather has become a television institution, and in most markets, more about the weather caster than the weather. The reason is that in the 1970's, surveys asking people why they watched the news found that a disproportionate number said they tuned in for the weather. The consultants took this to mean that people wanted more weather reporting, so weather casts were expanded to several minutes, and the weather caster became a station icon.

Where once weather was delivered by a cute-young-thing holding a pointer, standing before a wall map featuring a couple of H's and L's, today's weather caster is more likely a friendly geek-type who holds a clicker to change through a lengthy series of visuals. Standing before a chroma-key flat, sometimes supported with Doppler radar and special satellite feeds, he shows maps and statistics and a variety of other visuals to dazzle his viewers.

Consider that the consultants might have misinterpreted the survey results; that while most people tuned in for the weather, it wasn't for more coverage of it, just the facts. But for many stations, it's too late. They've made the weather caster one of the "family" and invested significant funds in his salary and accessories.

But some stations now facing tougher economic realities might think to give up the extravaganza and shift to simple and concise weather reporting.

For news directors dealing with shrinking budgets, letting the weather caster go and handing over his time and duties to the anchors could make considerable sense. The fact is that people watch the weather for three pieces of information. What will the weather be when the go outside, what was the weather today, and was there any interesting weather elsewhere. Many travelers would also like to see a national weather view. All of that information, even in a market where there are considerable meteorological variances, can be fully broadcast in thirty seconds with the aid of a few graphics.

In addition to saving an often sizeable salary, you could also recapture several minutes per newscast into which you might insert a significant number of news stories without neglecting your viewers' desire for weather information. That would give you important marketing points, i.e., the weather you need plus a higher story count. This is especially an opportunity in a down economy at a station where your weather caster is drawing only minimal ratings.

Another reason to consider such a move is that with The Weather Channel and the Internet, people can get weather reports 24/7 from the same sources that a local weather caster would use. They can get the precise information they seek, and not have to wait, or wait through several minutes of palaver to hear what is likely an hours-old forecast.

If you decide to take the plunge and convert the weather budget—money and time—to news, you should always know how to reach a weather expert on short notice. As with any expert, he should have a promote-able forecasting record, be able to speak clearly and intelligently, and offer expertise that will enhance the viewers' understanding of a special weather situation.

Whether you have your own weather caster or not, if you are anywhere near either national border (and even if you're not) it's a good idea to have your weather descriptors extend into the neighboring country. People from those countries— Canada and Mexico—may well be watching your newscasts. There may be people from those countries traveling through your city. There may be people from your city traveling to those countries. It doesn't cost anything to extend the map weather coverage and it demonstrates a broader scope of coverage.

If you are losing ratings to a another station, you might commission a study by local students of the forecasting effectiveness of the weather casters in your market. That is, if you know their guy to be wrong frequently, especially if you're right frequently.

And finally on the subject of weather casting, whoever does it on your station should stay away from the long-range weather forecasting. Since forecasts twelve hours out are so often wrong, the idea of spending time on five-day and longer range forecasts is cockeyed. Keep your weather forecasts to the next twenty-four hours, and you'll still be going out on a limb.

35. Sports

The importance of sports in the traditional newscast is declining. While it's not time to send the sports guy looking for a new gig, probably, the fact is that it's mostly men who are interested in sports coverage, but most women—who are the target audience of most advertisers—aren't. Most women view sports coverage in newscasts as excessive and a waste of their time. Not all women, of course, but more than 80% according to one survey. And there are also a lot of men who turn back to their newspaper rather than watch the same-ole shots of the baseball flying over the fence or the drive to the basket.

While it's true that sports highlights can be very exciting, they have become such an industry that they have lost much of their zing. Add to this the fact that most sportscasters fill their three or four minutes with as many video clips as they can find, and many sports casts have become something of a blur. The problem is that with some notable exceptions, most sportscasters lack editorial judgment, and few can write. They were hired because they used to play in the pros, usually for a team that was popular in the market.

Most sportscasters tend to erode the tenor of a newscast. They are rah-rah types who appeal to the same audience the beer-makers target with their advertising. They rarely appreciate nuance and are inclined to provoke a visceral response in their viewers. There are exceptions but not many.

Howard Cosell, Dick Schapp, and a few others knew how to cover television sports in a journalistic fashion most of the time. They produced coverage that was both significant and engaging, and not just to sports fans. But there are not many today who have that kind of ability. Most sportscasters are loud and inarticulate, and on local newscasts, they cheerlead for the local teams.

I had the pleasure of working with Jim Bouton when he was starting out as a sportscaster for WCBS in New York. The former Yankee pitcher and author of <u>Ball Four</u> was a bright if quirky fellow, who seemed to think that most people who watched sports were more interested in sports than they should be. He was more entertaining than most sportscasters because he didn't take himself or his subject too seriously, most of the time. That was probably a good attitude, but it didn't help the newscast.

So sports is still part of a local newscast, and it is not likely to disappear any time soon. The truth is that some of sports is legitimate news and should be reported, even if most of the audience is turned off to it. After all, most of the audience is also turned off to international news and reporting on cultural issues. Regrettably, many stations have all but dispensed with the latter, while allocating substantial blocks of time to sports.

Some envelope pushers suggest that local stations should save the sportscaster's salary and hire another reporter instead, and while the idea has some merit, few news directors would consider it, even less than they would think of dumping the weather caster. That's because at most stations, they promote their "talent" rather than their coverage. Watch the news promos in virtually any market, and they feature the smiling shots of two anchors, the sports guy and the weatherperson. They are marketing the personalities.

But if suddenly the news budget were slashed at the number three station in the market, their sportscaster might be in trouble. The news director might find that he could cut the sportscaster, his producer, and his assistant and be able to keep away the corporate wolves—all without sacrificing ratings, especially if research showed that his sportscasts weren't drawing viewers.

Instead, the budget-conscious cutting-edge news director would hand off the sports coverage to the anchors. Let them deliver the scores and major sporting news. Instead of spending three or four minutes on sports, he could get the sports news covered on most nights in less than a minute, often less. Since there aren't really that many sports stories that are important to the local audience, and since most people tune into the sports simply for the local scores, such a move could probably keep or even increase his ratings. Of course, when there was a spectacular throw or catch or run or goal, by all means they would show it; even non-sports enthusiasts appreciate an outstanding play. And television is a visual medium.

At most stations, a news director is not going to dump or even limit his sportscaster. But he might think to "encourage" him to make sports more relevant to a wider audience, expanding his vocabulary and occasionally broadening his perspective. There are a lot of people in the audience who have questions that sportscasters have never or rarely asked. Does the right-fielder ever find his mind wandering? How does a batter get over the fear of being hurt by the ball? It would be a thoughtful diversion from the standard one-of-the-boys flatulence that bores all but the obsessed.

Indeed, sportscasters should all be pushed to take a broader view of sports—that it's about the playful, physical side of life. It's about competition, with ourselves and others, and it's about our physical health. Sports coverage today is focused, for the most part, on the vicarious thrill of professional sports. It's about the viewers just watching others playing. Taking a more expansive look, sports could reach a much broader audience if the narrow-casting that is done today were replaced by more reporting on what we can do to improve our health and enhance the physical nature of our own lives.

A final issue with sportscasting, regardless of who does it, is how much support one gives to local teams. It is regrettable but common in small markets, that the sportscaster also does play-by-play for local teams. While most of the audience are rooting for the homies, many are not. We live in an increasingly cosmopolitan society, and many people relocate without giving up their team loyalties. Also, there are lots of people traveling from city to city on business. They may support different teams. They want the sports news, but do not want to hear a rant in favor of what for them is an opposition team. Just as a newscaster should not show favoritism to local politicians, sportscasters should be newscasters first, and leave their favoritism at the door.

36. Formatting the News

The content and pacing of newscasts will vary depending on the time that they are aired. People have different information needs at different times of the day. Different people are watching. There are also variances based on the time zones. When you are designing the formats for the different newscasts, think about the lives of the people in your market, what information they need, and what's on their minds at the different times of the day.

For instance, if you are a network affiliate, and you are integrating your schedule with theirs, you might have the resources to produce an early morning newscast that comes on before *Good Morning America*. Or you may only have the money and facilities to produce hourly cut-ins. In either event, in any market, your audience will be grateful if you tell them (1) what the weather will be that day, (2) if anything happened in the community that they should know about, and (3) is there anything on tap for the new day of which they should be aware.

That's pretty much what all newscasts are about. What happened, what's going to happen, and do I need an umbrella? The divergences from morning through noon to early evening and then late evening are significant, however, and are addressed in the following pages. What is laid out is not dictum, of course, but a framework for thinking about what kind of newscasts would best fit your target quality market. Adjustments to the schedule should be made if you are in the Midwest or the Mountain Time Zone because life is on a different clock there. And on the West Coast, being three hours "behind" means that you may be required to update the newscasts that originated an eighth of a day earlier.

If you want to dominate the television market, it has to be your early and late evening newscasts that people are watching. That's where you find your largest news audience, and your most news-conscious, respectively. Stories you have on those newscasts are what people will have on their lips around the watercooler the next morning. The morning and midday newscasts are important, but the evening newscasts are where a station makes its ratings and reputation.

Because of the profusion of choices, even in smaller markets, it is practical to allot two hours of the late afternoon/early evening programming time for the news. Particularly because most stations are going to air either news or something syndicated, and the syndicated program is often competing against itself where cable and satellite systems reach most of the households.

Those two hours will likely consist of ninety minutes of local news wrapped around a half-hour of news from the network. The networks feed their evening news twice, at 6:30 and 7:00 Eastern, with the second feed going out on tape if no corrections are needed and the news doesn't change. Which feed you take depends in large part on your time zone. If you have the option, you will want to go with the first feed for freshness and the second feed for the cleanest show.

37. The Early Evening News Hour

The news programs outlined in the following pages are based on line-ups that are designed for a quality television news audience. [See sample formats on line at dontmesspress.com.] They are certainly not etched in granite, but are presented as a starting point from which news directors and show producers might design their own programs based on their own unique market, talent and facilities considerations. Discussed first is outline of an hour newscast that would precede a half-hour network newscast which would be followed by another thirty-minute local newscast.

Since many people live by a routine between five and six, you might consider a radio news drive-time approach, i.e., one that is tightly formatted and the schedule adhered to with such zeal that the news cast can advertise itself as "you can set your watch by us." The news, weather, stocks, sports and special features should all air at the same time every evening. People at home—taking care of the children, getting dinner ready—will see the news segments timing out in conjunction with their own set schedules every evening. Indeed, as many people do with the morning news, they will often adjust their routines to be able to tune in to a particular part of the newscast.

(In small markets in particular, it is often possible to find a radio station that will be interested in simulcasting your news. They might take some of your commercials or roll in their own. It's excellent visibility for you, especially among commuters. People driving home listening to your news on the radio will find themselves at the same point in their journey home when the scheduled segments air.)

Let's make the presumption that there will be only twelve minutes of commercials per hour, six in each half-hour plus a minute-thirty station break at the end of the broadcast. That commercial load may be less than what other stations are running, but if the premise of quality television news is correct, you will soon be able to charge higher rates for the better audience you are drawing and will thus enjoy a rich(er) revenue stream. And one reason you will be drawing that news-hungry, consumer-oriented audience is that you will be providing them with more news in place of the extra commercials.

You will have a clean look. Your set has only two primary positions; they are for your anchor team, the two best television journalists in the market. They are the only people to deliver the news from the set, except on the rare occasion when a reporter sits in with them in a side position for a special or team report. The extra chair on the side of the set is primarily for the Newsmaker interview. You won't need a slot for a sportscaster because one of your anchors handles sports, and does a very good job of making less sports news more interesting to more viewers. Nor do you need a chair or a chroma-key wall for weather caster, since the weather is now more ably handled and in far less time by one of the anchors.

This means that the set is considerably smaller than most, and thus is less complicated to shoot, reducing the number of production errors. It is also less expensive to operate and maintain.

Because most of the audience tunes in to get the weather, in addition to the news, it is important to report the weather news they seek close to the top of broadcast. You might slot it in your line up for the thirty seconds going into the first commercial break. It would include the meteorological details of that day, including the highs and lows and any records approached or broken, plus the forecast. Finally, you might also show a national weather map, with forecasts for the next day; it makes a good bumper going into the commercials.

If people ask why you don't have a separate weather caster, you might point out that on the other stations, they have a weather person who gets paid a not insignificant salary to be a personality who takes six to ten times longer than need be telling you to bring an umbrella tomorrow or not. And you might point out that your viewers get to see the whole weather map, not just the part the weather person isn't blocking with his body.

You might also note that you didn't want to squander the resources—time and money—when the forecasts are so often wrong. Especially when so many weather casters deliver their reports with such pomposity. One Sunday night, the KRON weather caster had been going on for several minutes, when he finally wrapped it up with "So Jim, no precip for the next twenty-four hours." At that point, they took a two-shot, and Jim Paymar was hanging up the phone to the control room. Looking incredulous, he said, "They say it's pouring outside."

You should also report the weather in full in thirty seconds at the end of the first news segment in the second half-hour going into the commercial break. And finally give the forecast during the goodnight at the end of the broadcast.

As discussed earlier, sports news is highly over-played in local newscasts. Most women, the target viewers of most advertisers, aren't interested at all. And most men who follow sports are looking to the news for local scores and highlights. The true sports afficionados tune to the sports networks to get their main sports fix.

Your anchor(s) can deliver the relevant scores and major sporting news in less than a minute, and should do so at the same time every night, leading into the last commercial break in the first half-hour. You can also insert a cut-back version, say thirty seconds, before the final commercial break in the second half-hour. Of course, if there is an electrifying play, by all means show it. Television is about pictures, and most people have at least a passing interest in athletics. Plus, everyone likes a good play.

A third element that should be reported nightly like weather and sports is business. (It's curious though probably not significant that there are aspects to the business world that are similar to both sports (combat) and weather (forecasting).) Business coverage should get a minute in both half-hours, going into the middle break. That minute should not be given over to a brokerage house "reporter," as some stations do, but should be delivered as a package, either by a business-savvy reporter or one of the anchors. It should include the major Wall Street indices, the price of gold, other major national and international business news and any important items on the local business front that don't warrant separate coverage.

There is a fourth nightly element if you are located in a major metropolitan area, and that is traffic. Most markets, while they will have occasional or even regular traffic snarls, don't need to regularly report on it. But in major markets, traffic is an issue, both to those trying to get through it, and those who await their arrival. It may not be useful for someone stuck just behind an over-turned big rig with nowhere to turn, but to those who expect him home at a particular time and know that his route would put him behind the accident, it is useful information.

Since thousands—even tens of thousands—of people can be affected by extreme traffic situations, these situations become news. Many people are not affected, of course, so traffic reports should be limited. One method would be to go to a full-screen map with grid-locked areas highlighted, and a short voice-over locating the worst problems. This report could play in the middle of the second break where it would be less obtrusive. If it's still an issue in your market, you could put traffic in the complementary position in the second half-hour as well.

In some coastal markets, the time of the tides are more important than the traffic and could be reported in that position in place of traffic.

Please note that with there being an audience for each of these three or four regular items of general interest, there are also likely some long-term sponsorship opportunities. Not only do advertisers like putting their message near segments that draw a regular audience, but they appreciate being able to tell people when their spots are running, which the proposed format enables.

*   *   *   *   *   *   *

Now for the news.... The hour opens with headlines and is then, with the exceptions noted above for weather, sports, business and traffic, news through to the end of the first half-hour. The second half-hour opens with four minutes of expanded headlines and short bites, and is followed by three minutes of secondary news, primarily readers because you want to cover a lot of territory. Weather leads into the fourth commercial break, which is followed by the Newsmaker segment.

The Newsmaker segment is primarily an interview, though it may be supported with a brief tape package which defines the subject under discussion in the interview. You can also use visuals during the interview, but more often than not the person will be interesting enough to keep on camera for most of the segment. (As discussed elsewhere in this book, you never want to use visuals as wallpaper.) The Newsmaker can be a political or civic leader, a business person, educator, scientist, or preacher. It should be someone who has information of interest and importance to the general public.

The Newsmaker should be announced at the top of the program, and the audience encouraged to email questions to the station (unless the interview is on tape, of course.) The audience should also be invited to recommend Newsmakers for interviews. The interview should be shot with the Newsmaker in a guest position at the anchor desk or on location. It should be done live, whenever practical, because most live interviews are more energetic. Presumably, your Newsmaker will be compelling, so you might want to go to just a clock bumper before the commercial break.

If traffic is still an issue in your market at that hour, you might insert an update map and report in the middle of the next break.

In most markets, financial matters are important to a significant segment of your audience, so it is recommended that you provide a business report in the second half-hour, perhaps coming out of the commercial break. It doesn't have to be as long, but should cover the day's markets and major business news developments.

Then you might move toward the end of the hour with a segment of Viewer Q's. For three minutes, the anchor(s) or a reporter will report answers to questions sent in by viewers. They may be a series of simple questions that need only short answers, but other Q's might require a couple of minutes. The questions should have general interest, at least, and might range from the date of the next city council election to how anthrax is stopped by antibiotics. The names and towns of the viewers with the questions might be read with each question; this is very appealing to the viewers. The participating viewers should, of course, be notified when their questions will be answered on the air.

Finally, wrapping up the hour is a minute of the top headlines, the Dow close, and the forecast, followed by goodnights. As you can see from the sample format, the newscast is scheduled to be off the air at 58:30, which allows for any necessary network and/or station identifications. If your station controls the time, you might want to add a community calendar after the close and credits. This segment, also sponsor-able, could be managed by the news department and would be collapsible should news requirements warrant.

This production note: to further enhance the ease of accessing the news the viewers seek, particularly for those who are attending with just half an ear, you might insert different audio beds under the weather, business, traffic, and sports to cue your audience to their particular interest. Also, add a short single-note tone to mark the top and bottom of the hour. These audio cues should be carried through all newscasts. It may sound Pavlovian, but it works as an aid to your audience and many viewers will respond favorably, every newscast.

The strength of this newscast is that it enables people to get caught up more or less fully at the top of the hour, again in an abbreviated version at the bottom of the hour, and finally in just a minute at the end of the newscast. Plus, with this format your audience can watch the full hour with minimal repetition. The viewers and listeners can know where to turn and when, every night, to get the information they seek. They can adjust their schedules so that they are free to tune in to get the news they want, which is an important selling point since not everyone is interested in the full menu of choices.

38. The Third Early Evening News Half-Hour

As the networks offer up their national evening newscasts every weeknight at 6:30 and again at 7:00 (Eastern), affiliates have the choice of taking the first feed, or waiting for the second, which is likely to have errors corrected and stories updated. The choice exists mainly west of the Eastern Time Zone, since most East Coast stations are unlikely to use half of their prime time access hour—one of their most lucrative times of the day because the locals own all of the revenues from the early evening hour—for a network newscast. They bring in considerably more revenues by airing *Spin City* reruns or *Access Hollywood* instead.

Similarly, moving westward into cities like Chicago, St. Louis, Dallas, and dozens of smaller markets, there is a choice of running the net news at 5:30 or 6:00. But in the Central Time Zone, prime time access begins at six, so most stations will run the network newscast at 5:30, leading up to it with thirty to ninety minutes of local news.

In the Mountain and Pacific Time Zones, prime time access ceases to be an issue; both feeds arrive before you would air them.

In any time zone, the third half-hour of local news might be programmed something like that outlined in the next couple of pages. The basic concept is that most people who watch you at five or at six-thirty—before or after the network news—are deliberately tuning in for a full hour of news, both national and local. There will be other viewers, of course, but because you have to make a choice, you should primarily target those who are just watching the one hour package.

That means that your half-hour will be solidly local and tight; no features, and the slimmest of national headlines at the top and bottom of your program. You will have less time for each story than you did on the hour newscast, and not enough time to run them all. Since you are trying to get in more stories in less time, you have to make sure that you provide enough time for your audience to get the facts before you move to the next story. It requires some judicious editing, not only cutting packages down to voice-overs, but also dropping video sometimes to make them simple readers. Voice-overs require more time and attention.

Also, you don't want the newscast to have so many different shots that it looks more like a light show than an information program.

You should always keep an eye out for something truly newsworthy from the Newsmaker interview in an earlier hour newscast to use as a sound bite for the last half-hour. The "truly newsworthy" will depend on (1) what your Newsmaker had to say, and (2) how heavy the rest of your news budget is that night. But if it is reasonable to insert a clip from the interview, you will not only cross-promote the earlier news program, but you will also enable people who couldn't see it to get a taste of it. You would position it in your news half-hour on the basis of its newsworthiness, with a softer cut playing deeper in the newscast.

Run the same schedule of weather, stocks and traffic bumpers as in the 5:00 half-hour. Many markets won't have traffic issues this late, and you can omit that bumper from the middle of the second commercial break.

Finally, consider that this is will be the last time many of your viewers get news before they get up the next morning. Many go to sleep earlier than your late evening news, and some simply choose not to go to bed on a news stomach. So make sure that when they have watched your last half-hour of local early evening news, they are fully informed about the day that's been. Especially for the clock conscious, there is no time for fluff. As they used to say on WINS, an all-news radio station in New York City, "Give us 22 minutes and we'll give you the world." In your case, make it a glimpse at the world and a good look at the community.

39. The Late Evening News

The Eleven O' Clock news has always been the signature local news broadcast for a television journalist. Even though it doesn't get the same size audience as the early shows, it is the showcase for the top news organization because it wraps up the day—locally and otherwise—in a half-hour and sends people to bed with a complete picture. Also, the late evening news is usually watched by people who are generally more interested in, and paying closer attention to, current events.

As with the other newscasts, the eleven should open with headlines, and then run with the top stories. As there is no network newscast to complement the local, your half-hour is a mix of local and non-local news. You will usually have a higher ratio of national and international stories to local, depending on events, than the early evening newscasts.

In addition to requiring a more precise, thoughtful choice of stories—you have only half the program time—the late evening news also demands considerable editing; like the third half-hour compared to the hour, but more so. Because you are under greater time constraints, you will want to get in more stories per minute than on the early evening broadcasts, which means that the stories will necessarily be shorter. Stories that might have run as a 1:20 package in the early news might not have the story value for more than a :25 voice-over in the late. Which means that you have to be particularly careful that the audience, which might not have seen your early news, still has enough time to assimilate each item. And obviously, many stories simply won't make the cut at all.

The weather, stocks and sports should be aired in the same positions as the earlier newscasts, so that people know where to get the specific information they seek. The format may seem pedestrian, but with a well-chosen story selection, you can cover a lot of ground, and leave your audience feeling fully informed about their world.

For stations producing an hour ten o'clock news cast, you might format it just like the 5:00 early evening hour discussed earlier; dropping the traffic bumpers, of course. A combination of both local and national and international news, everything by the clock, answering all of the major questions, and adding some breadth with a Newsmaker interview and Viewer Questions. The ten o'clock hour is generally a more relaxed time for people but they aren't ready yet to turn in. Their minds are still awake and hungry; feed them.

The Linda Ellerbee Story

Life presents curious opportunities, often when they are not expected—sometimes not even invited—and you have a chance to reach for the brass ring. A better metaphor, to my way of thinking because it's not about luck, is jumping up to grab the bars on the overhead horizontal ladder, across which you can pull yourself on the basis of your own strength. If you don't grab right, if you don't hold on, if you don't keep up your momentum, you don't make it across. In my years of television news, I've had a number of opportunities to jump for the chance, and I took every one of them. Not all carried me a far distance, but I didn't regret a single jump.

One such moment was in February of 1974. I was part way through my first night as a free-lance news writer for WCBS television in New York. I'd never written news copy before, but I knew how, intuitively and from paying attention. It also helped that I'd been writing, sometimes for money, since I was sixteen. Besides, if you know what you're doing, news writing is a virtual sinecure. Also, no one at the station had a clue that this was my first time writing news; they knew I'd been with ABC News in Washington and made some presumptions. They weren't disappointed.

At one point while the early show was still on the air, the news director came into the newsroom and asked if any of the regular writers or producers knew how to produce a videotape spot. No one raised so much as an eyebrow, and then I raised my hand. "I can," I said casually. Actually, I'd never produced a tape spot either. I'd seen it done a few times at the ABC Washington news bureau, and in earlier times I had watched David Buksbaum, a legend in his own time at ABC News in New York, produce some tape stories, though never from start to finish.

Okay, I was told, here's the situation. Linda Ellerbee and a crew are going to a meeting of gas station owners in the Bronx. They'll shoot it on tape and feed it back to the tape room. There not being enough time for her to come back to the station for the editing for the eleven o'clock news, she'll write a script and feed a standupper and voice-overs to the tape room.

That would be a reasonably simple procedure for two people who knew what they were doing, and Linda knew how to write and report. It was presumed that I knew how to put her piece together.

We started by taping the ninety-minute meeting of the gas station owners, who were mostly complaining about unfair prices and angry customers; fallout from the ongoing OPEC machinations. When they were done, Linda and I discussed which sound cuts to use, and she sat down to write her script. At 9:30, she called back and we went over the script. Then she fed a standup open and close, followed by some voice-over bridges. Then she hung up and headed back for the station.

In those days, we were using two-inch tape on 90-minute reels. It took a considerable number of minutes to get from one end of the reel to the other, and we had shots and sound scattered over two reels. On top of that, the tape editors were not familiar with news editing, and had never done it for local news. Did I mention that Linda's spot was slated to run at the top of the newscast? No extra time, and even less time when you consider that I would have had to tell them considerably in advance that the spot wouldn't be ready in time. It's one thing to lose a spot at 11:20; it's another to lose your lead.

While it wasn't a complicated process—and it would be much less so with the improved technologies today; the standuppers could have been live, for example—producing that kind of spot would still require ability and focused attention to get it fed, cut and ready in that kind of time.

We made it back then, too. The spot ran cleanly, and on time; it was cued ready for playback about ninety seconds before it was to roll. The WCBS people were delighted and the news director singled me out for praise the next day before the entire newsroom. I must have known how to produce a videotape spot, as I had claimed; what I hadn't learned by observing, I had intuited.

40. The Midday News

The midday newscast should be designed for people who stay at home, especially retireds, but also for many business people who take their lunch at the same time every day, often at their desk. In most markets, some of the audience will watch the entire midday newscast, but most will drop in for an update on the news and/or weather or for particular features. Therefore, it makes sense to produce a format like the five o'clock news. Both of the primary midday viewer groups are interested in the stock market, so it would serve them if you featured a business update in both half-hours.

Because the audience is probably thin numbers-wise, and they are mostly just checking in, you can usually rely heavily on material already in-house for the bulk of the program after you've reported the new news. For instance, you can re-air the Newsmaker interview and Viewer Q's from the evening (or the Friday) before. Also you can use reporter packages from the night before, with updated tracks sometimes, or you can cut them down into voice-overs, as is news-appropriate.

Of course, on an overnight or breaking story, you'll need fresh footage and information, but for the most part, unless you are a sizeable operation and/or your midday news garners a significant audience, you are going to leave most of the day's coverage for the early evening newscasts. One reason is that most of your people are still out in the field, and it would disrupt coverage of that or succeeding stories to have them return to the station to prepare a report. Of course if the opportunity is there to feed some footage and perhaps a narration, that would certainly enhance the program, but that will rarely be practical.

Sometimes your people who are out covering stories in the morning can drop off cassettes on their way to afternoon assignments. They should certainly be encouraged to think about servicing the midday newscast as it is a promo, in a sense, for the full blown coverage of the early evening newscasts. This does not suggest producing teases, but rather excerpting voice-over material and/or sound bites that would inform the audience, perhaps enticing them to tune in for more later; as if they weren't already planning to do so.

There is another advantage to relying primarily on features and previously-aired reports and that is it reduces the staff requirements to produce the midday newscast. Most of the video has already been edited, and the scripts have been written. The features are also on tape. It is important, though, with all of that done for you already that you make sure to correct any errors that might have gotten by in the earlier newscast. Bad edits or misspelled supers should never be repeated, and it is the obligation of the people involved in both newscasts to make sure that these errors not go through again. Otherwise, the audience—and there will be a number of repeat viewers since most who watch the midday will watch other newscasts—will think you're lazy or incompetent, twice.

41. The Morning News

There are some places in the country where a lot of people are up early but don't have the time or interest in knowing what happened in the world over night, but those places are few and far between. The morning is a quiet time for some people; they might not speak a word from the time they get out of bed until they arrive at their desk. For many people, however, there is the usual daily routine of rushing around to get themselves—and their children and spouse, as well—out the door. For everyone, however, the morning schedule is an agenda of many separate chores, including cleaning, dressing and feeding, not to mention preparing the food, checking the email, taking care of the pets and leaving a note for the housekeeper.

Whatever their routine, the point is that people usually have one in the morning, and of those who have some latitude in their schedule, many will vary it to accommodate their assimilating the latest news, weather, overnight scores, and/or the opening market. Therefore, it is important for the local newscaster to format a program that stays on schedule, day after day, so that people know how to accomplish the rest of their morning duties around the task of accessing the information they seek.

This is not unlike the other newscasts you are producing, of course; the reasons are the same, with circumstances only slightly altered by the clock. So you want to present a tight newscast to people who can pay only so much attention. Even if you are programming an hour instead of just a half-hour, the same access limitations apply because very few people have the time in the mornings to dawdle before the television set.

Because the morning news staff may be the thinnest of all, you're going to use packages and voice-over material—and often re-polished readers—from the night before. Your latitude depends, of course, on how, if at all, the stories have changed since they were last on the air. If you have the time, you will want to rewrite everything, perhaps putting a "today" spin on the story. This does not mean simply changing "tonight"s to "last night"s, or "tomorrow"s to "today"s.

You will also be using cut-down versions of reporter packages and voice-overs. Make sure that the scripts are both current and accurate. If you opt to use a piece of them, make sure that you don't omit critical details setting up the pictures or sound bites. You can also usually use the Newsmaker interview from the night (or the Friday) before, but you will probably want to cut it, maybe in half, depending on how much time you have and how much news there is to cover. You may ask that the Newsmaker producer provide the editing information, or an actual new version, before she leaves the station the night before.

Also available, and appropriate for morning audiences are myriad syndicated features on health care, consumerism and similar feature topics. In the final segment before the close, it would probably make sense to air one of the syndicated business reports on the overnight Tokyo and London numbers and opening domestic markets, depending on your time zone. Also included would be any expected significant business/economic announcements for the day, e.g., major earnings reports, labor and inflation statistics, et cetera.

Remember that most viewers are tuning in for news developments in an expanded headline fashion, and for the weather, to know what they should wear that day. If you use a lot of pre-edited material from your evening newscasts the night before, plus some informative syndication features, you can produce an hour morning news with very few people at relatively little expense.

Even if you are in a smaller market, you are going to want to produce a morning newscast to run before the network morning shows, if not for an hour, then for a half-hour; and if not a full program, then at least the morning show news cut-ins. The cut-ins alone are important, providing the essential local news developments overnight, if any, the home team sports scores, and the weather forecast. (On the West Coast, you want to add the stock market opening numbers which wouldn't have been covered in the East.) The cut-ins work not only for the people who turn the television on as they get out of bed, but also for those people who just want the latest local headlines and weather.

It should be noted that because cut-ins attract both of these audiences, they can similarly attract lucrative sponsorship. Even for a station with very limited resources, the cut-ins are simple and easy to produce. At a minimum, one person can do a series of readers without tape or graphics in front of a slave camera, punched in and out by a computer clock in master control. Plus the cut-ins serve the public need to be informed, as they further extend your station's identity for being on the job from before dawn to after dusk.

42. News Briefs

A station that is able to dominate the news market has more revenues and more options. One option is to launch a news brief. Practically speaking, news briefs are not going to be a 24/7 event. More likely, you are going to want to air them hourly starting with morning programming and run through prime time.

You don't need video for news briefs. In fact, you should avoid it, since the stories are necessarily short, and you don't need to complicate the production. Graphics are nice but not essential. You're most likely talking about an anchor or reporter sitting at a desk in the newsroom.

Any news brief format you choose should be simple and constant, featuring the top local, national and international stories, presented in order of importance. An effective approach might be to run :57, which started at a minute before the hour would allow for a three second station ID at the end before straight-up.

The news brief would include an opening billboard and ten-second commercial, allowing about :42 for news. If you cover the weather and the Dow in ten seconds, with a hello and good-bye, you have time for about five, tightly written (:05) headlines.

That would tell people in your area that they could tune in your station at 59:00 throughout day and evening and know the general shape of the world, the community and the skies in less than a minute.

You might also choose to run news briefs only during prime time or at nine in the morning and three in the afternoon. It would all depend on your resources and the appetite in the market. You might further explore partnering with a local radio station.

News briefs should not be taken lightly. Many viewers will make them a habit, at least at certain hours. Others will stop in when there is a breaking story they want to stay on top of, and many will tune in just for the weather. But because they are inexpensive to produce and air, they can also be a significant source of revenue for the station, as they are often an easy sell to sponsors. You might also consider marketing them to your local cable system to run on their Headline News channel.

43. Long-Form News Reporting

Back in the old days, networks aired documentaries because they had to in order to stay in good with the FCC. Documentaries were money-losers, and the only benefit the networks saw in them was that they might earn them some prestige by winning awards. In truth, some of the documentaries helped to define—and in some cases to change—history. Work by Edward R. Murrow, Fred Friendly, Walter Cronkite, Howard K. Smith and Av Westin, among others, drew attention to some of the critical issues of the time, and forced examination and fresh thinking, and sometimes prompted action that altered U.S. policy.

Many of the documentaries of the past were long and ponderous, more like what is seen on public television these days; they drew relatively small audiences. Today, their successor news magazines are ubiquitous, popular and immensely profitable. They are doing well because they deal with prime time subjects like sex, crimes, scandals and violence. They are usually light fare, compared with the lengthy investigative work of the past, and though they frequently reveal public failures and miscues, they don't move many mountains, either legislative or intellectual. There are exceptions, but they are few.

Producing long-form news broadcasts is little different from producing packages for the evening broadcast. The same rules for good writing and tight editing apply, only you have more time, which allows you to cover more ground and enrich the story with a broader scope and/or more details, and produce a meaningful report. Sound cuts can run longer, more people can be interviewed, and you can take more time with your script, allowing visuals to play out more of your story.

For the networks, compared to the sitcoms and police shows that comprise the bulk of prime time, news magazines are much less expensive to produce and are very popular with advertisers. That means significant profit margins. Plus, there is little lead time or investment in a magazine. And there is the added benefit that if someone doesn't find one of the stories interesting, there are usually more to come; and every week's show will be different.

While the news magazines are profit centers for the networks, the same is not the case for local stations, because they produce very little of their own programming outside of the news windows. They are not trading down costs from high-priced sit-com salaries. Also, there aren't a lot of local advertisers with the money to float the costs associated with producing an hour—or even a half-hour—news magazine. Some syndicated magazine shows succeed, but they are usually fluff—Hollywood, animals and sports—and don't serve to significantly expand the awareness of the audience.

Successful news operations can sometimes convince well-heeled advertisers to swing a monthly hour magazine, with lots of sponsorship promotion for it. Another avenue in larger venues is to appeal to an advertising agency with multiple appropriate clients to sponsor a series of extended news reports, i.e., in a magazine or single-story format, on a regular (e.g., monthly) basis.

Some stations air special reports, usually one-time shots, on a pressing local subject. Often these programs are on stories that have been receiving heavy local news coverage, and so the assembly of footage, the writing and the reporting is not very complicated. These programs are usually pre-sold to major local advertisers for the prestige value. Mostly they focus on covering an historic array of facts, rather than plowing new ground. Sometimes this is just what the story and the community need.

If you go this route on a story and find you have drawn a significant audience, you might go back to your sponsors and ask them to support more such efforts. One route for the cost-conscious news director might be to start with a town hall meeting on a particular subject—or not—to gather ideas and maybe pick up some sound bites as a foundation for a larger report. Remember that some of the cost could be mitigated by re-editing material shot and run on your regular newscasts.

Finally, local interview programs, usually produced by the community affairs department, could probably also be considered long-form news reporting. Regrettably, at most stations, these programs are aired purely to show that they are community-minded. They are often hosted by the least efficacious reporters and are aired early Sunday mornings.

At some point, a news director is going to remember that the networks' Sunday morning talk shows used to be a step below obligatory, and today they are the sources of many Monday headlines. It wouldn't take much to juice up their community programs, getting the true decision-makers into the studio to answer important questions, with their feet held to the fire.

Again, the success of such an effort would depend on the particular market, the potential audience, the time slot, and the quality of the personnel arranging, hosting and promoting the programs. But it is certainly not implausible that a local Sunday morning interview program could earn a significant audience, and occasionally generate some headlines.

44. Making Mistakes

If you ever have doubts about the "facts" you are reporting, as tempting as it might be to get out in front of the competition with a scoop, stop and check. If you are wrong, you can damage your reputation as a journalist, as well as that of your entire news operation. While in the smaller markets the viewers may be used to the news people making mistakes, the higher up the ladder you climb, the longer the memory the viewers have—and should have—and the harder it is to recover from mistakes. Especially mistakes in judgment. Factual errors—e.g., mispronouncing a name or mis-locating an event in time or space—are usually easier to overlook.

All errors need to be corrected. With air time precious, unless you have made a serious error, you're not likely to want to go on the next night and say that you meant the North Dewdrop Landfill instead of the West Dewdrop Landfill, unless that distinction is significant to the substance of the story. All corrections that need to be made on air should be done the next day in the same time slot as when the error occurred; probably at the end of the segment. An alternative to an on-air correction—for minor but factual mistakes—is to put your errata on your web site, and every week, maybe in a voice-over at the end of the broadcasts, tell your viewers to go to your website for updates and corrections.

Make every effort to keep the errata section small. The fewer nicks in your armor the better. A further protection is to have every line of the newscast copy proof-read before you go on the air by someone other than the writer, but someone who is familiar with the facts.

There is something regrettable in our nature that likes to see people pulled down from pedestals, and a reporter making mistakes is more than the usual entertainment for much of the audience. People will more easily forgive you being late than being wrong. Remember, it can take years to build a reputation and only seconds to destroy it. Don't take being right lightly.

Seton's Law

There are many stories of how even the best laid plans—even the tightest line-ups—can be overthrown. Here are a couple that explain why you need to be ready for anything, and it still may not be enough.

In my early days with ABC, I worked as a desk assistant on the late weekend newscasts when Sam Donaldson anchored the broadcasts from New York. Sam loved the opportunity to anchor, but at the same time, he appeared very nervous. He also exposed a bit of his paranoia when things didn't go well, which often happened on the weekends, in part because like most seven-day operations the news was in the hands of the second string.

Another problem he faced was that the weekend news was often used as a place to burn off spots that had been assigned for the *Evening News* but which hadn't made it on the air and were going to be out-dated and wasted if not run on the weekend. One such film spot—this was in 1971—was coming out of the Middle East; it was being shipped from Tel Aviv to New York, in plenty of time for processing and editing. In plenty of time, that is, had not a camel run across the tarmac as the TWA flight carry the film was racing down the runway, forcing the plane into the sand. The flight was canceled. Donaldson wondered aloud, joking, if it weren't some kind of plot against him.

A number of years later, I was on the front lines myself, confronting a series of problems. It was a few days before Christmas in 1978 and I was acting Operations Producer for *World News Tonight*. My job was to make sure that every package and voice-over was transferred to tape and readied for air. This night I found myself in production hell, as one piece after another came in by satellite or land-line with a problem in it. One piece was out of synch and required the audio to be re-laid. Another came in only twenty minutes before it was to roll, and still needed to be assembled. A third was fed to us in chunks, during commercial breaks in the local newscast; their master control played the commercials while their control room fed us the story.

When a fourth piece got stuck in traffic on the way to the office, we loaded up a bank piece. And about twenty seconds after it rolled, for reasons no one but The News Gremlin could explain, the tape machine—they were the two-inch variety back then—kicked itself into low-band. Since no one had used low-band in years, it took a moment to realize what had happened. A savvy operator pushed the toggle button, and the machine returned to normal high-band playback. After feeding a cleaned up version to Los Angeles for the West Coast feed, we all adjourned to a local watering hole to drink martinis and shake our heads over the proof of Seton's Law that sometimes, if nothing can go wrong, it will.

What can go wrong? Ron Moses, a top-notch director in Providence, was walking through the WPRI control during one late newscast when he witnessed someone else suffer the director's ultimate nightmare; the director was also the technical director. The microphones crackled and died; the film spooled out of the projectors. The slides jammed; the tape machine wouldn't lock up, and the anchor's camera was shifting phase and changing colors. In desperation, the director/TD pushed his thumb down hard on the switcher button marked "House Black" and killed the broadcast. "You saw what was happening," moaned the semi-hysterical director to Moses, "Everything was broken! Nothing worked! I took black. What would you have done?" Ron replied calmly, "I would have dissolved."

IV—Managing The News Operation

The newspaper should be more than a business enterprise. It should also be the champion and protector of the public interest and defender of the people's rights.

—*Theodore Bodenwein*

Section Four of *Don't Mess with the Press* looks briefly at television news as a business. It does no good to have a brilliant newscast every night if no one is watching it. Once you are producing quality television news it is necessary that the public finds out so that they can watch so that your sales people can go to the cream of the advertisers and say, We have the cream of the community watching the best newscasts in the market.

How do you get those viewers? Word of mouth is useful, and because quality television news will stand out so starkly in most markets, at least in the early years before the competition catches on and joins you, it will be a highly visible new commodity that will earn attention from viewers and newsmakers alike. Still, it will need to be promoted and advertised.

It will take a little time, but less than you think, to get your new approach up and running. You shouldn't be discouraged by some of the pot-shots that critics will likely fire at you. It seems intrinsic in our culture that innovators are attacked because they bring change. You may actually benefit from the criticism; at least listen to it. Pay less heed to the ratings, however, because at least initially, they will be an undependable gauge of your audience and your staying power.

It may take a leap of faith for station management to try quality television news, but some of those mired in second or third place in the ratings—in a business where news could be the source of 60% or more of your revenues—should find the risk a reasonable one. Especially because quality television news costs less to produce. That should be very appealing to the top corporate people. Instead of carrying expensive star-quality talent, you can hire less expensive journalist-quality reporters. And because your focus is on the news, you don't need to spend unnecessarily on live remote trucks, Doppler radar and other extraneous sizzle. At some point you may let go your consultants, and not even bother with a ratings service.

Quality television news will benefit everyone involved, on both sides of the screen, producing high revenues for delivering important information to a news-hungry public.

45. The Television News Business

The business of television has changed dramatically over the past twenty-five years. Whereas it used to be that ownership of a television station was a license to print money, nowadays running a station requires finesse. A principle cause of this transformation is the proliferation of competition from other stations and channels, particularly outside of the market, distributed via cable and satellite. Where once a station might have had to compete with two other network affiliates, a usually-weak PBS outlet, and at most a couple of independents with "I Love Lucy" reruns and old movies, now most Americans have access to hundreds of different channels, dramatically diffusing the viewership, ratings and revenues.

The ability of viewers to record/playback programs has also created problems. Not only has this meant a further decline in station viewership as people buy and rent videos and DVDs, but it has threatened the very foundation of commercial television. People who record programs for later playback don't sit through the commercials, and advertisers are not getting their money's worth when viewers fast forward through their commercials.

News advertisers, however, are most likely to reach viewers because most people watch the news live.

News advertisers are not insulated from the problem of remote controls, which have also dramatically shifted viewing practices. Even if the viewer is planning to come back to a program, when the commercial hits, he is likely to click to another channel, or at least to hit the mute button. As quality television news draws a quality audience, so the advertisers trying to reach these viewers will need to produce quality commercials that stand out from the typical spots, perhaps by using humor or otherwise presenting their messages in a clever way.

So with all of the choices facing viewers today, the advertising revenues for local news may account for two-third of a station's revenues, in an arena where competition is back down to two or three stations. Some stations, accepting new latitude from the FCC and not having the perspicacity to recognize the opportunity to compete, have simply cut back or cut out their news programming entirely, when the revenues from being number three or worse were inadequate to cover their costs.

It means that the massive shake-out that began in the mid-Eighties is continuing. Indeed, it has accelerated. Where once station managers had the revenues to hire over-priced consultants, build *Star Trek*-like sets, pour money into the latest gadgets, fire and hire with wild abandon, today their hands are tied by corporate accountants. And because most station managers came up through the ranks of the sales department, they have little working knowledge of what makes a successful news program, let alone what makes it journalistically sound.

In the early days, television news was almost as much news television as it was news. But the level of sophistication among news viewers is increasing, in large measure because of the Internet. While the majority may still tune in to a newscast for glitz and glamour rather than the information, it is more out of habit than discernment. As quality television news becomes a factor in more markets, the viewing public will realize that it is wasting its time watching shoddy news programs for their entertainment value, and many will change their viewing habits.

This is not to say that news must be dry and boring; quite the contrary. But viewers who want to be informed will demand more than the blood-'n-sperm pandering that masquerades as news on many stations today. They want information…substantive, useful accurate information. They don't want to simply zone out; they want to be able to take something away with them. They will insist upon a quality news product instead of an empty box.

Revolutions

One reason why the world sometimes seem so chaotic today is that our society has experienced enormous change without fully or consciously digesting it. The people who were born after the Second World War were reared under remarkably different circumstances than the generations before them, because of six revolutions that were launched in the Sixties. The six were Environmentalism, which got its start with Rachel Carson's book *Silent Spring*; Consumerism, which arrived with Ralph Nader's book on the Chevrolet Corvair, *Unsafe at Any Speed*; Civil

Rights, with Martin Luther King's "I have a dream" speech; An End to War, birthed in the anti-Vietnam War movement; Women's Liberation; and the Sexual Revolution.

Each in itself would have been enough to transform a society or upend a government. We Americans started six in a single decade. More important is to realize that those revolutions are still underway. We still wage wars, though not the same kind as the masses of frightened young men in trenches facing off against each other as cannon fodder. Racism is more deeply embedded in our social fabric than can be eradicated by law, but we've made a great deal of progress in breaking down racial barriers. Consumerism is virtually inherent in our commerce; at least to be accessible, once the need is revealed.

Environmentalists have won major battles, lost some, and remain an indomitable force in our country and worldwide, but with lots of work yet to be done to clean up our messes and prevent others. As regards the revolutionary realignment of the genders—partly due to the Free Love or Sexual Revolution and The Pill—women seem to have thrown off most of the shackles of second-class citizenship that were their lot not so many years ago. The changes this has wrought have yet to be fully felt and examined. For instance, what has it meant to our society that the women left home and went to work? How has that changed the way children are societalized? What has it done to the relationship between men and women? How has it affected us as individuals?

If you want a sense of how different the world is, when I was a desk assistant at ABC in New York City in 1970, I took the privilege of being a member of the fourth estate up to Yankee Stadium one evening to catch a game from the press box. Nineteen at the time, I and another desk assistant hopped the subway to the Bronx, brimming with self-importance as we showed our ABC News ID cards and went through the special door to take the elevator up to the press level. But we were stopped from entering the press box by a crusty, unpleasant version of Oscar Madison. I could go in, he said, but not my colleague, Kathy Johnson. Women weren't allowed. We watched the game from the stands.

By the way, I think it would be reasonable to add a seventh revolution to the Sixties panoply. The Communications Revolution. Television exploded onto the scene in that decade and has changed the whole world forever. TV was followed by satellites, computers, cellphones and the Internet. It is difficult to fathom the enormity of the effects the new technologies will have on who we are, how we see ourselves, and how we relate to the rest of the world. The boys in the press box were all banging away on portable typewriters then. Now women are in the locker rooms, for better or worse, writing stories on notebook computers and feeding them in on cellphones.

The point to be taken and remembered is that change is endemic to life, and we should never be too certain that we know how a day's events will fit into the big picture. Humility is a sounder wrap than bravado.

Perhaps in time we'll gain perspective on what has happened and is happening now, but for the moment, its almost too frenetic to see many of the patterns. Consider that with the Internet putting all of the world's information at the fingertips of all of its denizens (hyperbole, of course), it means that we will be leveling the playing field, and everyone may soon be defined by what information they select, and what they do with it.

It's a constant job to stay informed about what is going on in the world or just your corner of it. You can't possibly have a handle on all of the important information, but the more sources you tap into, the better perspective you will generate. When you have the time, you might check out alternative publications, stations, and/or websites that challenge the status quo and question presumptions. Often they will indicate change, some time down the line, and you will already have a background on who's doing what, where, when, how and why.

46. Baseline Performance

It starts with an idea…that quality television news is the way you want to go, and while the details are important, it is that approach that will make what is possible happen. In order to implement this approach, you need good people who share your vision. This mean creating an environment of collaboration rather than competition, where everyone, to use Edward R. Murrow's term, is "a laborer in the vineyard." Yes, titles and responsibilities are different, but when you are respectful of a shared purpose, the team functions better.

It is axiomatic that news departments are underbudgeted and under-staffed. One way to increase staff is to hire or apprentice interns. There are a lot of people who would be glad to work for nothing—but minimum wage is more practical— just to get a start or to be around the news. Whether you bring them on as a go- fer, to answer phones, or degauss tapes, you expose them to the operation in a way that they can't do much damage, but they can discover if they have the makings of a television newsie. They can plug some holes and be trained at the same time.

Another way to leverage your resources—and expand your scope—is to create a partnership with a radio station and/or a newspaper. While there is usually an incipient sense of competition among the different news media, cooperative or pooling arrangements can be practical for all concerned, especially in a small market. Why should everyone try to cover 24/7 when you might share the duties with the promise that all participants get the same information at the same time?

Orientation

You will get more out of your employees when you make them a part of the team from the outset. Too many new hires are simply shown a desk and phone and then sent out to cover a story. Every new employee—reporters and photographers especially—should be given a full orientation. They should go out on stories with veteran staffers to the learn the ropes of your television news operation, to see how coverage is implemented, to understand the protocols between the field and the station and just how stories make it from assignment to broadcast.

You should also take your new hires around the station, introducing them to everyone with whom they might have contact, e.g., the receptionist who takes the viewer callers, the bookkeeper who tracks time sheets, and the comptroller who issues the checks; also the station manager, because ultimately, she's the person they have to please.

If the new person has a family, it would be helpful to your ultimate goals to make sure that they have help adjusting to the (new) surroundings, perhaps driving them around to show them neighborhoods, shopping and schools. It also makes sense for the spouse to meet at least the people who answer the phone, the news director and some of the news staff; it helps to smooth the transition.

When you bring in new people, make sure to get them press credentials. If there is nothing official provided by local or state authorities, produce your own press passes for the individuals and for their cars. They provide quicker access when time is important. Since much of your coverage is probably going to involve the police, i.e., crime and disaster news, you might also send your new hires down to the police department to introduce themselves to the public information officer.

Also, make sure that they understand both the official rules and the unwritten agreements between the people who report and those who enforce the laws. It would make sense, too, to have your rookies get a tour of the other major city operations such as fire, paramedics and city hall. Think of it as an investment.

You should also consider advising the staff about the various costs of production. If your reporters understand how much it costs to cover the news, they will have a better grasp of what is involved and how their work fits into the big picture. When they have an understanding of the different expenses of studio versus field production, for example, you can expect them to make a better use of scarce resources. They will know to employ production techniques that are perhaps more cost-effective. While they should be assured that you will spend what you must to cover the news, if they realize that they can get the same effect shooting an extra half-hour in the field as would take an hour of more expensive studio time, you enfranchise them with a sense of value and participation in the overall news operation.

Bare Bones

It doesn't matter how small your station is, you can always put on a quality television newscast. You work with what you have. For instance, if you have only a single-anchor studio with two cameras, set one for straight-on head shot, and the other 45 degrees off line and slightly tighter. That way you can transition from a chroma-key shot with a graphic, for example, to a simple head shot.

Today, few television stations lack the capability of going live virtually immediately, and most can feed a live signal from anywhere in their coverage territory in about as long as it takes to drive there. But back in 1970, two weeks after I started in television news, the Apollo 13 crew ran into trouble late one night and all three networks had to scramble just to get on the air.

Even though they significantly trailed the competition in news ratings, ABC did better in space coverage because of its Science Editor, Jules Bergman, who knew the subject and many of the people involved in the space program. The night of the first trouble with Apollo 13 found Jules reporting live into a black-and-white flash camera mounted on the wall near the network news assignment desk. It took hours, literally, to get the space coverage studio up and on the air. If you saw the Ron Howard film, *Apollo 13*, you could see the coverage as it happened, on the fly so to speak, that night in April of 1970.

Error Checking

For a community that would like to, and needs to, be informed, the more mistakes they witness from a news operation, the less faith they have in the information coming to them. As one might expect and as it should be. When you lose the confidence of the audience, you might as well close the doors and not re-open until you have a competent team truly committed to the task and capable of informing the community.

Accuracy in news coverage is vital. Because there is naturally some celebrity attached to news personnel, when they err, their mistakes are often magnified well out of proportion.

It is the obligation of station management to hire only those people who are capable of doing the job, i.e., presenting the news fully and accurately. That is often tough in smaller markets where salaries are too small to attract seasoned journalists. Smaller markets are viewed as the lower end of a farm team system for larger markets, training grounds for aspiring reporters. It is in the smaller markets where they are expected to learn their craft and make mistakes doing it.

Too often, media outlets in smaller markets explain their lapses by claiming to be too low on the ladder to have more talented news people. There is some legitimacy to this excuse, but it is overused. Most news operations have the option of paying more to fewer people and hiring better reporters, but ours is a culture that tends to value quantity over quality, and so more people with less ability are brought on board. That leaves many stations in small markets with people who have little or no training, and who don't know what they don't know.

Worse are the operations that hire people without any interest or ability in journalism simply because they are looking for work. People who view journalism as a 9-to-5 job don't invest the kind of attention needed to properly inform the community. They are drawn by a paycheck, not driven by purpose.

Considering the low starting pay scale, one might think that few people would be attracted to reporting if they didn't hear the calling of journalism, but some are attracted to the celebrity. One might think that they would evince some interest in the news, but that isn't always the case. If people don't catch the news bug, they are not likely to perform according to high standards.

Even in the smallest of markets, it's important to require of news people that they keep themselves informed; about current events in general and their market in particular. They should also have a facility for expression. They should be clean and properly groomed, and demonstrate an ability to assimilate, manipulate and disseminate information. Most of all, they should have a hunger in their belly to observe and report history being made, as a service to the people who will, in our precious democratic republic, help to shape the future.

47. Website

A website is a wonderful adjunct for a news operation, not only for enhancing your presence as a source of information, but also to solicit ideas from your news audience. The Internet makes it much easier to elicit information about on-going stories, including personal perspectives that help to put an issue before the community in a more thorough way.

Bulletin boards on issues can be constructive in providing new information and contexts, enabling readers to get more depth in, and understanding of, the issues, even when there isn't time to provide such scope on the air.

A good website will parallel the station's news coverage and then expand with other news sources and links. Archives are also important, and you should consider putting on your site all correspondent reports in a searchable format, so that viewers can find information they might have missed during a broadcast.

You also want to have bios on your news personnel and, of course, a schedule of newscasts,

If you have the resources, you might also run contests based on knowledge of news reported in the previous weeks.

You could develop special sections, rife with links, on health care, education, the environment, or matters of local special interest.

Other website features might include a calendar, clock and weather; emergency phone numbers, links to public officials, and links to community sites like the public health office and the schools.

As mentioned earlier, the website is where you might have a section correcting errors on your broadcasts. Also, make sure that any errors in scripts are corrected in the versions on the website.

You should provide email links to all of your on-air and management people, and encourage your people to respond to as many notes as possible. Also, ask them to keep their eyes open for any unusual comments or trends that they might pick up. In that vein, it would probably be useful to ask them for a sample of comments that are coming in to them, to get a better picture of how they are perceived, at least by this segment of the audience.

The success of the website in generating a dialogue with viewers will depend on the Internet nature of the community, who's on and who's not, and how they use it. In some markets, you may get just the same-ole cranks complaining up one side and down the other, which might be useful for a day or so and then not at all. But in other markets, you will find that the interactivity can bring about a wealth of tips on news stories and alternatives to a mired status quo.

Without selling your soul, you might have a suggestion box and a tip hot-line, both of which might earn contributors a prize of some sort, or mention on the air. The website would be another vehicle for people to contact the station with Viewer Questions and suggestions for Newsmakers.

It should be noted that while there are a lot of self-important folks writing a lot of notes to a lot of people, you might remember that this is a new medium of communications, and there's considerable settling out to be seen. So don't put up with harassment, but always keep an ear cocked when you hear something only slightly implausible.

Websites can take time to maintain, but if your staff is properly involved in the process, the workload is spread around. To cover some of the costs of the site, you might involve your program advertisers in purchasing sponsorship billboards. You also might consider partnering with an ISP to offer connections for your viewers, with your site as the default home page.

48. News Promotion

In the old days, the news and sales departments—at both the networks and local stations—were barely on speaking terms. The former scorned the latter as pimps, even though that's where their salaries were generated, and the latter would have been happy to sell without ever having to mention the news. Then the two sides decided that they could better work together than fight, and in no time, there was considerable collusion. Not only did the news department fully support promotional efforts of their newscasts, but many local station news directors went so far as to solicit story ideas for sweeps from the sales department; sometimes at the behest of the general manager.

While it's not hard to understand how this symbiosis came about, it is still an unfortunate acknowledgment that the news is merely a commodity, and in the corporate mind, sales come before journalism. With quality television news, the sales outlook actually improves because (1) in most markets there is no competition, (2) the audience is upscale and thus more attractive to more top drawer advertisers, even during downturns in the economy.

Also, quality television news is more promote-able. It has a higher story count, it attracts the top whistle blowers and best sources, and it scores the best interviews. It is also formatted for the most effective, community-minded news consumption. What's not to like. Promotion is a snap: it's the best written, produced and reported news in the market. It will attract the cream of the audience and the cream of the advertisers.

There are some issues to be resolved. First, advertisers who have been trying to reach a broader audience will probably want to redo their commercials. The audience attracted to quality television news does not buy into staccato editing, bright lights and lots of noise. It is attracted by clever messages, humor and complementary high quality commercials.

Second, unlike many stations, the staff would be barred from joining civic organizations or engaging in sponsored events. If they felt a need to contribute to the community—certainly a healthy instinct—it might be through teaching, or speaking appearances at a wide enough variety of public functions that there could be no question of their objectivity.

The reason for what might seem a rather austere policy is that such organizations are occasionally in the news, for better or worse, and a reporter's allegiance to the news should never be the subject of speculation. Some top charities, including United Way and the American Red Cross, have gotten into trouble, and even being a member of, or contributor to, such an organization could compromise a journalist's reputation.

It should then go without saying that direct endorsements of products and/or services are inappropriate. A journalist needs to have an arms length relationship with people and things that get reported. To be associated with companies or products necessarily will raise in the public's mind a question about the ability of the newsman to be objective. Theoretically, this policy should include a prohibition against sportscasters doing color commentary at local sporting events, but in many markets, that practice would be very difficult to curtail.

The fact is that with quality television news you don't have to use your reporters as shills. Their journalistic talent is the draw. They don't need to be hyped. They work for the top news operation in town.

Finally on the subject of promotion, many stations feature promos throughout the day and evening which are designed to draw audience to the next newscast. All too often, they are teases which promise "the latest" and "new developments" and "we'll tell you why." Of course they will tell you all of those things; that's what the news does. But this kind of packaging cheapens the news.

A better approach would be to eliminate these teases and invest the time in news briefs instead. News briefs, unlike promotional teases, actually generate revenues, while they are keeping the audience current on events in between newscasts. And its stands to reason that anyone watching a news brief does so because of an interest in the news, and doesn't have to be sold on the idea of tuning in to the full newscast.

49. Criticism

"You know, Antoine," said the public relations director of ABC television news, "not all of the reviews that come in will be favorable."

She called me that because we were friends. I had dropped in at the office of Av Westin, then an ABC Vice President and my mentor in television news, and my friend the PR lady was also there. I was the business/economics producer, and Westin as VP had the oversight of an unprecedented series of programs we were doing on the state of the economy. It was March of 1980; inflation was high and recession was looming.

We had aired several special reports on *Good Morning America* and *Nightline*, which had debuted that week. There was also an eight-minute report on the *World News Tonight*, and a half-hour special at noon on the set of *The $20,000 Pyramid* game show. I had come to his office to tell Westin that the ABC affiliate in Jacksonville, Florida, had received more than a hundred calls regarding our noon special.

My PR friend wasn't trying to deflate me, just protect me. Unnecessarily as it turned out. The final report from her department included comments from newspapers around the country and all of them were complimentary. I recount this not to clap myself on the back; rather to report the answer that I gave to her at the time. "The only review that counts," I said, "is mine."

It was a brash statement for someone not yet thirty. It didn't mean that I always did my best work, since there were times when I'd been lazy, or had settled for second best. But I knew those times, and didn't have to be told about them by anyone else. I knew every missed shot, every wrong edit. I knew when my efforts really hit the mark, and when they didn't.

The thought reminded me of a discussion between the two friends from the theater in the film *My Dinner with André*. By the time the reviews come in, the director said, you're already moving on to the next play.

It is important to get feedback, but it should be from those whose opinions you respect for their discernment and high standards. You want people who understand the challenges you face and how you meet them. You're not looking for someone to excuse your work, but people who understand the exigencies of the news business.

You shouldn't listen too closely to those who make a living criticizing the work of others. Most critics have their jobs because they attract readers based on their negativity; our society is one that enjoys watching celebrities be pulled down to earth, and then interred alive. However, it is worth familiarizing yourself with the professionals, so that you understand their perspectives. Some may be as good at their job as you are at yours, and thus worth more attention. Others are just whiners, who occasionally make a trenchant observation that is also valuable.

You will find self-styled critics among politicians, people in civic affairs, and others in the business community. You will undoubtedly meet people who watch your broadcast with an eagle eye and feel a need to comment on minutiae. Again, they sometimes will have a valid point, but even when they don't, it is often worth keeping channels open so that you don't miss the times they get it right.

A better source of criticism may come from your viewers, especially the ones who rarely call or write. Usually they have seen or heard something that most people missed, but which you'd want to know.

Remember, that ours is a rapidly-changing society. What was unacceptable behavior only a few years ago is not any longer. What might be taboo in another part of the country may be sanctioned somewhere else. And not just a matter of right or wrong, but also levels of appropriateness or simple cultural differences. For example, while it might be all right to speak of Orientals in New York City, in San Francisco, it seems the term Asians is preferred. You might not know that until you're called to task by a viewer.

Ratings

Ratings are another form of criticism. Depending on their accuracy, they can provide a clue as to your success in the marketplace. Ratings aren't always accurate, however. Despite the new technology, there are often glitches. You should not put any faith in numbers that spike—up or down—in the midst of an otherwise flat trend.

Some news and station executives check ratings every morning, and if they do so with other than the most casual attention, they are likely to read too much into them. There are myriad reasons for ups and downs, one day to the next, and at least as many ways to interpret the numbers. By and large, ratings are only meaningful in the long-term, as in a six-month climb or slide.

Yes, keep an eye on trends in the ratings, if only to check the pulse of the community. But a good reporter or producer knows what are his options in getting on the air, what shortcuts might be taken, what risks chanced. When all is said and done, he alone knows every idle slip, missed opportunity, choppy script, failed choice, bad edit, sloppy mix and otherwise weak effort. If such becomes a pattern in newscasts, the ratings will likely reflect that, but they won't be news to you.

Anyone who has studied the subject of television news knows the phrase, "If it bleeds, it leads." It reflects the choice of producers, usually dictated by management, that the newscast is targeting the prime time audience with stories that grab the viscera—crime, tragedy, scandal and sex. Newscasts that load up with stories from the police wires and gossip columns fail on two levels, first by not measuring up to the prime time fare, and second by not delivering the news. Or is it the other way around?

To format this way indicates that the news director doesn't think the audience is bright enough to be watching the news for the information; that the news must be full of the same stories that were on the laugh-track and detective shows. The problem, besides insulting the audience and eventually losing ratings to a competitor that takes journalism seriously, is that you leave the community ill-informed, which is dangerous with our form of government.

Finally, on the issue of ratings. Most stations schedule special reports and features during sweep periods to attract larger audiences, often producing reports that tie into entertainment programming or follow similar plot lines. If you are producing quality television news, you don't have to alter your approach during the ratings periods. You're already giving your viewers the best. They know it. You don't have to sell them with hype.

50. Marketing Quality Television News

Quality television news is on the verge of a resurgence. Of sorts; it didn't used to be called that. When it first appeared, it was simply television news. It was stiff, simple, and journalism. Those readers of you who remember what news was like in the 1960's will appreciate the comparison. To younger people, it will seem an innovation.

There are several reasons why certain station managers will embrace the concept of quality television news. One is that they feel a need to serve the community. Another is that they need to reduce their overhead. A third is that they are mired in last place in the news ratings, and have to try something because their market is saturated by cable, making competition almost impossible except in the area of news, and the current market leader is drawing more than 55% of its revenues from their news programs.

For whatever motive, if they take a serious run at quality television news, they will discover that their costs of producing the news will, in fact, decline, and some of the savings they will want to put toward promotion of their new approach to news. They will find that they have a far more substantial product to promote, and that their primary target audience are discerning consumers who have high standards for substance and quality.

This is significant because in a down economy, many businesses cut back on their advertising. Those that continue to advertise try to reach the upscale audience that is still buying. The discerning viewers of quality television news have a significantly higher level of discretionary income than the common viewer. Many of them stopped watching television news years ago because the quality had fallen to the point that there was little point in watching it. Some migrated to pubic television and NPR, others spent more time with the local newspaper, and some searched the radio airwaves in vain for a dependable source of news about their community. Few were satisfied and many shifted to the Internet to stay informed, though many again failed to find a strong source of local news.

But these people would return to watch quality television news because they appreciate it as an efficient way to stay current on events, especially local events, since not that many markets have significant local news delivery on line. The issue is, how can you reach these people to tell them why they should come back to watch your news. The answer is that there are a number of ways, but you shouldn't start your marketing effort until you have at least a month of polished newscasts under your belt. You don't want to cry News! and not deliver to their satisfaction.

The points that need to be addressed are not only how to reach them, i.e., through which media, but also what kind of message will catch them. They've heard all the promises of first, fastest, action news, et cetera. They've been drowned in a sea of smiling faces. But the people you expect to watch your newscasts stopped watching television news because they weren't getting significant, relevant, accurate information about their world and their community, at least not on a regular basis.

So the message you want to put out is that you are producing quality television news that will sate the appetite of the news-hungry viewer with professional writing and reporting, a better story selection, and a higher story count. They, the viewers, will be delivered the news goods in journalistic fashion. Their time will not be wasted. No more Chatty-Cathies; an end to the fluff. When the news is over, the audience will know what every responsible citizen should know about their community, their country and the world.

Your first target with this message is the cream of the audience, and then the masses will follow. So how do you reach the viewers at the front of the herd? Once you have gotten your newscast to journalistic trim, you tell your reporters—who, after all, are speaking with the newsmakers in the community—to spread the word about what your station has done, and why they should watch. When they see these people again, in a private situation, your reporters should ask them outright if they have given your news another look. They should ask this after they have gotten their news work out of the way, of course. In all likelihood, they will say yes or promise to do so "tonight."

Once you've gotten a bunch of significant public figures to say that they'll be watching your station, without ever naming names, you can promote your station as the news the newsmakers watch. You will start a buzz—on local talk radio, in the local newspaper TV column and throughout the community. The business people will be interested because you'll be trying something different. The politicians will wonder how the new approach will affect their relationship to their constituents.

At the outset, you may be a curiosity. Then, as more people catch on, your quality television news will be heralded as an innovation. And soon people will flock to your channel at news time. They will tune you in because they know that the newsmakers are people don't have time to waste and they are people who truly need to know what's going on in the community.

If you're Joe-Q-n'-Martha-Public, don't you want to be watching the news that the newsmakers watch? Okay, some will want to stay with their favorite weatherman, but most people like to be associated with the best.

Once you are the best, and people know it, you won't need to spend much time or effort on promotion. After all, you are serving the public better than the competition and you have the facts to prove it. If you're not outright capturing the largest number of viewers, you will certainly own the smartest and the wealthiest. From a beancounter point of view, it doesn't matter if you get the most viewers as long as you are attracting the ones with money who in turn attract the advertisers who are willing to pay premium rates to deliver their message to the only people left who can afford their goods and services.

Also, promotion works only if (1) people are dissatisfied with what they're watching, and (2) the competition offers something better. That would seem unlikely if you are presenting quality television news.

At the outset, you might want to spend some of the money you save on lowered overhead on advertising. Some bus signs and billboards; maybe buy some ads in the newspaper. You might use some trade with select radio stations to spread your word. You might even try to buy some underwriting time during the public television nightly news broadcast and on NPR. Maybe you'll want to run ads comparing your newscast to the competition. "If you didn't watch us last night, you didn't discover that the city is missing an opportunity...." More news, better coverage.

*   *   *   *   *   *   *

As mentioned earlier, quality television news will save you money because it is less expensive to produce. When you're not going live for the sake of saying it, when you are more focused on the script than on how many clips you can cram into a half-hour, you spend less money shooting and editing. That's a marketing point for a news director pitching a station manager.

She might add that the pace of the news-gathering also changes. There's less rushing, and more attention to detail. People enjoy their work more, feeling a greater sense of purpose. The accountants will appreciate the fact that absenteeism and sick days drop dramatically. Staff turnover also declines. Productivity rises. All generating important cost savings.

And it gets better. The top talent from the competition will want to work with you, along with quality journalists from larger markets. They will knock on your door, some ready to take a pay cut to work for your operation. You don't have to wait at the door, however. You already have enough on your plate. It is a wonderful meal that nourishes your colleagues, your bosses and the entire community.

V—Appendix

A. My Network News Operation

Every so often, sitting in the hot tub under the stars, I've thought about how I would run a network news operation. The ideas that have come to mind generally follow those presented in the preceding pages on how to produce quality television news at local stations—straightforward coverage and simplified reporting of the facts in context. It could be done far more effectively and far less expensively than the commercial networks or cable channels do it; with a considerably smaller staff and a minimum of rushing around the globe.

I would start with the premise that a news-hungry audience that wanted to be informed had the appetite for an hour program. Formatted like the local early evening hour newscast, it would be designed for people to watch the news they wanted to see at the same time every night, so they could get the pieces they wanted if they didn't have time to watch the whole program.

The second premise is that it is more important to have talented people producing the coverage than a stable of pretty faces. One of the "givens" in television news is that you should have lots of reporters, but this is a throw-back to the notion that reporters were there as much to be personalities to attract more viewers. And the unexamined presumption that the audience wants to see reporters on scene.

In fact, especially at the network level, a newscast could get along fine with more voice-overs and sound cuts and fewer correspondent reports. Since most reports are voice-over, sound bites and a standupper, the job can easily be done—and with less coordination—by a producer and the anchors. Which is why I suggest that anchors carry more of the program.

First, there would be the saving of all of that time now consumed by introductions and sign-offs. Second, the audience would find it easier to assimilate the news from fewer sources. Third, producers are less expensive than reporters, since you don't have to pay extra for their looks.

I would close all of the domestic bureaus except Washington because it's the nation's capital and there's simply too much news generated there. Instead, I'd put the top producers at a half-dozen affiliate stations around the country to funnel net-worthy information and pictures from the different regions to the main office.

Similarly, I'd eliminate the international bureaus, and station the other top producers at the major local news organizations like London's BBC, RAI in Rome and NHK in Tokyo. There they would monitor coverage in the region, and pass along important stories and production elements to the U.S.

These changes would result in huge financial saving, because today most of the expense in news coverage is personnel, and traveling five-person teams here and there. For a pittance, we could obtain the local coverage, which would be more timely, since the locals would be on the scene or closer to it, and it would be more accurate, since they would know better the territory, people and background. Some judicious editing for the American audience supervised by our producer, and bang-zoom, the report is on the air before the other network crews have even been dispatched.

Other benefits of tying in with various foreign news organizations is that they have the contacts and the file material that can significantly enhance coverage. By having an on-going working relationship with the locals, you can be assured of getting an early break on a story, along with greater depth in the coverage.

On the domestic side, putting a producer at a desk at major regional affiliates would provide better overall coverage than having a bureau, for a fraction of the cost. That person would have a geographical network of stations with whom she would maintain active contact, not only about breaking stories, but about developing issues, changing trends, and new ideas.

By the way, I would make every effort to place all of the camera crews, editors, reporters and other personnel not needed at headquarters or at the Washington bureau at the affiliate and overseas operations. Those working abroad would need to know, or immediately work to become fluent in, the local language. No ugly Americans on our staff.

The affiliated stations would also be used as a farm system, as in professional baseball, where people who showed significant talent would be encouraged to learn how to be better broadcast journalists and to move up to larger stations. The best people would be followed along their climb, directed to markets where their talents could be honed, and real training provided. The network would offer regional seminars, and individual instruction to those who showed promise.

This would be a far cry from the current rat race, of people jumping stations and markets, without regard for true ability or knowledge. They may know how to jut out their chin or razmataz the audience, but many don't know about journalism, integrity, or informing the public. They receive little if any instruction; rather, they arrive in a new town and are sent off to cover a story.

Imagine a reporter arriving at a new station and he receives a week of orientation to travel about the area with and get briefed by other reporters. He's sent to meetings of the city council, chamber of commerce and school board to get a flavor of the community. He's given a stack of back newspapers to read, and provided with file footage of public players and issues. The more context a reporter has, the more effective would be his reporting.

Also at our network, the anchors would have a critical role in determining both the content and line-up of the newscast, and would be responsible for writing much of the script they would read. They would screen the voice-overs, not see them on the air live for the first time. They would also see all correspondent scripts, so that if there were a technical glitz, they could explain what was in the report.

The news would be called the news, not the news with the anchor's name in the title. Even with more responsibility put on the anchors, it would still be a team broadcast. Besides, if you're anchoring the top national newscast, that should be enough for your ego. And if you are committed to quality television news, your interest is being known for your work, not for your title.

Not everyone would watch this network news. It would draw an audience of people who felt obligated to be informed and were willing to do their part, i.e., to pay attention. When they finished the hour, they would know what they needed to know, and much more. They would have a sense of the world and the nation. They would have a context for their lives as citizens of this planet.

Expanding from this basic premise for how to organize and deliver a nightly network newscast wouldn't be very difficult. There are plenty of serious, talented broadcast journalists who could staff morning and midday newscasts, or even a 24/7 quality television news channel.

B. Finding Work

If you are thinking about becoming a TV news reporter, first make sure that you are considering this work for the right reasons. If you are choosing the profession because you want to be recognized at restaurants rather than to serve the community, then think about another line of work. But if you hear a calling, consider your skills and instincts and how they would support you in the job.

Ask your trusted friends and relatives what they think of your intentions. If they don't dissuade you, or even go so far as to endorse your plan, ask them for their views, e.g., what they like about the news coverage they watch, who comes across most effectively and why, and what they would like to see different.

On the basis of this research, consider which stations in the market would provide the most conducive working environment for you.

Don't rush it. Take some time to watch the news of the station you're applying to, to get a sense of their styles of producing, writing, editing, reporting and directing. See what kind of reporting is most effective, and which writing styles work best with which types of stories. What editing is the least jarring? How stories lead from one to the other? What is important and what is extraneous?

When you've watched for a while, and gotten both a feeling for, and a picture of, how they assimilate, manipulate and disseminate the news, then think about how you would approach the news director.

If you're applying for your first position in television news—on air or not—and don't have a lot to say on your resume, don't lie, but make the most of what you've done. If you don't have a lot of experience, you might make up some ground by showing that you are clever. Be creative to catch the news director's eye, but always tell the truth.

If you want to be a reporter, you should try to produce a demo tape that would be compatible with their approach to the news. An important qualification is that you be realistic; don't try to get too fancy. Shoot a tape that represents who and where you are, not your aspirations.

If you are just starting out in television news, or are seeking your first on-camera position, you might arrange with a friend who has a video system to shoot a very basic resume tape. If funds are tight, you might check with the local educational facilities to see if they have video equipment available to the public, and perhaps some students who have the ability to shoot and edit for you.

Most news directors of stations where you would be seeking your first on-air job will take into account your tyro status and will be less concerned about the technical quality of your tape. At some stations, you may even find a news director who will be generous and patient enough to let you go out with a staff photographer. But more often than not you will have to first impress her with a resume and interview.

As you gain experience and move up the ladder, make sure that you keep copies of your work. Even if you are not a reporter, there is plenty to tape as a writer, field producer, or show producer. You don't have keep everything, but certainly you want to build a library of your best work.

An obvious advantage to this ongoing practice of preserving your work on tape is that you have the material for a demo reel in the event that you suddenly find yourself having to look for work. Most newly-former bosses are going to be inhospitable to the notion of your building your resume tape after they've fired you.

Even if you're not looking for a new position, it is useful every so often to run through some of the major pieces you have done to mark your growth. It will also show you how your criteria have changed.

It is also recommended that you keep scripts and line-ups of shows that have meant something to you. The thinning out process can come every year, or when it's time to move, but hold onto what you consider even marginally important. When it does come time to prepare a resume tape, you know that you have all the clips already.

And here's how you might present yourself. Pick three stories, the ones that best represent you and your work, preferably different types of stories. Even if you are looking for a specialist's position, you want to show that you are multi-faceted. The three might be a hard, breaking-news report; a deeper, think piece; and a spot that shows the ability to take a lighter approach, perhaps featuring special production techniques.

Arrange to shoot some standuppers—perhaps calling in a favor from one of the staff photographers where you work; in his off hours—to bridge these spots. All should be shot in the same location to keep your presentation simple. The first should run fifteen to thirty seconds: give your name, the position you seek, and an introduction to the first spot. The second and third standuppers should be equally brief, introducing the other two spots, explaining if necessary why you chose them. And finally, shoot a :45 close explaining who you are, your principles, your goals, and close with a "Thank you for watching." The final shot should be a still frame of you with your name, address, phone number and email address supered across the lower portion of the screen. If you have a website, put the URL. Let it run for thirty seconds.

Make sure that your tape is crisply edited, that you have no excuses to make about its production. Your opening should begin cleanly, without color bars, and within seven seconds of the beginning of the cassette. Use the highest quality cassette, and remove the record tabs to prevent accidental erasure. Put typed name/address/phone/e-info labels on both the cassette itself and on the box.

You might also produce a DVD or CD version instead.

Don't expect to get your demo back. The copies don't cost enough to even ask.

With your tape should go a resume, equally professionally done. It should be one page, and include the highlights of your career—and/or related experience—to date. If you are going for your first job, it won't impress anyone that you were a summer checker at the local supermarket, unless perhaps you are trying to become a produce reporter.

You should also state your formal education, including any degrees, your hobbies and interests and your personal situation, e.g., marital status, race, age, height, weight. While some states don't allow an employer to ask some of these questions, it shows the potential employer that you are aware of your own situation and want all your cards on the table. Also, since most news directors are concerned about diversity, you may have just the attributes she seeks.

A resume should lead with a brief—brief!—summary paragraph that illuminates your character. Be honest; you don't want to trick the wrong person into hiring you. If you have goals, state them. A news director is going to want to know if you're aiming for the 25th market hoping to make the network in two years or you want to settle in his town. Writing this piece also helps to frame your own thinking, to make you more aware of your own needs and expectations.

Need it be said: send your resume and tape to the right people. When it is time for a change, don't rush into the process. Go through your old tapes and resumes and see where you've been. Clear your mind and reconsider who you are. Think of where you are in your life, how your old goals serve you now, and how your descriptions of them might need some tweaking. Think about the geographical and environmental situation you want. Market size is less important than your health.

Find out by talking to colleagues and reading trade papers which news directors (or general managers) you might want to work for, which newsrooms would provide the kind of atmosphere for growth and exploration that you now need. And then call the market, maybe a competitor or the local newspaper and find out what people think of the potential employer. What is it like to work at the station? Do the reporters there seem involved in their work or are they in it for the money or glamour?

By taking time to find out more exactly who you are and who are the people with whom you wish to spend half of your waking hours for the next year or two or longer, you will be making a key investment in your own contentment.

Another consideration that can be more or less of a factor—or none at all—is unions. Regrettably they often generate a division between talent and producers, and between editorial and technical people. It cuts into the effectiveness of team-work when it is invoked. So be aware of what the rules are governing a particular station where you might be considering a job. If the unions are strict, it could be unduly unpleasant.

Agents

A good reporter should be able to represent himself and his value clearly to an honest prospective employer. The basis for an employment agreement should be a clear understanding of

—What the station expects of the reporter in the next six to eighteen months;

—What the reporter expects from the station during that time;

—What resources the reporter brings with him;

—What facilities and resources the station will provide.

The formal agreement should be a straightforward letter or a simple contract in regular language written by the news director and the reporter. If you need a lawyer to look it over, it may be that you are not sure of either yourself or the station and perhaps you want to re-examine your agreement. Confucius said, a person makes a second mistake by not admitting the first.

If for whatever reason you decide that you should have an agent, find a company or individual who will represent you scrupulously. Make sure they understand who you are and what are your personal needs. A single person in her late twenties is going to be more flexible than a man in his mid-forties with three children. Be certain that the agent will know, for instance, that you are simply not a morning person, that you hit your stride in late afternoon and are burning up the track at eleven. Or that you like getting up before the sun, watching it rise and taking your time after the morning news in preparing a think piece for the evening broadcast. In other words, find someone who will draw out of you the details of the kind of position you seek and will find the right one for you. But be clear that whatever advice you receive, you make the final decision yourself.

C. Author's Experience

On April Fool's Day 1970, while enrolled as a full-time political science major at New York University, I began my career in television journalism as a $73-a-week copy boy on the overnight shift of the network television news assignment desk at ABC. I shuttled back and forth from Washington Square to West 66th Street on the subways at midnight and then at the end of the morning rush hour. I knew immediately that I had found my calling, and classes didn't hold much interest or require much attention.

Journalistically, it was the beginning of the extraordinary Seventies, and mine was a baptism by fire, with the space emergency on the Apollo 13 flight, the invasion of Cambodia and the killings at Kent State in the first five weeks. My job as desk assistant was to rip the wires, answer the phones, mimeograph, Xerox, collate and run errands. While the Assignment Desk required the most constant work, it also meant being in the middle of history being written in the moment, on the wires, the telex and the phones.

Giving up the *Front Page* atmosphere of cigarettes, coffee and shouts of "Boy!" that summer, I went downstairs to work for the *Evening News*, under the rich tutelage of Executive Producer Av Westin and Show Producers Dick Richter (editorial) and David Buksbaum (operations). The *ABC Evening News* back then was a lean and hungry operation committed to journalism. I was there only a few months before my organizational talents were (er, hem) recognized and I was transferred to the Elections Unit as Senior Desk Assistant for the coverage of Elections '70.

ABC's coverage of the elections was excellent, with our outfit making more first-calls than either NBC or CBS. The next morning, Frank Reynolds, who had done such an exemplary job anchoring the elections coverage, was informed that Harry Reasoner would be replacing him on December 7th.

In 1971, I was promoted to Production Assistant, which had me coordinating the graphics presentation for the *ABC Weekend News* and then the week-day show. Working with Richter and Art Director Ben Blank allowed a peek into the weaving of still visual images of a story with a full script.

In the fall of that year, I quit ABC and went off for a brief stint in public television as an Associate Producer on the WNET consumer program, *Up Against New York*. It was a very different environment where a volunteer unit manager would try to hold down costs by refusing to buy enough film for a shoot, and videotape edit sessions were scheduled for midnight because consciousness-raising group meetings earlier in the evening took precedence.

I was desperate to return to ABC, even though it meant a 50% pay cut, but for some reason the corporate personnel director blocked my re-hiring. As it happened, my grandfather played cards on the commuter train out of the city every evening with, Jim Haggerty, a former Eisenhower press spokesman and a vice president with ABC. Haggerty intervened. I got back to ABC.

Returning to the Special Events Unit at ABC at the end of the year, I worked on the coverage of President Nixon's trips to China and the Soviet Union and on the '72 Primaries. I received an Emmy Award for being part of the production of the China trip; I was the graphics production assistant in the New York control room. My job was to keep track of all the still visuals; we produced thousands of dollars worth of graphics, pictures and maps on cards and transparencies, and then only used a few pieces as the live and taped coverage from China was far more exciting. The Emmy didn't mean much when it was explained to me that they were dealt out, with CBS getting one for a space shot or the primaries and NBC getting the Emmy for the Moscow trip.

Then a month after the Watergate break-in in 1972, I was transferred to the Washington bureau as a Production Associate, a new title that meant assistant producer. For political reasons, as tend to exist between the Washington bureaus and the New York headquarters, I was ostracized because I had been sent down from The Big Apple. It was a remarkably unpleasant time, but was mitigated by the fact that I was working on one of the biggest stories of the century, Watergate, starting with to the coverage of the trial of the original burglars. In retrospect it was quite an assignment, but at the time, it meant frigid mornings around the Federal Courthouse trying to catch pictures of the defendants and the witnesses.

In the Summer of 1973, I covered the Senate Watergate Hearings. When the committee broke for summer recess, I was assigned to the Agnew investigation. Despite the historical significance of these stories, I was aching to get out of Washington. The climate there, particularly the political infighting at the bureau, was terribly unpleasant to the point of being unhealthy. Company political machinations prevented me from securing a transfer, so I quit and moved myself back to New York.

It was not good timing. Not only did I leave some major stories behind, but I returned to a recession-shuttered job market, and without the formal writing or producing credits I needed. After five months without work having sent out 80 resumes for news, marketing, writing, advertising jobs—and being nearly out of money—I was given a week of freelance work as a newswriter at WCBS Television. This led to more freelance work both as a Producer and an Assignment Editor.

Finding myself unemployed again at the end of 1974 and on into February of '75, I received an offer from News Director Andy Fisher to produce the Six and

Eleven O'Clock News at WPRI in Providence; I had produced a couple of his spots when Andy was a reporter at WCBS.

I had been at WPRI for less than a week when I got an invitation from Dick Richter to come to work for him again at ABC in New York, this time on the new morning show, *AMAmerica*, as a producer/newswriter. At several times what I was earning in Providence, and without the 180-mile commute twice a week.

A few months later, I became News Operations Producer when the program became *Good Morning America*. For two more years I worked the overnight shift, responsible for all of the satellites and line feeds, as well as the bulk of the editing of the morning news tape.

In 1977, when ABC corporate decided it needed to be competitive in news, it put sports division president Roone Arledge in charge of news as well, and thus started a new era. Arledge brought back Av Westin who had been forced "out into the cold" as he called it, consulting for the Capital Cities stations. And Westin brought me back from my "overnight purgatory" to be Associate Operations Producer for the ABC Evening News.

In 1978, I was put in charge of the six-person unit that produced Barbara Walters' news appearances. This was a bone thrown to Walters' because she had been dumped as co-anchor. Because the climate was so hostile after the anchoring failed, my assignment and duties were often more political than journalistic. It was no-win, and stayed ugly because Barbara and the news executives refused to be honest with each other.

But there were some wonderful times, and among the interviews I personally produced were those with Israeli Defense Minister Moshe Dayan, U.S. Defense and Energy Secretary James Schlesinger, German Chancellor Helmut Schmidt, New York Yankees owner George Steinbrenner, Iran Ambassador Ardeshar Zahedi, National Security Advisor Zbignew Breszhinski, NYC Consumer Commissioner Bess Myerson, White House Counselor Midge Costanza, Anne Bancroft, Liv Ullman, JFK assassination attorney Mark Lane, Secretary of State Cyrus Vance, Romanian President Nicolae Ceaucescu, Economics Advisor Barry Bosworth, FAA Administrator Alfred Kahn, Treasury Secretary William Simon, scientist Barry Commoner and heart surgeon Christian Barnard.

Just writing that list reminds me of the excitement, and there were indeed wonderful moments, but it wasn't really news, and the office political situation was deteriorating. A year later I threatened to quit if they didn't give me a new assignment; I gave them 60 days to act. Four days shy of the deadline, they made the Business/Economics Producer, the position I had long sought because it meant I would worked exclusively with Dan Cordtz, a highly-respected veteran print reporter who knew his subject as well as I knew producing.

Dan and I had a grand time for over a year, preying off soaring and plummeting numbers that few in the newsroom understood. In addition to extensive daily coverage of the deepening recession and double-digit inflation, we produced special reports on The Subterranean Economy, The Japanese Auto Invasion, The Chrysler Bailout, Silver Thursday, The Credit Crunch and Recession in the Rust Belt.

In 1980 we created a landmark in economics reporting, with special multi-segment, day-wide network programming under the heading "Inflation: The End of the American Dream?"

And three weeks later, from five cities in six days, I produced and co-wrote a prime time special called "Recession: Bitter Medicine for Inflation." The following week the US Treasury Secretary used that phrase during a news conference. That sort of recognition of our coverage was icing on the cake; that year we won a Janus Award, a Gainsbrugh Citation and a Judges' Award at the North American Consumer Film Festival.

In 1980, with both New York City and ABC sliding toward some bad decisions, I wrangled a transfer to KGO television in San Francisco. The two months that I worked there were among the most unpleasant of my life, dealing with smug incompetence and some news decision-makers who should have been locked up for mental defect. The few people who did have any journalistic awareness at KGO had given up or pretended not to see the disgrace.

In January 1981, I was fired by the news director who thought I had been sent from New York to replace him. It wasn't true, but my dismissal and some other of his other shenanigans induced New York to fire him shortly after I left.

So I began a second career as a consultant on marketing, advertising, public relations, and corporate communications, ventures that included long distance telephone service, riverboat gambling, medical equipment leasing, taquerias, matchmaking and computers. I also kept my hand in broadcasting; as Director of Marketing and Research for KXTC, a Monterey lite rock radio station, I doubled revenues, produced a series of highly-praised environmental minutes, and another series of interviews with local business, political and civic leaders.

In 1992, during a three-year exile from California in the Chicago area, I directed the Barry Watkins for Congress campaign against Henry Hyde, with Barry winning 80% more votes than any previous Democratic candidate in the history of the district, but still losing two to one.

I returned to the Bay Area, and in 1995 partnered with my long-time friend, veteran radio talk show host, Peter B. Collins, to form *Wins of Change*, a political consulting firm specializing in media and message. In the first three election cycles, we produced television messages for a number of federal, state and local campaigns. We also produced radio spots for three U.S. Senate and two House races in five states. Clients included Rep. Nancy Pelosi (D-San Francisco) and

U.S. Senate candidate Rep. Tom Campbell, a Republican who represented Silicon Valley.

Offered the opportunity to get back to broadcasting, I debuted *Tony Seton's InFORMATION*, on KBPA radio in January 1998. The show reached thousands of upscale Bay Area listeners, appealing to those who were bored with NPR and who tuned in for scintillating, relevant conversation, news2use and thoughtful humor. The gig was short-lived because I got married and moved out of the Bay Area.

After moving to Redding in 1998, I worked briefly on radio KQMS radio, where my *SetonnoteS* commentary and *Newsmaker* interviews won their time slots by 50%. I traded commercial time for flight instruction and wrote a series of reports on the experience called *From the Ground Up* which were later reproduced for national syndication. (I earned my instrument rating in 2001.)

In 2001, I wrote, produced, directed, and reported a half-hour public television program on child-rearing called *Mother Nurture*. And in 2002 applied similar efforts to another half-hour program called *Divorce—Collaborative Style*.

I have published two books *Right Car, Right Price* and *The Under $800 Computer Buyer's Guide*, a passel of poems, a volume of book reviews and a sheaf of essays. My writing has appeared in publications across the country. I also taught *Documentary Film Writing* at Monterey Peninsula College and occasionally lecture on "The Truth about Television News." I have also instructed in *Creative Writing* at the women's federal correctional institution in Dublin (California).

D. Glossary

ADI—Area of Dominant Influence. A term to describe the geographical area reached by a television signal. An ADI is often referred to as a market and differs from a city proper where the signal extends beyond the city limits. With cable system proliferation, ADI lines are becoming fuzzy and signals from one market are being made available in another. (see superstation)

Advisory—A wire service term telling the subscribers that the copy is informational and not a news story.

AFV—An abbreviation for Audio Follows Video. A control on a video switcher which couples the same audio to the video output.

Air check—A recording made from a broadcast signal, as opposed to from an internal line. An air check records what a viewer sees at home.

Ambush interview—Popularized by Mike Wallace, Geraldo Rivera and their proteges, it consists of surprising an interviewee, rather than scheduling an appointment. It is done in cases when the interviewee is unlikely to want to speak on camera. The presumption is that even if the person won't speak—or say more than "Get lost!" or "No comment!"—then at least the general hubbub will convey it's own meaning, usually evasion.

Anchor—"Any instrument, device, or contrivance that holds something else secure, keeps it from giving way, etc." (Webster's unabridged.) Also, a television journalist who delivers a newscast from a base.

ANNC—An abbreviation for Announcer, often used in scripts to designate a narrator outside of the piece, i.e., other than an anchor or reporter, who reads billboard, bumper, ident and closing copy.

Arbitron—A broadcasting ratings service.

Aspect ratio—The relationship of horizontal to vertical in a television picture, roughly four-to-three. Screen sizes are measured in the length of the hypotenuse, i.e., the diagonal. A 25" screen, for example, would have a 25" diagonal, a 20" horizontal and a 15" height. When you are selecting or composing a shot, you need to consider this window.

Associate director—The person who assists the director. The duties of an AD might include screening and timing pre-recorded material, back-timing, count-downs in and out of segments and other such duties as designated by the director.

Audiotape—An outgrowth of Edison's invention of phonography and formally called magnetic tape, audiotape is a "thin plastic ribbon coated with a suspension of ferromagnetic iron oxide particles" used for recording of sound. In the television business, audiotape is most frequently found in cassettes, micro-cassettes, cartridges and 1/4" reels.

B-roll—A term from the days of film, it means pictures to cover a narration or sound cut. The "A" projector would be loaded with the narration track, standup-pers and sound cuts. The "B" projector would have a reel of pictures (usually with natural sound) to cover the track in the appropriate places. The projectors—and sometimes there would be more than two—would be rolled simultaneously, and the director would cut or dissolve back and forth between the projectors. The term today refers to pictures used to cover narration.

Background (BG or b/g)—A description of what is behind the primary visual. Also a reference to secondary audio, sound other than the narration, e.g., the noise of a crowd at a demonstration while the reporter is telling the story.

Backgrounder—A report that provides background information to a situation; an explainer.

Backlight—To put light behind a subject, either on the subject itself or on the background. Backlighting a subject without normal lighting in front creates a silhouette, thus hiding the person's identity. Backlighting the background provides depth to the picture.

Back-timing—Timing from the end of a spot or show to where you are at the moment. Back-timing enables you to know how much time you have left. If you find yourself half-way through a thirty-minute newscast and you know that your remaining tape and live segments run 18:30, you know that you're going to have to drop something, or run over.

Bank—As a verb, it means to put away a report for later use, as in banking an evergreen. As an adjective with piece, it means a spot that has been shot for future use. As a noun, it means a collection of pieces that are to be run at another time.

A piece can be banked for a specific occasion, e.g., a fireworks story to be held for the Fourth of July, or it can be (relatively) timeless, as might be a profile of the local ice sculptor.

Beta—A videotape format.

Billboard (BB)—A "brought to you by…" commercial announcement usually at the top and/or bottom of a broadcast or segment, referred to as opening and closing billboards respectively.

Bird—Slang for satellite, used as both a noun and a verb.

Black—A visual image devoid of light, not to be confused with a lack of picture.

Blanking—A technical term regarding videotape.

Bounce—The path of a microwave signal when it is focused on a building, for example, so that it will change directions. Also used as a verb, as in bouncing a signal off the Empire State Building so that it will hit the receiver downtown.

Boxcar numbers—A term meaning numbers in the billions and trillions; the triple zeros are like boxcars following the significant number or engine.

Break-up—Visual hash created when the video signal fails to lock up.

Bridge—A copy transition between two segments or ideas, e.g., "In other news…" or "Back at the ranch…."

Brite—A light story, often funny, generally used to close a segment or a broadcast.

Bulletin—In television, it is the interruption of normal programming with a story of major importance. (see Special Report) In news-wire jargon, a bulletin will interrupt the normal sequence of stories with a news report of major importance. (see Urgent, Snap, Flash)

Bumper—A segment between a broadcast and a commercial. Often a "coming up" announcement, with a super over a still frame, graphic or set shot. A bumper might also be news information, e.g., stocks, scores, etc. (see tease)

Butt cut—To edit film or tape segments together directly, as opposed to setting up a dissolve or using a cutaway.

Call letters—The three- and four-letter designations of broadcast frequencies. Stations east of the Mississippi begin their calls letters with a "W"; west of the Mississippi the call letters begin with a "K". There are exceptions, e.g., WOI in Ames, Iowa, WFAA in Dallas. The Canadians use "C", and in the Carribean the first letter is "X".

Chain—A reference to a film or slide projector or a multiplex. Tape has multiple channels that take the place of chains.

Character generator (CG)—An electronic supering device. It replaced slides and the old system of hand-set white type on black cards, the CG started out only being able to insert words—usually names—over the television picture. That was in the early Seventies. Today, it is a generic reference to any device that provides supers.

Chyron—A type of character generator, and also a generic reference to supers.

Clear—The verb referring to gain clearance, as in clearing an affiliate to carry a late night weekend news cast.

Clip—As a verb, slang meaning to cut off. Usually used in reference to an audio source, as in a director shouting to the audio engineer "Clip his mike!" when someone says things that shouldn't be on the air. As a noun, clip means segment, as in a film clip.

Clip reel—It used to be back in the old days of film and two-inch videotape that segments would be kept together on a reel. They could be entire reports, as might be kept on a bank clip reel. Or they might be the highlights of a person's career. Clip reel is also used to describe a reel—or cassette, these days—that would have insert materials to be assembled into a larger piece.

Close—The end of a spot or broadcast. On a spot, it would usually including a culminating thought and a sign-off, e.g., "The city council will meet next Thursday to take up the issue. I'm Sterling Tarnish, Channel One News, at City Hall." For a broadcast, the close would include the credits, copyright information and probably theme music or sound effects. Some producers will include the anchor/host's "goodnight" as part of the close segment.

Cluster—As in cluster point, a secondary control room acting as an organizing center for bringing in remotes from a particular region and readying them for the main control room. A cluster point might be a control room in Los Angeles, for instance, bringing in all of the election night remotes from the West and Southwest.

Cold open—The beginning of a report or broadcast with sound and picture from the story itself rather than narration. It might be the racket of riveters or the chanting of a crowd, with the narration picking up a few seconds later to explain.

Control room—The production command center where audio and video sources are integrated and put on the air. It is where are located the switcher and audio board, director, TD, audio engineer and an assortment of other engineering and production equipment and people.

Control track—A band on videotape that keeps the program tracks in synch. Without control track, you are unable to edit. A break in control track will often result in break up on the screen.

Correspondent—An on-air network reporter. At the network, there is sometimes a distinction between correspondent and reporter, with the latter often performing most of the same tasks as the former, but behind the scenes.

CPB—The Corporation for Public Broadcasting. An agency of the federal government that uses tax revenues to fund television and radio programming.

Crawl—A horizontal strip of super information running from right to left, usually along the bottom of the screen, as in a "stay tuned" announcement or weather bulletin.

Credits—The list of people responsible for a program, usually supered at the end of a broadcast. Non-news programs will often have some credits at the beginning also. There are certain union regulations regarding credits which govern the length of time and exclusivity on the screen, particularly in relation to positions represented by other unions.

Cross roll—To roll a second tape or film projector after rolling a first, for example, when you have a series of tapes or when you have a single tape but a single cutaway shot that can be rolled in late into the report.

CRT—Short for Cathode Ray Tube, it is a the device through which the electronic signals are projected to produce a television image.

Cue—(1) A signal from the control room (usually through a floor manager or studio camera operator) to the anchor or reporter, e.g., to begin or stop talking or to throw to the anchor. (2) An electronic signal set by an editor in a tape to show the tape machine where to make an edit. (3) Cuing (up) a machine means preparing it to play back. (4) As in roll cue, a tape machine or film projector would be backed up a number of seconds before the on-air element would begin to make sure that picture had time to lock up; for the film to stop fluttering and for the tape to settle electronically. In the old days when directing required a real sensitivity for pacing, the film projectors were set :03 from first picture, and the two-inch tape machines were cued up :10 seconds back. Cartridge tape machines were usually :02. Today's playback devices, tape and disc, can usually be rolled on a :01 cue, referred to as "instant"-roll.

Cumulative time—As the words imply, the total time of the elements in a broadcast up to a particular point; running time. Most news run-downs will have a column noting the time allocated for each item, and next it the accumulated time to that point in the broadcast. For example, if you have played three tape reports averaging 1:30 each and five :15 readers, you have accumulated about 5:45 of news.

Cut—(1) A segment, usually of audio, as in a sound cut. (see sound bite) (2) The order, usually by a director, to end a segment. A director might yell "Cut!" to the audio engineer when referring to the sound coming from a remote microphone into which a drunk is yelling obscenities. (see clip) You can cut out of something, or you can cut to something else, e.g., cut from the anchor's microphone to the tape machine. Cut can also be used in the same context to refer to video.

Cutaway—As in a visual cut away from the person who is talking, usually to a shot of the interviewer listening or to a two-shot, used to cover an edit in the sound of the interviewee. It was devised in the days of film when the audio track preceded the picture track by 28 frames. When two pieces of an interview were edited together—by physically cutting the film at the end of the first audio and at the beginning of the second and then taping or gluing them together—the picture change when it played through the projector would be more than a second earlier, making it very jarring for the viewer who would see the speaker's lips saying something other than what was being heard. Covering the jump cut, as it was called, entailed putting a listening shot in the b-roll just before the first cut ended to just after the second cut began, usually several seconds. With tape, the audio and video edits occur at the same time on the air, but as there is still a shift in the picture of the person' speaking if non-contiguous segments are edited together, a visual cutaway will be over-laid upon the edit point. The term cutaway is also used to be mean set-up shots, e.g., wide, tight, profile, that would be different from the shot from which the sound cuts will be pulled. Cutaways often enhance the visual presentation, but there are some news operations that prohibit the use of cutaways because they "distort" the true picture.

Cut-in—A segment of a network show that is to be filled by the local stations, e.g., during election night coverage, or the local news and weather cut-ins during the morning shows. The networks run programming to cover the hole if the local stations choose not to cut in.

CX—A frequently used line-up or script abbreviation for "commercial".

Dead pot—To roll an audio source without playing it to air. Say the news theme for your broadcast is supposed to culminate one second before the show is off the air. But the amount of time you have at the end of the broadcast varies by a few seconds each night. If the theme runs 1:00, the audio engineer can roll the cartridge (or tape machine) 1:01 before you're off the air. Then no matter what time your anchor finishes talking, you already have the theme running and can take it or fade it up when you want, knowing that it is set to end on time. (see pre-roll)

Defame—To slander or libel. To make or publish statements impugning someone's character and reputation.

Degauss—To neutralize a tape, erasing all recordings.

Desk assistant (DA)—The television version of the copy boy. Errand-person, gofer, menial, hazing victim and general target. Also a great position in which to learn how everything works without being responsible for it.

Director—The captain of the control room. The person who calls the shots, audio and video, usually working from a producer's script. In smaller markets, the director often doubles as the technical director, running the switcher, and sometimes the audio board as well.

Dish—Slang for a microwave transmitter or a satellite transmitter/receiver.

Dissolve—To put two video sources together on the screen at the same time, fading one out and the other in. Different from a take (or cut) which replaces one source with the other instantly, a dissolve can take as long as you want, blending the two images. Unlike a wipe which replaces one picture with another completely in a particular shape (or pattern), a dissolve affects the entire image over the full screen. A dissolve can be used to mix pictures softly and create a particular mood for a report, or to transition between sound cuts. Also, many directors will dissolve to black out of an obituary. A dissolve will be used to show the passage of time.

Down cut—To bring in an audio source prematurely so that it overrides the previous audio.

Dub—Both a noun and a verb meaning a copy or to copy.

Editing—The process of editing—whether film, tape, a script or a broadcast—is to make certain that the most critical information is included, and is presented in a coherent fashion. We usually infer that editing means only to take out. Many editors forget that editing means to revise and refine. Sometimes a story will need more information on a particular aspect that, thinly written, can leave a viewer guessing. As one editor put it, "I understand what you're saying, but Joe Six-pack out there isn't going to get anything after 'Good evening.'" Good editing shows a sensitivity for pacing, order and content. In film and tape, it means creating a sequence of shots that enables the viewer to grasp the detail of, and the reason for, the report. Thus, be sure that you provide enough of a shot for the viewer to understand it clearly, and that you change visuals before they get boring.

Effects(FX)—It originally referred to a deck on the switcher where you could combine video sources, e.g., through a dissolve, matte, wipe, or key. When a script calls for FX, it may mean taking a shot of the anchor with a graphic keyed in over his shoulder, or a reporter with a "Live" super. It is frequently used to call for a split-screen or a graphic preset with a super. Effects can also refer to sound effects (SFX). Sound effects are pre-recorded audio not directly linked with the video source, as opposed to a live microphone or a tape machine or film chain.

EIC—Short for Engineer-in-Charge, the person in charge of the technical side of a production.

Electronic wallpaper—Video that is used as background, often just as fill; the source could be tape or graphics. The term degrades the importance of the visuals.

Establisher—A shot used to identify a person or scene, particularly a wide shot before a close-up.

ESU—A relative anachronism, it stands for Engineering Set-Up and refers the time allocated before a broadcast for preparation. With new equipment, actual set-up time is negligible or greatly reduced, since there are no tubes to be warmed up and camera registration is not as time-consuming or as frequently required as in the days of yore.

Evergreen—A report that will (virtually) never be outdated. Often a piece produced and held in the event that an unexpected hole is created in a broadcast. Often soft news, an evergreen may be a profile of a town founder or a retrospective on the meanderings of the local river.

Fade—To reduce the video level of a picture, as in dissolving out. Often used in the expression, Fade to Black, a direction issued at the end of a segment or broadcast.

FCC—The Federal Communications Commission. The federal agency which oversees the telecommunications industries.

Feed—As a verb, it means to transmit or send. As a noun, it means a transmission, as by telephone line, microwave, or satellite.

Field—(1) In the field means outside of the broadcast center; remote position; on location. (2) A half-frame of videotape.

Filler—Material—usually copy stories of secondary news value, or brites—inserted into a broadcast to plug holes left by a piece or copy failing to make air. Also called pad.

Film—Once the standard recording medium of the industry, it is rarely on television news these days, replaced by tape and disk.

Flack—Derogatory slang for a public information person.

Flash—An American wire service designation for an interrupt of the utmost importance, e.g., assassinations, invasions and natural cataclysms. Equivalent to a snap on Reuters.

Flavor—Ambience; mood. Adding flavor to a report means providing a more vivid description. A flavor piece is report that sets a mood, an atmosphere. A flavor piece would be a companion piece, perhaps describing the surroundings for upcoming negotiations.

Flood—The status of a spotlight when the beam is diffused rather than focused. The opposite of spot.

Font—A type face.

Format—(1) Also called a line-up or rundown, the format is the outline of a broadcast, listing information such as order of news items, stories, reporters, item times, running times and sources, e.g., tape machines, remote, studio. (2) The technical design structure of a videotape, e.g., VHS, Beta.

Frame—One picture. There are thirty frames in every second of video (24 per second in film).

Fresh—Live; for the first time. An anchor is reading fresh if she delivers copy on the air without reading it in advance.

Frezzi—Short for Frezzolini, a type of portable light used in shooting news film and tape.

Fringe—Local programming time in the early morning and late night.

Genlock—An electronic pulse that keeps each of the 525 lines that make up U.S. broadcast in alignment to make a television picture.

Goodnight (GN)—The signing-off of a broadcast, usually by an anchor or host.

Hash—A slang term for an unusable picture.

Head clog—When dirt—often flakes broken off from an overused tape—adheres to a head in the tape machine, interfering with playback or recording. If the clog is on the playback head, a simple cleaning should regain the picture. If it's on the record head, the recording may have to be redone.

Headlines (HL)—A title or caption, abbreviating a story. An abbreviation used to tease an upcoming story.

HUT—An acronym for Homes Using Television, a ratings term describing the size of the potential audience.

Ident—Short for Station Identification, the time set aside for local stations during network programming to give their calls letters and run commercials.

IFB—An acronym for Interrupted Feed Back. An audio line, usually to the earpiece of an anchor on set or a reporter at a remote. The way the line is wired, the director and or the producer have the capability of interrupting what the talent is hearing—usually live programming—to give instructions. (see SAR)

In-house—At the broadcast center or station. In-house can describe the location of someone (a reporter or photographer) or something (a tape or a camera) that sometimes operates outside of the broadcast center. In-house can also be a description of where a service might be done, e.g., the stations promos are done in-house, using its own facilities and personnel.

Insert—A source usually meaning other than the original report, usually graphics or another tape, that is imbedded into the middle of a tape report. It can be audio and/or video.

Intro—Short for introduction, describing copy that will precede another segment, e.g., a lead-in for a tape report or for a broadcast.

Investigative reporter—A redundancy; every reporter worth his salt is investigating his story.

Jump cut—When two pieces of tape of the same subject but not recorded contiguously are edited together so that the subject shifts visually in a jerky manner. Often seen in an interview when a cutaway isn't used.

Key—A verb meaning to mix two video sources electronically, by inserting one into part of the other, as in chroma-keying.

Kfc—An abbreviation for news conference.

Kinescope—The process of making a film copy of a videotape; also used as a noun.

Lead-in—Same as intro. A lead-in can refer to the anchor copy that leads in to a reporter's tape story, or to a set-up for a sound bite.

Libel—Used as a noun and a verb. Any false written or printed statement or depiction which tends to expose someone to ridicule or contempt, or to damage their reputation. Written slander.

Lighting—A critical facet in the production of television pictures, and one usually overlooked or undervalued. Lighting is an art, and with careful attention can be used to create and enhance mood and other effects to more fully explain a story.

Line-up—Same as format or rundown, it is a list of the news items, participants, video sources and timings in a broadcast. A line-up aids the director, producer and staff in maintaining control of the elements in a program, particularly in readying facilities, moving cameras and on-set talent and back-timing.

Location—As in on location, outside of the broadcast center; in the field; on a remote.

Log—To register times, e.g., the length of tape segments or the appearance of particular events at particular times to help with later editing or identification.

Macro-micro—An approach to reporting the big picture and bringing it down to the local level, e.g., an end to federal revenue-sharing means that North Slopefall will have to get a quarter of their income from somewhere else.

Master control—The super control room of a broadcast operation through which all other control rooms feed. The place where a station or network selects its output to the transmitter.

Matte—The electronic mixing of one video source over another, as in matting supers.

Media event—A publicity term meaning a situation designed to get news coverage. This, as opposed to a public event that would be covered by the media because it was a news story in itself. A photo op is a media event.

Micro-macro—An approach to reporting a single or small component and then extrapolating to the big picture, e.g., to look at what will happen to one person who will be laid off and then note that 4,000 are also losing their jobs.

Microwave—A type of broadcast transmission signal, usually for distances of under fifty miles. The term is also used as a verb.

Mix—The combining of one or more video and/or audio elements. You go into a control room to mix audio channels, e.g., narration and background and video sources, e.g., separate tapes, graphics, CG material.

Monitor—A high resolution CRT, usually without a tuner, that is connected directly to a video source, e.g., a tape deck or remote feed.

MOS—(1) An expression meaning "without sound" or video only. (2) A reference to man-on-the-street, as in the kind of interviews.

Multiplex—A projection island containing two 16 millimeter film chains, two slides projectors and a 35 millimeter projector. A mirror is switched to select the source. An anachronism.

NAB—Acronym for the National Association of Broadcasters, the largest of the industry associations.

National—As a noun, short for a nationally-run commercial, as opposed to a local or regional.

NATPE—Acronym for National Association of Television Programming Executives.

Narration—The audio track of an anchor or reporter. The track that tells the story around sound cuts in conjunction with background audio.

News director—The person in charge of a news department, sometimes an obstacle, always a teacher. A position of questionable power. A person caught in a morass of ratings and budgets, squished between the staff and management, often a target of the program director, and an unwilling co-pilot with the promotion manager.

Nielsen—As in A.C. Nielsen, the major television ratings service.

NTSC—A U.S. standard of broadcast transmission.

O-&-O—An acronym for owned-and-operated stations. Usually referring to the networks' own stations.

On-camera (o/c)—It means that the person reading the script is also in the picture.

180-degree rule—Less a rule and more of a suggestion, it means that you should see in your mind's eye a geometric plane which exists for your viewer that runs straight across your scene from one side to the other and to infinity. For discussion's sake, call the left side zero degrees and the right side 180 degrees. You can shoot pictures from on any and all points of that line. But if the arc inscribed from the furthest left camera position to furthest right is more than 180 degrees, then you run the risk of confusing the viewer. If bent carefully, however, you can provide an interesting new dimension to a report.

outro—A short tag to a package, which might end with a feed to another reporter or anchor, as in "The trial resumes tomorrow. Back to you, Lorna."

Package—A complete report, as opposed to merely a sound cut or voice-over clip.

Pad—Extra material, usually secondary copy stories; filler.

PAL—A European (primarily) broadcast transmission standard.

Pan—To shift the direction of a camera from one side to another. The horizontal version of tilt.

Parallel construction—A term from junior high grammar meaning to use the same style throughout a composition or paragraph. Say "The trees were green, the sky was blue and the earth was brown." Rather than "The trees were green, blue was the sky and the earth was brown."

Patch—Slang for an electronic connection, as between two links in an audio and/or video chain, e.g., the plugging of a video source into the switcher or the cabling of a tape machine to a monitor. Used as a noun or a verb.

(in) Pattern—A network term meaning that a broadcast will play through the normal time zone structure, e.g., at 10PM in New York and again at 10PM in Los Angeles. In pattern means that the same show is seen at the same clock time on both coasts, though three hours later. The alternative is to go live across the board, as is done in coverage of an Inauguration. If you are a West Coast programmer, it means that Monday Night Football—seen at 9:00 in the East—goes on at 6:00 which forces you to truncate your early local news, perhaps 5:00–5:30, with the network news to follow from 5:30–6:00. But unlike the situation on the East Coast, your late news will play in its regularly scheduled time slot. This is important to network news executives who interrupt programming, because if they go live to every market, they will be interrupting different programming in each time zone.

Phase—A term meaning the synchrony of two video sources, e.g., a camera in phase with the studio means that the signals are locked and will play without break-up.

Photo op—Short for photographic opportunity. A photo op provides set-up or voice-over shots for a reporter to describe the purpose and/or content of the meeting. (See media event)

Piece—Slang for a spot; story; report.

PIO—Abbreviation for Press Information Officer.

Pix—Slang for pictures; video.

Pool—News coverage by different companies, in which one crew covers and shares the coverage with all the participants. Often done in covering the President on Air Force One or in courtrooms where there is limited space for journalists.

Post production—The final mixing of a report or broadcast, when special effects, dissolves, wipes, keys and other visuals techniques and audio sweetening are added. Graphics and other non-tape visuals like supers will also be inserted. Most news operations are too pressed by time and facilities to do much post production. The exceptions are documentaries and special reports aired during ratings periods.

Pot—Slang for an audio source.

Pre-roll—To start a tape rolling before you will use it, e.g., in anticipation of a dissolve. (see dead pot)

Pre-set—Cued and ready to go. Also, used before "control room", pre-set means the operation that readies tapes and remotes for the main control room in major coverage, like a national election.

Prime time—Prime time is the period between 8:00 and 11:00 (Eastern/Pacific) every evening. It is prime because it gets the most viewers.

Prime time access—The hour before prime time; 7:00 to 8:00 (Eastern/Pacific) in the evening.

Producer—In the world of entertainment productions, it is usually the producer who raises the money and handles the administrative side of a production while the director does the creative work. In television news, the producer is responsible—with occasional and particular exceptions—for the whole production, including the content of the script, visuals, facilities, staff, budgeting, logistics and direction. Whether producing a spot or a broadcast, the producer is the final authority beneath top management.

Production assistant—In most news operations, it is a person who helps both producers and directors to organize the news for broadcast by collating scripts, ordering supers and tracking graphics.

Promo—Short for promotion or promotional announcement.

PSA—An acronym for Public Service Announcement; commercial messages for non-profit organizations. They usually run free of charge, and often during the early morning hours.

Rack focus—To focus a camera simultaneously with—or immediately after—a major zoom, e.g., from a tight shot close-up to a wide, distant shot. Used, for example, to show a relationship between two distant or contrasting elements.

Ratings—A measurement system used by the broadcast industry to count viewers (and listeners) by polling a selected sampling and extrapolating.

Reader—A copy story, usually for the anchor.

Regional—A network description for a broadcast to a particular section of the country, as in regional football games. Commercials are also sometimes bought by regions and are called regionals.

Remote—A transmission point away from the broadcast center; location.

Reporter—At the local level, it means the journalist who covers a story, writes the script, reads it on air, and often on camera. In most cases it is used interchange-ably with "correspondent", but at the networks, a reporter may be more of a researcher and interviewer for a correspondent or producer who will less often voice a piece or appear in a standupper.

Reprise—To bring back up; to play again. In a documentary, you might go back to an early speaker for another sound cut, reprising that person. You can reprise, people, ideas, themes, images, etc.

Roll—(1) An order from a direction to set a tape machine in motion, as in "Roll it!" (2) A vertically run super. (same as scroll)

Room tone—Generic background sound recorded at a particular location, usu-ally inside. Not used much in spot news but useful in providing a fuller presence in special reports and documentaries, room tone is inserted to help cover edits and/or to maintain background audio continuity in a narration track.

Routing switcher—A panel of buttons through which input and output trans-missions are directed, e.g., to a tape machine or studio.

RTNDA—An acronym for the Radio Television News Directors Association.

Run-down—Same as line-up or format, it is a production outline for a broadcast, usually showing order, story, talent, video source, item and running time.

Running time—Cumulative time. The total time for all of the segments of a broadcast to a particular point in the rundown.

SAR—An abbreviation for Selected Audio Return. It is an audio circuit with certain channels cut out. This might be used in a remote interview situation, for example, where the interviewee would hear questions from the anchor in the studio, but not the directions from the producer in the control room. SAR might also be used to keep a reporter from hearing his own voice coming back. It is particularly useful if the remote is a long way for the broadcast center—across the country or overseas—in seeing to it that the audio delay doesn't unnerve the person while reporting. (see IFB)

Scroll (also roll)—Matted CG running from the bottom to the top of the screen, as in credits; a vertical crawl. Also used as a verb.

SECAM—A European broadcast transmission standard.

SEG—An abbreviation for shit-eating-grin. A posed smile; not a candid shot.

Segment—A section of a broadcast, usually between two commercial breaks. A segment can also be an editorial delineation of information in a script, e.g., a segment on reactor meltdowns in a report on nuclear power.

Segue—The mixing of two audio sources, one's sound increasing, the other fading out. The audio version of a dissolve.

Set-up—A type of shot which establishes a scene, e.g., a wide shot that puts in context the subsequent close-up.

Sign-off—The final words of a report, usually a reporter's name, station and location. Also the final minutes of a broadcast day, with the national anthem and the announcer saying that the station was going off the air until such-and-such a time.

SIL—Abbreviation for silent, found on scripts and log sheets.

Sked—Short for schedule. In newswire parlance, a day sked means the list of news events for a particular day.

Skycam—A camera system operating on a series of wires which position the lens on a horizontal and vertical grid parallel to the ground, as for football games. Also, used by stations to refer to cameras mounted in helicopters and planes.

Slander—Both a noun and a verb. The making of false and/or injurious statements about a person's character that could damage their reputation. Oral libel.

Slate—An audio and/or video announcement of what is to come. Slate originated as a feature film term to describe the action of holding a slate board marked with the movie title, director's name, scene and take numbers in front of the camera and then slapping the clapsticks together. The clapsticks, by the way, made a clear snap so that the editor had a point at which to synchronize the sound and picture reels. Also used as a verb.

Slave—An unattended, mounted camera, usually on the wall of a newsroom and used for emergency coverage.

SMPTE—A form of encoding tape with time reference points.

Snap—The Reuters version of American wire category Flash, the highest priority level a new story.

SOF—Abbreviation for Sound On Film; from the old days when a lot of film was shot without sound (MOS).

SOT—Abbreviation for sound on tape, found in scripts and log sheets.

Sound bite [cut]—A segment of audio, usually from a person speaking, e.g., an interviewee. A sound bite could contain a single statement or can be two or more segments edited together.

Special Report—A network designation for a news interrupt, a level less urgent than a bulletin. A Special Report might be used to provide an update on an ongoing story. A Special Report might also be used to interrupt regularly scheduled programming for an expected event like the State of the Union address.

Spec footage—Short for footage submitted on speculation; a freelancer photographer will submit spec footage of an overnight fire, for example. If it's used, he's paid for it. Some of the most significant footage ever aired has been spec, when nature has struck suddenly, or when a major news event occurred unexpectedly in a distant and/or unstaffed location.

Specialty reporter—A broadcast journalist who has the credentials to understand and report on a particular area or field, e.g., business, consumer affairs, medicine, health, science, ecology, etc.

Spot—(1) Slang for a report; piece; story. (2) A light beam set to its tightest focus. Opposite of flood.

Stake out—Used as both a noun and a verb, it means to be in position to capture someone on tape at a particular location, for instance, people on their way into a grand jury.

Standupper—A report delivered on camera from the field, live or on tape.

Static—A non-moving element, e.g., a slide or a graphic, as opposed to rolling video.

Station identification—The time set aside during network programming for local stations to give their call letters. (See ident)

Steadicam—A shoulder-rig camera mount that keeps the lens motion calm despite the action—running, jumping, ducking, etc.—of the photographer. Used for walking interviews, for example.

Sticks—Slang for a camera tripod.

Studio—Sometimes used to refer to the broadcast center or station, but specifically a large, sound-proofed room especially designed for television production. Usually featuring high ceilings to make room for sets and lights, different staging areas and special outlets for audio and video lines. Studio is also a term for an audio recording facility.

Super—Short for superimposition, it usually refers to a name, title, or some other verbal identifier that is superimposed electronically over another picture. Originally hand-set white letters on a black card shot with a separate camera and matted over another video source, today's supers can be multi-colored, multi-font affairs created and manipulated by computers generators to move in various manners, directions and at different speeds across the screen.

Superstation—A station which transmits to an audience substantially beyond its own ADI or market. WTBS in Atlanta, WGN in Chicago, WOR in New York are all television superstations.

Survey—To check out a shooting location in advance to ascertain necessary logistical information, determine camera angles and scout possible advantages and potential obstacles. Also used as a noun.

Sweeps—As in "sweep weeks" it refers to the major ratings periods, when surveys are conducted of the ADI to determine audience size for television programs. Advertising rates are based on sweep statistics. The major sweeps run four weeks in November, February and May. Many news directors program special reports during sweeps in an attempt to boost their news ratings.

Sweetening—To improve the quality of the audio through electronic tuning.

Switcher—The technical director's board, a series of buttons, levers and dials wired to load, select and manipulate video sources to create a television picture. On some switchers there is an AFV control which locks the Audio in to Follow the Video selected on the board, otherwise the audio is usually controlled separately.

Synch—Short for synchronous, meaning at the same time; simultaneously. Synch-sound is a film term meaning that the audio is recorded separately but directly coupled to the camera. Lip-synch means that the audio and video of a person talking is occurring simultaneously.

Syndication—A distribution system to a group of stations, operating outside of the major network routes. The majors also have syndicated services of their own, but the term usually refers to an independent distribution network.

Tag—The end of report or broadcast; outro; close. Tag is also used to describe copy that may follow a report or tape cut, often to complete the story. A tag is frequently used to give the viewer a chance to adjust from one picture to another before changing stories.

Take—As a noun, a take is a version of the same piece or standupper or narration, as in take two is the second version. As a verb, it is an order to switch to another source, e.g., "Take camera three". A take is a direct, full-screen, instantaneous cut. (see dissolve)

Talent—Sometimes used pejoratively, it refers to the people who are on-air; usually anchors and other studio personalities; sometimes also correspondents or reporters.

Tape-roll—euphemism for a lead-in to a package, from the days when it took ten seconds for a tape machine to lock up for air.

Tease—A promotional piece, often voice-over tape; sometimes just video with a super. A tease may end a news segment and promote a story to come out of the next commercial break or sometime later in the broadcast. A tease can also refer to those :03 bits that are placed at the end of station identification breaks promoting news coverage later, e.g., "Frogs loose in Calaveras; film at eleven."

Technical director (TD)—In the larger markets and at the networks, the person who sits at the switcher and manages the video part of the broadcast under the command of the director. The technical director is usually the highest ranking of the engineering types, other than the Engineer in Charge (EIC).

TelePrompter—The equipment that projects a script onto clear Plexiglas panels in front of a public speaker or anchor, enabling him to look as though he is speaking when he is actually reading.

Think piece—A report that is less about a day's events and more designed to create a context for the news; an explainer.

Throw—To verbally hand off to a reporter or an anchor; toss. Also used as a noun in the same context.

Tilt—To move the camera lens up or down; the vertical version of a pan. Tilt up means to raise the lens, which means lowering the back of the camera; and vice versa.

Time base corrector (or TBC)—An electronic devise for controlling and refining the video signal, assuring synch between, for example, a tape machine and the studio.

Time code—An electronic time reference system on a videotape used to facilitate logging and editing.

Toss—A verbal hand-off; throw. Used as both a noun and a verb.

Track—(1) The recording of a narration; used both as a noun and as a verb. (2) An audio recording. (3) A band on a video tape, e.g., control track. (4) To follow, as the developments in a story.

Traffic—(1) The name for a network operations department that handles incoming and outgoing transmissions, e.g., a satellite feed from London or a microwave feed from a remote truck. In some news operations, traffic means the department that handles the dispatching of couriers, e.g., for tape pick-ups from a camera crew. (2) A description of incoming and outgoing transmissions.

Two-shot—A picture of two people, often in interview situation. The two-shot is often used to set up a sound cut or as a cutaway.

TX—An abbreviation for time.

UHF—Short for Ultra High Frequency, a section of the television band which you access through channels 14 through 83. Developed for television use after VHF, UHF signals have a shorter range.

Up and under—Audio that begins loudly and then is lowered to background level, e.g., music starting at normal level and then lowered to play beneath a narration track.

Urgent—A wire service designation for a story of importance and off the regular schedule. More important than an advisory but not as serious as a bulletin.

Vanda—A traffic term standing for Video-and-Audio. Vanda lines might be drawn on a technical wiring diagram, or to show the flow from remotes to cluster points and the broadcast center.

VHF—The abbreviation for Very High Frequency. The channels 2 to 13. The older brother to UHF on the television band. The first channels allocated were in the VHF band, and is why so many of the network affiliates have VHF band locations.

VHS—A popular tape format. (see beta)

Videotape—(see audiotape) Videotape comes in a number of sizes and specifications. Until the early Seventies, the predominant format was two-inches wide; it was originally edited using a microscope, a razor blade and sticky metal tape. There was high-band and low-band and other details that are of interest only to nostalgia buffs. Then came 3/4" tape which was much more portable and easier to edit. One-inch and half-inch tape followed quickly. Now there are significantly smaller formats, like mini-DV, and the technology is moving to non-rolling media, like discs.

Voice-over (v/o)—Audio that is coming from other than the video source, as in a narration with b-roll.

White balance—A verb meaning to show an electronic camera the color white, from which the camera can then define the rest of the color spectrum and adjust appropriately the signals that it reads and transmits, based on existing lighting conditions. Also used as a noun.

Window—A time frame with set start and close, e.g., a time slot when an affiliate's facilities are able to feed a network spot, e.g., 5:00-5:20 would be a twenty-minute window.

Windscreen—A cover—usually foam rubber—for a microphone which reduces wind noise.

Wipe—A technical term for changing the picture on a screen by replacing one video source with another through a patterned insert. Wipes can be of virtually any shape, size and speed. A wipe can be hard or soft, bordered or clean.

Wire—Slang, a verb meaning to put a microphone on someone, e.g., wiring an interviewee.

Wires—Slang meaning the news services, e.g., Reuters, AP, Dow Jones, etc.

WX—A line-up abbreviation for weather(cast).

Y—A cable that splits in two, e.g., for tying two microphones into one input on a tape deck.

Zoom—To adjust a camera lens to create a tighter or a wider shot, e.g., to go from a close-up to a wide shot calls for a zoom out, and vice versa. Also used as a noun.

Zworykin—Russian-born American physicist Vladimir K. Zworykin invented the iconoscope (1923) and other major components involved in television production.

0-595-28781-6

Printed in the United Kingdom
by Lightning Source UK Ltd.
120211UK00001B/190-192